2

Greenhill Books

FIGHTING IN
NORMANDY

WORLD WAR II GERMAN DEBRIEFS
PUBLISHED BY GREENHILL BOOKS

THE ANVIL OF WAR
German Generalship in Defence on the Eastern Front

THE BATTLE OF THE BULGE: THE GERMAN VIEW
Perspectives from Hitler's High Command

FIGHTING IN HELL
The German Ordeal on the Eastern Front

HITLER'S ARDENNES OFFENSIVE
The German View of the Battle of the Bulge

THE LUFTWAFFE FIGHTER FORCE
The View from the Cockpit

SPEARHEAD FOR BLITZKRIEG
Luftwaffe Operations in Support of the Army, 1939–1945

INSIDE THE AFRIKA KORPS
The Crusader Battles, 1941–1942

FIGHTING THE INVASION
The German Army at D-Day

FIGHTING IN NORMANDY

The German Army
from D-Day to Villers-Bocage

by
**Heinz Guderian, Fritz Krämer, Fritz
Ziegelmann, Freiherr von Lüttwitz et al**

Edited by
David C. Isby

Greenhill Books, London
Stackpole Books, Pennsylvania

Greenhill Books

Fighting in Normandy: The German Army from D-Day to Villers-Bocage
First published 2001 by Greenhill Books,
Lionel Leventhal Limited, Park House, 1 Russell Gardens,
London NW11 9NN
and
Stackpole Books, 5067 Ritter Road, Mechanicsburg, PA 17055, USA

© Lionel Leventhal Limited, 2001

British Library Cataloguing in Publication Data
Fighting in Normandy:
the German Army from D-Day to Villers-Bocage
1. Germany. Heer – History – World War, 1939–1945.
2. World War, 1939–1945 – Campaigns – France – Normandy
I. Guderian, Heinz. 1888–1954
II. Isby, David C.
940.5´413´43

ISBN 1-85367-460-5

Library of Congress Cataloging-in-Publication Data available

Designed and typeset by Roger Chesneau
Printed and bound in Great Britain
by CPD (Wales), Ebbw Vale

Contents

Contents

Illustrations

The developing situation, 15 June
The developing situation, 22 June

Maps and diagrams

Note: The maps on pages 40 and 118 are reproduced directly from original and surviving maps and sketch maps held in the National Archives.

PART ONE

7 June, D+1

After 6 June the Germans had three objectives: to bring up forces; to contain the invasion with those forces already in contact; and to prepare for a decisive counterattack. On the 7th, von Rundstedt gave the mission of a decisive counterattack to General Geyr's Panzer Group West.

But with the 21st Panzer engaged in defensive combat and Panzer Lehr unable to reach the battlefield in time, the decisive counterattack was revised to a limited attack by elements of the 12th SS Panzer Division during the afternoon. While the attack—which led to the Battle of Broun against the 9th Canadian Brigade—was soon forced on to the defensive, it helped prevent the advance on Caen from gathering any momentum until more German forces could arrive. I SS Panzer Corps took over the sector from LXXXIV Corps.

East of the Orne, elements of the 21st Panzer Division and the 346th and 711th Infantry Divisions counterattacked the British airborne and commando forces without success.

To the east of Omaha, elements of the 352nd and 716th Infantry Divisions, along with the 30th Mobile Brigade, launched their own counterattack around Bayeux. The attacking units made little progress and were soon ground down between the advance of the veteran US 1st Infantry and British 50th Infantry Divisions. This attack, however, helped delay the link-up of the US and British forces until 8 June.

Opposite Utah, the 709th Infantry Division's units—especially Günther Kiel's 919th Grenadier Regiment—were able to improvise effective bocage fighting tactics to defend Montebourg against US forces advancing from Utah Beach. But elsewhere the 91st Luftlande Division proved to be no match for the 82nd Airborne, who were able to link up with 4th Infantry Division forces advancing inland.

Another front was opened up on the roads as units and supplies moved on to the routes towards Normandy in the face of Allied interdiction efforts. This was no less a battle than that against the beachhead.

D.C.I.

OKW War Diary, 7 June

by Major Percy E. Schramm

In order to establish a uniform command, Panzer HQ West (General Geyr von Schweppenburg), with three Panzer and two infantry divisions subordinated to the Seventh Army, took over the command in the Orne–Vire sector. General Marcks (91st, 709th and 243rd Infantry Divisions) was in command on the Cotentin peninsula, while southwest thereof General der Flieger Meindl, commanding general of II FS Corps, (17th SS Panzer Grenadier Division, 3rd FS Division, 37th Infantry Division) was in charge.

On the evening of the second day 10–12 enemy units, among them three airborne divisions, were spotted. These strong reinforcements offset the successes which had been achieved against the already landed forces. It was hoped that the British parachutists who had been squeezed into an area 6 by 6 kilometers could still be annihilated. The intended attack against the main bridgehead was somewhat delayed. The fact that the enemy's situation at the mouth of the Vire river was bad was considered advantageous for our side. Enemy tanks penetrated during the night into Bayeux in order to establish contact with the east. The American parachutists could likewise be squeezed in, but the landing of an additional division made it possible to open a narrow strip toward the coast which permitted the enemy to bring up reinforcements. The sorties of our own Luftwaffe, which was to be reinforced according to an order of 6 June, amounted to 400 on this day. The promised reinforcements arrived on 7 June. The Navy continued to participate with motor torpedo-boats and destroyers from Cherbourg and Le Havre. The Marcouf heavy naval coastal battery, which periodically had been inactive, could again partake in the battle.

LXXXIV Corps Counterattacks on 7 June

by Oberstleutnant Friedrich von Criegern

On 7 June the counterattacks against the beachheads were again resumed. During the night the mobile 30th Brigade was brought up to the 352nd Infantry Division from the Coutances area and assigned to the counterattack against Colleville. The division with its only remaining reserve, 352 Pi Battalion, conducted a counterattack against the beachhead near Masnières, which reached the locality but finally failed against enemy supremacy. The rest of the the Corps which was deployed at Ryes on 6 June was forced on to the defensive east of Bayeux and then were thrown back in the course of the forenoon by a strong enemy force with tanks. At about 1200 hours enemy tanks penetrated into Bayeux. The telephone communication to the 716th Infantry Division, running through Bayeux, was disrupted. In the morning the division had told the Corps about the events in the Caen area. According to this information, I SS Panzer Corps had not yet launched the counterattack there and the enemy was about to widen the beachhead.

During the morning the enemy forced a new landing near the 352nd Infantry Division along the rocky coast of St-Pierre-du-Mont, where rangers with special equipment conquered the cliffs. At first the battles for the beachhead of Ste-Mère-Église seemed to take a favourable course. Here began the ordered counterattack after a regrouping during the night. The regiment from the 243rd Infantry Division which had arrived in the evening from the west coast was committed by the 709th Infantry Division from the north along the coast. The forces adjacent to the west—elements of the 709th Infantry Division and of the 7th Assault Battalion—were concentrated under a regimental staff of the 709th Infantry Division. An additional grenadier regiment of the 243rd Infantry Division had been brought forward during the night by Corps and assigned to the 91st LL Division, which attacked with both regiments from the west. The 1058th Grenadier Regiment of the 91st LL Division captured Ste-Mère-Église during the forenoon but lost it again by reason of enemy counterattack. The attacks from the north suffered from heavy ship gunfire, especially a regiment of the 243rd Infantry Division which had been pushing forward along the coast but was finally stopped.

Only in the morning was Corps informed that the 6th FS Regiment had lost all the gains they had achieved during the night. A night air landing in the attacking area of the regiment north of St-Côme-du-Mont had brought confusion and cut off the advanced battalions. The battalion which had penetrated into Ste-Marie-du-Mont was lost, while

16

the bulk of the regiment were able to assemble around St-Côme-du-Mont and established themselves there for defense.

With the failure of the counterattack, the last hope of success was lost. The attacking troops had suffered such high losses that it was doubtful whether they would be able by attacking to prevent a widening of the beachhead. Each hour brought reinforcements to the enemy while our own reserves were used up and fresh ones were not to be expected yet. The enemy ship guns played a decisive part in the failure of the counterattack. We had no means of eliminating the ships. Each hour brought further advances for the enemy. The more clearly friend and foe became defined within the beachheads with their increasing distance from the coast, the greater was the scope offered for ship guns and the air force to take an effective part in ground combat.

7 June: 709th Infantry Division

by Generalleutnant Karl Wilhelm von Schlieben

On the evening of 6 June I reported by telephone to the Commanding General, General der Artillerie Marcks, on the development of the situation with regard to the 1058th Grenadier Regiment and my plans and preparation for 7 June. The Commanding General expressed his approval, particularly of my intention to increase the fighting power of the regiment by the assignment of the two motorized artillery battalions and the self-propelled gun company of the 709th Light Battalion. Into the evening of 6 June I learned that the commander of the 922nd Grenadier Regiment, Lieutenant Colonel Müller, who had been assigned to the 243rd Division on the west coast, had been transferred by the "Senior Officer of the Garrison on the Cotentin Peninsula," Generalleutnant Hellmich, with regimental troops of the 922nd Grenadier Regiment, the 3rd Battalion 922nd Grenadier Regiment, one battalion of the 920th Grenadier Regiment, and the engineer battalion of the 243rd Infantry Division, to Montebourg by night-march (night of 6–7 June). The regiment was to advance south with its left wing along the St-Floxel–Fontenay-sur-Mer–Ravenoville road. I do not remember what its mission was. I presume it was to prevent a widening of the enemy bridgehead to the north and to support the left flank of the 1058th Grenadier Regiment.

I also had moved the 3rd Battalion of the 729th Grenadier Regiment, commanded by Major der Reserve Elbrecht, who was killed in action later on, from the area of Height 180.2 southwest of Cherbourg to the area east of Montebourg.

Generalleutnant Hellmich also dispatched the 3rd Battalion of the 243rd Artillery Regiment (less the 10th Battery) from the west coast via Bricquebec to Valognes. The two batteries took up position during the fight of 6 June near Écausseville (3½ kilometers south of Montebourg). They were assigned to Regimental Staff Seidel and supported the attack of the 1058th Grenadier Regiment on 7 June.

In the night of 5 June the Seventh Army assault battalion was placed into such a difficult position by an encircling movement that its commander decided to withdraw west to the Montebourg–Neuville-au-Plain road. There the battalion supported the 1058th Grenadier Regiment, which throughout that day had fought with varying success to capture Ste-Mère-Église.

On this day a number of enemy tanks made their appearance. The fire of large-caliber enemy naval guns and strong mortar fire added further to our discomfort. The heavy fire of the naval guns also prevented an attack by Regiment Müller (3rd Battalion 922nd

Regiment, 1st Battalion 920th Regiment), which had been tired by its night-march, from making progress.

In the afternoon of 7 June, at a location north of Neuville-au-Plain, I gained the impression that the 1058th Regiment was no longer even able to capture Ste-Mère-Église, much less hold it against the fire of the enemy naval guns and tanks. The AT Battalion of the 709th Division had suffered considerable losses, but on the other hand had achieved good results. Enemy tanks fired from Neuville at the highway leading to Montebourg. Together with retreating units of the 1058th Regiment, men of the Seventh Army assault battalion and artillerymen of the 3rd Battalion 243rd Artillery Regiment, I succeeded in stopping the beginning of a panic caused by the enemy armor and to establish a makeshift defense line on both sides of the Montebourg–Ste-Mère-Église high road, 1,200 meters to the north of Neuville-au-Plain. It lacked, however, any antitank defense.

During the afternoon of 7 June I clearly saw that the enemy beachhead could no longer be eradicated by counterattacks of local reserves. This would require an organized attack with strong artillery support and a Panzer formation, and for this purpose the strong enemy air forces and naval guns would have to be neutralized. But the enemy air forces and navy were entirely unopposed. Neither our own Luftwaffe nor Navy rendered any assistance.

Therefore I decided to assume the defensive, and try to prevent the enemy from breaking out of his beachhead in a northerly or northwesterly direction. My impression, which was that the enemy intended to advance quickly north from his beachhead at Ste-Mère-Église and try to capture Cherbourg, proved later on to be correct. On 6 June an operational order of the American VII Corps was washed ashore. In substance the order said that the US VII Corps with four divisions (of which two airborne divisions were in the first wave) had the mission of turning to the north from the Quineville–Carentan beachhead, which was protected on the south, and of taking Cherbourg from the landward side while . . . At that time I hoped that Panzer Group West, which had been mentioned in orders before the invasion, could appear supported by 1,000 German fighter planes (this figure had actually been given me before the invasion) in order to stamp out the enemy beachhead.

I organized a task force under Colonel Rohrbach, the commander of the 729th Grenadier Regiment. I did not assign this task to the commander of the 919th Grenadier Regiment, Lieutenant Colonel Keil, who was closer, as at that time I expected further landings between Quineville and St-Vaast-la-Hougue. Nevertheless I took away his third battalion, assigning it to Colonel Rohrbach, to whom furthermore the 100th Smoke Battalion (less one battery), which was employed at Morsalines with the beach as its field of fire, was attached.

In the evening of 7 June there was a makeshift defense line on the Montebourg–Ste-Mère-Église road, 1,200 meters north of Neuville-au-Plain and on the Fontenay-sur-Mer–Ravenoville road, without support on either flank. The 1058th Grenadier Regiment had suffered badly and was in a confused condition. Its commander, Colonel Beigang, was and remained missing.

At this time the absence of a corps headquarters staff near the front was badly felt. The divisions received little orientation on the major situation. It was difficult to get in touch by telephone with LXXXIV Corps headquarters at St-Lô. The distance was 60 kilometers and the enemy was in between. On the evening of 7 June I decided to weaken the garrisions of the bases and islands of resistance of the seafront, which had not been attacked, and to leave only emergency garrisons there. Such a measure had been provided prior to the invasion by a printed directive. When the catchword "emergency garrison" was given, only a few men remained at the bases and islands of resistance, whereas all the others assembled inland in reserve.

In this connection the complete lack of mobility of the stationary infantry divisions was particularly unpleasant. Men who had been assigned to the northeast coast had to walk more than 30 kilometers to reach the area south of Montebourg. Supplying them became a problem, as each company had only horses for its field kitchen, which, however, had to feed the emergency garrisons remaining at the bases.

Although the daily reports of higher headquarters mention fighting by the 709th Infantry Division at Montebourg, it must be made clear that during the first days after the enemy landing the bulk of the division was tied to its bases and islands of resistance along the coast from the mouth of the Vire river half way to Cherbourg–Cap de la Hague. The bringing up of the men from the bases and islands of resistance, which had not been attacked, was made more difficult still because the enemy air forces completely patrolled the high roads and fired unopposed at the smallest formations. Not even single men or cyclists could move freely on the road in broad daylight. I myself was fired on on 9 June by two P-47 fighter-bombers at a few seconds' intervals when driving to a troop unit. My car was burned and I had to walk several kilometers. In this way the enemy air surveillance was a great handicap to the German commanders and their troops. Even if a motor vehicle was not hit, it was not possible to drive straight to the destination in broad daylight, as again and again the car had to be stopped and the personnel take cover quickly when enemy fliers attacked.

7–8 June: Cotentin Coast Artillery

by Generalmajor Gerhard Triepel

The batteries—of the 101st Rocket Projector Regiment—were committed along with the three battalions, one after the other, south of Montebourg, on 7 June; but some of them were recognized at once and suffered heavy losses to aircraft bombs. On 7 or 8 June the 4th Battery destroyed another torpedo-boat which had approached Quineville. The 709th Infantry Division was forced to defend the east coast sector—from the mouth of the Vire river to the north—as well as the north coast.

The Infantry Regiment of the 709th Infantry Division, which defended the sector from the mouth of the Vire river as far as Quineville (Commander Oberstleutnant Keil), employed all reserves on the southern front, generally along the line Fresville–three kilometers north of Ste-Mère-Église as far as to the east coast to Ravenoville. From the 709th Infantry Division, committed on the south front one after the other, were also those battalions of the Infantry Regiment (Commander Oberst Rohrbach) which held a sector from Quineville across Barfleur as far as to the north coast. Every day, and more than once, unit boundaries had to be fixed anew.

Apart from the 101st Rocket Projector Regiment, the three battalions of which were committed one after the other south of Montebourg, a large number of heavy projectors were emplaced on the east, north and west coasts. Ammunition was there for two salvos.

The chain of command for artillery was somewhat complicated. Army coastal batteries were subordinated to the naval commander at Cherbourg for fire against targets out to sea. The Army Coastal Artillery was subordinated to the divisions for fire against an enemy who had already landed.

All anti-aircraft batteries which could fire beyond the shore line were brought up for barrage fire in defense against landing troops.

7–8 June: Kampfgruppe Keil Opposite Utah Beach

by Oberstleutnant Günther Keil

In the night of 6 June Oberstleutnant Müller, commander of the 922nd Infantry Regiment, arrived in the area north of Azeville–St-Marcouf with the 1st and 3rd Battalions of the 922nd Infantry Regiment, the 243rd Engineer Battalion and the regimental units of the 922nd.

In the morning of 7 June he attacked, the 3rd Battalion of the 922nd Infantry Regiment on the left wing operating against St-Marcouf. He succeeded in taking St-Marcouf. Under the pressure of the heavy fire of the enemy ship-based artillery he had to give it up again; in other respects he had not gained terrain by his attack. Making connection with the 3rd Battalion of the 739th Infantry Regiment, Müller then entrenched, his front facing the south.

On 7 June the 3rd Battalion of the 919th Infantry Regiment was taken away and shifted to the area south of Montebourg. When on the evening of 7 June I met the divisional commander in Montebourg, I suggested that, in addition to the 3rd Battalion of the 739th Infantry Regiment, the adjacent 3rd Battalion of the 922nd Infantry Regiment of Oberstleutnant Müller be subordinated to me and not the newly formed Rohrbach combat team, since the signal communication lines of the two battalions were going through my command post. On my request the division decided that the battalions were subordinated to me under the command of Oberstleutnant Müller, whose regimental units were also subordinated to me. Under my command, then, Oberstleutnant Müller took over the southern front as far as the Rohrbach combat team, his units being the 3rd Battalion of the 922nd Infantry Regiment and that of the 739th Infantry Regiment. The boundary with the Rohrbach combat team was the western edge of the park of Fontenay. At the coastal front there was still employed the 2nd Battalion of the 919th Infantry Regiment; apart from the Engineer Platoon of the 919th Infantry Regiment, I had no reserves at my disposal.

The enemy had not recognized our weakness in the morning of 6 June. On this morning, advancing to the north with tanks, the enemy could have rolled up the entire front, which had no depth, just passing along the nests of resistance. Nothing would have been there to face it. Now we had succeeded in forming a defensive front toward the south.

7 June: 243rd Infantry Division Elements Committed

by Hauptmann Herbert Schoch

At about 2300 hours in the night of 5 June the first enemy combat formation effected an air landing on the Cotentin peninsula. An alert was ordered between 0100 and 0200 hours on 6 June. The units assigned to coastal defense were in full preparedness a short time later. But as the main landing had been effected on the east coast in the area Carentan–Baupte–Chef-du-Pont–Ste-Mère-Église, the advance elements of the divisions were committed on 6 and 7 June in the area Ste-Mère-Église–Amfreville–Gourbesville–Grainville–Le Ham–Montebourg. The enemy units were American. The strong hostile pressure made it necessary to give up the initial attempts to take the offensive and to act on the defensive instead. As the enemy formations committed on the peninsula very soon attacked, more and more troops were withdrawn from the west coast and committed to reinforce the defense front in the area Ste-Mère-Église–Valognes. As the units were committed one after another, the regiments were torn apart and the fighting was by combat groups.

After a few days the enemy succeeded in pushing from Carentan to the north and in making contact with the formations which had landed from the air at Ste-Mère-Église. The American combat group developed two spearheads, one in a northwesterly direction toward Montebourg–Cherbourg, the other via Pont-l'Abbé in the direction of St-Sauveur–Le Vicomte–Barneville. By employing large quantities of matériel (naval guns, bombers, fighter-bombers, and increased artillery fire) the enemy succeeded, though with heavy losses, in gaining ground to the northwest and west. Only a few supplies had arrived. After the bulk of the 3rd Battalion 921st Regiment, under the command of Oberstleutnant Rüffer, who was subsequently killed in action, and units of the 91st Infantry Division had been dispersed in operations around and just west of Pont-l'Abbé, there was an acute danger of the Cotentin peninsula being cut off and the troops who were still north of a line Pont-l'Abbé–Barneville being trapped. The 3rd Battalion 921st Regiment consisted of the 9th and 12th Companies and the battalion staff. The 10th Company had been assigned to the division and the 11th Company to coastal protection.

7 June: 6th FS Regiment

by Oberstleutnant Friedrich, Freiherr von der Heydte

On the evening of 6 June 1944 the regimental commander was informed by LXXXIV Corps that an attack coordinated by the Seventh Army and with strong artillery support was planned for 7 June, to be launched from the north, from the area of Montebourg, against Ste-Mère-Église. The regiment was given the mission of joining these elements in the area of Ste-Mère-Église. A defensive front was to be established on the Merderet river west of Ste-Mère-Église.

In attempting to recall the events of the night of 6 June 1944, it appears to the author not unlikely that the American air landing operations that night may have been intended to supply the troops who had jumped and landed at the beginning of the invasion rather than to reinforce them. However, this was not apparent at the time, and the regimental commander therefore had at least to consider the possibility that these forces were combat troops presenting a serious threat. Consequently, during the early morning hours of 7 June he instructed the 1st and 2nd Battalions by radio to halt the advance, to re-establish at any cost contact with the regiment and with the adjacent battalions on the left and right, and after reorganization to redeploy in defensive positions in a semicircle around St-Côme-du-Mont at a distance of about one kilometer east and about three kilometers west of the town.

The 2nd Battalion, stationed north of St-Côme-du-Mont, acknowledged receipt of these instructions and at daybreak reported that they had been executed. It had not, however, been possible as yet to establish firm contact with the 1st Battalion. The radio station of the 1st Battalion made no response, and the order was sent blind.

Since it was impossible to reach the 1st Battalion by radio, the regimental commander made attempts immediately after daybreak to reestablish contact with the 1st Battalion by messenger and, when this also failed, by strong reconnaissance patrols of the bicycle reconnaissance platoon. However, about 500–800 meters east of St-Côme-du-Mont these reconnaissance patrols encountered enemy resistance which increased in intensity as the day went on. The elements of the Seventh Army reserve battalion committed east of St-Côme-du-Mont reported contact with the enemy and strong pressure; about noon the hostile forces, at first in small numbers, infiltrated their positions, bypassing them on the south, and reached the St-Côme-du-Mont–Carentan road. In the early afternoon it became necessary for the regimental commander to move two companies of the 3rd Battalion from the Carentan area to the front, in order to strengthen the main line of resistance and extend it to the south and to repulse the enemy troops who had pushed forward along the St-Côme-du-Mont–Carentan road. At the cost of heavy losses, they succeeded by nightfall in establishing a thin line about 300–500 meters east of the St-Côme-du-Mont road. There was still no response whatever from the 1st Battalion.

The 2nd Battalion was engaged in combat between St-Côme-du-Mont and Ste-Mère-Église on both sides of the road with American units attempting to advance southward. On 7 June severe clashes took place principally in the area of Addeville, which was held by the enemy.

After nightfall, enemy pressure increased in the east. Enemy reconnaissance patrols succeeded in infiltrating the weakly held German main line of resistance in terrain hidden from observation. At about 2200 hours two American armored reconnaissance cars broke through and succeeded in reaching the Carentan road. A regimental messenger destroyed one of them directly in front of the regimental command post with a magnetic antitank hollow charge, and the other was put out of commission at the southern exit of St-Côme-du-Mont by antitank fire.

352nd Infantry Division on 7 June 1944

by Oberstleutnant Fritz Ziegelmann

Fighting on 7 June 1944

Course of the combat day: During the night of 7 June naval artillery continued its bombardment. [There was] vigorous air activity, [and] bombing in rear areas. With the beginning of the forenoon [there was] increasingly lively fighter-bomber activity over the Bayeux area and the St-Laurent bridgehead.

At 0700 hours the adjutant of the 915th Grenadier Regiment reported that the enemy had crossed the Seulles with tanks at St-Gabriel, had shattered the remnants of the 352nd Fusilier Battalion and was advancing farther south. The sound of fighting was also to be heard in the Esquay area.

At about 0800 hours it was established by the 726th Grenadier Regiment (right) that a stronger enemy attack was in progress at the moment at the crossroads southeast of Ryes and that weaker enemy groups had crossed the Cronde creek and were advancing upon Arromanches. Countermeasures were in progress with hastily collected groups.

Toward 0900 hours the 916th Grenadier Regiment (center) reported that its own counterattack upon Vierville was making progress. It had been possible to push the enemy to the extreme northern part of Vierville. Our own attack from Vierville on St-Laurent has begun with elements of the 352nd Pioneer Battalion. The losses in Vierville were described as considerable on both sides. A telephone conference with the commander of pocket of resistance 76 (Pointe et Raz de la Percée) confirmed the report of the 916th Grenadier Regiment and disclosed that, during the night, and now also, the enemy, almost undisturbed, continued unloadings, including tanks and artillery. The 914th Grenadier Regiment (left) reported no change in the fighting for the Pointe du Hoc strongpoint. In the morning hours the enemy had again dropped parachutists (one company?) at the Brévands bridgehead.

Toward 1200 hours the 726th Grenadier Regiment (right) reported that enemy elements had reached the Bayeux–Caen road in the vicinity of St-Léger and that in Ryes and just east of Sommervieu there had been heavy fighting. The 3rd Battalion 1352nd Artillery Regiment was fighting with its last ammunition in direct fire. In the 916th Grenadier Regiment (center) the 2nd Battalion 915th Grenadier Regiment had succeeded in penetrating in the northeast part of Colleville; on the other hand, the enemy had launched an attack from St-Laurent to the south, using for the first time field and coastal artillery. In the distance there was heavy naval artillery fire and fighter-bomber activity.

After a briefing of the noon situation the General commanding LXXXIV Army Corps reported that the 30th Mobile Brigade with the 513th, 517th and 518th Battalions had been placed under the control of the 352nd Infantry Division, effective at once, and would be placed in the first line for the protection of the right open flank. The 30th Mobile Brigade, less the 517th Battalion, was placed under the control of the 726th Grenadier Regiment and the latter was ordered to prevent, with the brigade, an enemy breakthrough on Bayeux. The 517th Battalion was attached to the 916th Grenadier Regiment (center). As a result of the vigorous activity of the fighter-bombers the battalion of the 30th Mobile Brigade arrived at the assembly points (517th in Formigny, 516th and 518th in the southwest corner of Bayeux) in the late evening hours only.

After the telephone conversation with Corps HQ, several fighter-bomber squadrons attacked the divisional CP with bombs and aircraft armament. The buildings around the church of Littry occupied by a few sub-groups of the tactical group of general staff sections were destroyed and casualties resulted. As G-3 echelon was located 500 meters away it remained fit for work. (This attack was probably the result of the data found on the 1:100,000 map taken from the fallen commander of the 915th Grenadier Regiment.)

Toward 1600 hours I drove in the "people's car" (general-purpose car) to the CP of the 916th Grenadier Regiment (center) and from there on the side road to pocket of resistance 76 (Pointe et Raz de la Percée). The trip, which usually takes 30 minutes, consumed five hours. The fighter-bombers forced us to take cover. The view from pocket of resistance 76 will remain in my memory for ever. The sea was like the picture of a Kiel review of the fleet. Ships of all sorts stood almost close together on the beach and in the water broadly echeloned in depth. And the entire agglomeration remained there intact without any real interference from the German side! I clearly understood the mood of the German soldier who was missing the German Air Force. That the German soldiers fought here hard and stubbornly is and remains a wonder.

At around 1700 hours, in the 726th Grenadier Regiment (right), the enemy had penetrated in the first houses of Sommervieu, was taking possession of Ryes and was advancing to the west. Another enemy Kampfgruppe stood just south of Arromanches. The 2nd Battalion 916th Grenadier Regiment and the 3rd Battalion 1352nd Artillery Regiment had been torn to pieces. In the 916th Grenadier Regiment (center) the enemy in his attack from St-Laurent had penetrated into the gun positions of the 2nd Battalion 1352nd Artillery Regiment (northeast of Formigny). In Colleville and Vierville heavy local fights continued, some groups of houses changing owners several times. In the 914th Grenadier Regiment (left) the enemy had broken through the ring of obstacles at Pointe du Hoc and had slightly pushed back toward the west the reinforced company of the 914th Grenadier Regiment. Fighting continued with parachutists west and north of Brévands.

After 2100 hours the picture was as follows. In the 726th Grenadier Regiment (right) sector weak enemy forces had crossed the Bayeux–Caen road toward the south and southwest. Remaining elements of the 915th Grenadier Regiment stood with weak security detachments northwest and north of Tilly-sur-Seulles. The division learned that the 716th Infantry Division, which could not be contacted by telephone throughout the day, still had a few security detachments on the main road from Caen to Bayeux at Bretteville, but no longer any troops farther west. Other enemy forces, including tanks, had surrounded Sommervieu from the north, had captured it from the west and were stopped west of Sommervieu by elements of the 3rd Battalion 1352nd Artillery Regiment fighting as infantry (the guns had been destroyed). The enemy advancing westward from Ryes had reached the Bayeux–Arromanches road and advanced on Bayeux, also pushing elements on Vaux-sur-Aure. The 726th Grenadier Regiment (right), with remnants of the 915th Grenadier Regiment, planned to occupy the line Cristot–Chouain–Nonant–St-Martin, and with the 30th Mobile Brigade the line just west of Sommervieu–Vaux-sur-Aure–Aunay–just south of Tracy, besides launching elements of the 30th Mobile Brigade to attack the flank of the enemy advancing on Bayeux. In the 916th Grenadier Regiment (center) sector hard fighting continued until late in the evening. The 517th Battalion (30th Mobile Brigade) was to relieve the completely exhausted 2nd Battalion 916th Grenadier Regiment in the darkness. In the 914th Grenadier Regiment (left) there had been no change in the situation.

At around 2200 hours the 916th Grenadier Regiment (center) reported that the 352nd Pioneer Battalion, in the hand-to-hand fighting in Vierville, had taken from a fallen American officer an extensive order of the (American) V Army Corps.

Winding up Overall Picture
in the 352nd Infantry Division on 7 June after 2200 Hours

Enemy: On 7 June the enemy succeeded in a deep assault in the right, open flank of the 352nd Infantry Division. It was to be expected that the forces of the (British) XXX Army Corps, located just northeast and north of Bayeux, would launch a strong attack on Bayeux from the north or perhaps also from the southeast. This attack would be successful if the German forces did not manage to stop the enemy by a counterattack (30th Mobile Brigade) from Vaux-sur-Aure to the east. The attack of the (American) V Army Corps from the St-Laurent bridgehead toward the south was not fully successful because of our effective attacks at Colleville and Vierville. Though it was not possible to fling back the enemy toward the sea, at least we managed to thwart his probable intentions of attack on 7 June. We expected, however, a further reinforcing of the occupation of the St-Laurent bridgehead and the continuation of the attack on 8 June.

A landing of other new fighting forces in the Grandcamp area on 8 June was also not out of the question. The overall picture disclosed that on 7 June, in the 53-kilometer width of the 352nd Infantry Division sector, the enemy employed in attack or counterattack the bulk of four infantry divisions—29th, 1st and 2nd (American) and 50th (British)—with at least two tank battalions (80–100 tanks) with continuous naval artillery protection (equivalent to two artillery regiments approximately) and reinforced throughout the day by constant fighter-bomber activity on a narrower front.

By comparing a few figures the following picture was reached at the two focal points of the defense on the evening of 7 June, taking into consideration the losses of 6 June and the replacements:

On the German side	On the enemy side
Combat infantry: 4,800 men	10,000 men
Artillery: 20 guns and little ammunition	Approximately 100 heavy caliber guns and plenty of ammunition
Tanks 6	Approximately 100
Fighter-bombers 0	24 during the day with continuous relief

Even the best soldier must, as an individual, feel overpowered by such continuous, varied superiority. Another "weapon," determination, could, moreover, no longer remain unmentioned on the second invasion day.

Own troops; adjacent troops: In the right regimental sector (726th Grenadier Regiment), after the enemy had crossed the Caen–Bayeux road, penetration to the east and the north and continuation of the attack was possible—even perhaps an advance to the south. Between the 716th and the 352nd Infantry Divisions a gap had been created in width and depth that the 352nd Infantry Division was powerless to close with infantry forces. The remnants of the 915th Grenadier Regiment, reinforced by alert units and Fortress Pioneers, formed in the Tilly–Bayeux line only a thin screen. Whether the 30th Mobile Brigade would be able until the early morning hours of 8 June to prevent, by a counterattack from Vaux-sur-Aure eastward, the enemy from reaching his objective, Bayeux, remained uncertain, for this troop was unseasoned (recruits) and exhausted by a 90-kilometer march on bicycles (low-flying planes activity!). Another decisive factor for this frontal sector was that only two batteries of the 1352nd Heavy Artillery Battalion, with scant ammunition, were available. The activity of the Army coastal battery at Longues had been cut down by further bombing so that the enemy (British 50th Infantry Division) was able to reinforce his troops without difficulty.

In the central regimental sector (916th Grenadier Regiment) it had been possible to crush in the shoulders of the St-Laurent bridgehead, but because of the enemy's superiority in men and matériel (bulk of the American V Army Corps) the reinforced 916th Grenadier Regiment had suffered considerable losses and was severely weakened physically and morally. Counterattacks could not be continued on 8 June. Rommel's tactics—the annihilation of the enemy at sea, or his immediate repulse to the sea—could no longer be employed in the sector of the 352nd Infantry Division. The question was, rather, to strengthen the newly formed defensive front, with the objective of preventing a breakthrough to the south. Therefore, in addition to the 517th Battalion (30th Mobile Brigade), two field replacement training companies were put in march to Formigny and the 4th Company (specialists) of the Field Replacement Battalion placed at the disposal of the 1352nd Artillery Regiment to move the guns out of battery. In this sector only one heavy and two light batteries with scant ammunition represented the artillery, along with a few guns from untrained antiaircraft battalions. When personnel and matériel are compared it seems improbable that these troops were in a position to withstand a strong enemy attack on 8 June.

In the left regimental sector (914th Grenadier Division), the breakthrough by the enemy, who had been surrounded at Pointe du Hoc, necessitated the reinforcing of the front east of Grandcamp by additional elements of the 1st Battalion 914th Grenadier Regiment. The fight against the parachutists around Brévands had caused further casualties in the 2nd Battalion 914th Grenadier Regiment and had not brought the expected result. In this sector the 1st Battalion 1352nd Artillery Regiment and the 3rd Battalion 1716th Artillery Regiment fought with their depleted ammunition the important landings at Pouppeville and northward (709th Infantry Division, with which telephone communication no longer existed). There was no substantial report concerning the rearward combat area except the continuous activity of fighter-bombers.

When the division, toward 0900 hours, received the captured order from Vierville, the situation could be estimated in a much clearer way. In my opinion, this extensive operational order disclosed that the invasion plan was far beyond the scope of the American V Army Corps. I admit that I, along with my division commander, did not have time to study this operational order in detail. This order covered every minute item from D-Day to D+17 (as far as I can remember), and contained much data on organization, armament, assignment, tactical intentions, radio plans, etc. On a sketch map (small scale) it could be seen that the boundary line between the British XXX Army Corps and the American V Army Corps lay at Port-en-Bessin (British), then along the course of the Drôme. According to the time schedule of the enemy, the latter intended to build a bridgehead on D-Day at St-Laurent with the American V Army Corps (codename "Omaha"). On D+1 he wanted to have reached the line Isigny–Bayeux, and on D+3 the line St-Lô–Balleroy. In this plan the area of the 352nd Infantry Division was given out as St-Lô. Next to the organization the names of the regimental commanders and their adjutants were given; of the divisional HQ the enemy knew only the name of the military law inspector (last data was dated January 1944). After D+2 (or D+3) the American XIX Army Corps was to begin pushing the 30th Infantry Division between V Army Corps and VII Army Corps. It showed also that, in addition to the army tank battalions, the subsequent employment of the American 2nd Armored Division was also planned for. Moreover, it was assumed that the establishment of a strongpoint transshipment port (called "Mulberry A") had been provided.

I must say that never in my entire military life have I been so impressed as in that hour when I held in my hands the operational order of the American V Army Corps. I thought that with this captured order the German Seventh Army and Army Group B (Rommel) would reach a decision—*the* decision. (I learned later that this captured order first lay around for days at Seventh Army HQ and reached High Command only after a long time. Even then it did not get the consideration it deserved, or else I could not account for the "piecemeal" bringing up of the divisions from the Fifteenth Army Zone etc. in July and August. To a young general staff officer the impression was more and more as if in highest quarters it meant "looking, but not jumping.")

After 0100 hours on 8 June LXXXIV Army Corps was informed of the situation and was given a camouflaged verbal report by telephone of the most important data in the captured order of V Army Corps. The division pointed to the fact that, according to this order, captured during the fight and therefore holding no deception, the enemy was not concerned with the establishment of a bridgehead around Bayeux but that he intended to build a much greater bridgehead in that area and then, from the Carentan area, get possession of the Cotentin peninsula with its important port of Cherbourg. The envelopment of the front which had begun in the divisional sector from east to west was covered in this plan. Corps HQ was notified that, as a result of the manifold personnel and matériel superiority of the enemy, the 352nd Infantry Division on 8 June would not be in a position to:

1. close the wide gap to the 716th Infantry Division (right);
2. cover the right flank just east of Bayeux (Bayeux included);
3. hold up for any considerable time the expected attack of the enemy from its bridgehead of St-Laurent.

After discussing other questions of reinforcements and support, especially by the air force, and rejecting them, the commanding general demanded the continuation of the fight in the defensive with the objective of holding the positions at all costs. It was intended to move in the general direction of Bayeux with armored forces brought up from the south. This would lighten the load of the 352nd Infantry Division considerably, especially as additional forces under II Parachutist Corps were on the approach march.

Evaluation of the Combat Day (7 June)

Infantry, including reserve: Our infantry fought with unexcelled courage and endurance. The effectiveness of enemy weapons and the numerical superiority of the enemy resulted, however, on 7 June in a flagging fighting strength, especially in the unseasoned units—all the more as the need increased for a commander and subordinate commander, who had become casualties. The structure of the front, the unity, began to break up. The questions: "Where is the German Air Force?" and "When is retaliation going to begin?" were often heard.

It was possible, however, to make up, numerically, for the losses sustained by putting in line the 30th Mobile Brigade and two field companies. But these soldiers had no combat experience.

Artillery and antiaircraft: On the evening of 7 June the German artillery (1352nd Artillery Regiment) was really already done for; its 36 guns (instead of the 60 guns it had heretofore) lacked the ammunition needed to smash strong enemy attacks. The 1st Antiaircraft Regiment of the German Air Force could hardly be described as of full combat value and reliable, and because of unskillful camouflage suffered heavy losses through fighter-bombers.

Antitank defense guns: The 1352nd Assault Gun Battalion (6 assault guns) had become wiser through experience and helped to stem the enemy assault in the 726th Grenadier Regiment (right). Fifteen tanks and 25 motor vehicles was the total shot down or put out of action on 7 June.

Signal troops: Listening troops continued to intercept current radio talk of the enemy. As he radioed "in clear," it was possible this way to confirm or correct our own reports and on the other hand often and easily to recognize his intentions.

Supply units (road system): The Bussy supply depot (right) and the Army field dressing station of Bayeux were evacuated. There was a new allotment of ammunition. The evacuation of prisoners (about 300 men) was carried out smoothly. It must be mentioned here that the prisoners behaved very well and observed such silence that could hardly be credited by the German interrogation officer. They became talkative only when captured papers made it possible to present facts from the German side. Otherwise [there was] nothing special in the rear combat zone.

Headquarters (command): Command became more difficult after further break-downs of means of communication. The attack of the enemy air force on the known division CP made it imperative for the future that subordinates be in ignorance of the location of all CPs. It was ordered that message centers be organized to check orders and reports (also callers) and forward them to the CPs. These measures had proved satisfactory in the East.

Enemy: In the villages the infantry fought stubbornly and skillfully. In open terrain the impetus of the attack soon came to an end when the infantry met with strong German defense. Then infantry fighting was replaced by fighting with heavy weapons, with matériel.

Losses: Our own losses in personnel on 7 June were 1,000 men; they were replaced by the 30th Mobile Brigade.

21st Panzer Division, 7 June 1944

by Generalleutnant Edgar Feichtinger

The regrouping that had been started during the night was finished off. The 125th Panzer Grenadier Regiment Combat Team was involved in heavy fighting with the 6th British Airborne Division. Particular difficulties were attached to regrouping II Battalion 125th Panzer Grenadier Regiment, which, partly surrounded, had been fighting since the early hours of the morning. [The enemy] was trying to extend his bridgehead in order to gain the important heights near St-Honorine, while on the other hand Combat Team 125 was trying to narrow down this bridgehead. Already at this early date the enemy's superior weight in men and matériel became obvious. He was constantly being reinforced by sea and air, while the division did not have any reserves worth the name to call on, and those units that were arriving the High Command had to commit northwest of Caen. Already on 7 June the task of Combat Team 125 was not only to prevent the enemy from extending southward, but also to prevent him from penetrating into the Bavent Wood. In the meantime the elements that had landed from the air in the Troarn–Trouffréville–Sannerville area had assembled and threatened the rear and the right wing of Combat Team 125. In order to eliminate these enemy troops the division freed the Engineer Battalion less its first company, and this battalion, reinforced by a Panzer rifle company, succeeded in beating the enemy and thus removing the threat.

In the Blainville area of the Orne Valley, heavy fighting developed between II Battalion 192nd Panzer Grenadier Regiment and the British 3rd Infantry Division. The enemy succeeded several times in cutting off the battalion. By evening, however, it had become possible finally to reestablish contact through Blainville as well as through I Battalion 192 Panzer Grenadier Regiment in Hérouville, and bringing the battalion into the Colombelles–Hérouville area undamaged.

Due to the lack of infantry forces the changeover to the defensive was particularly difficult for the armored group. It had to defend a sector over 5 kilometers in width, for which it had only two Panzer Grenadier companies, one heavy Panzer Grenadier company and one engineer company. As the whole antitank battalion, with the exception of three guns, had been lost through its subordination to the static division on 6 June, but the enemy had already tried breaking through at Caen with tanks on 7 June, the two battalions of the 22nd Panzer Regiment had to be pitted into the defense somehow.

The whole day long it was difficult to cover the left wing of the division, as the 3rd Canadian Division was trying to envelop it, the 12th SS Division not having arrived yet.

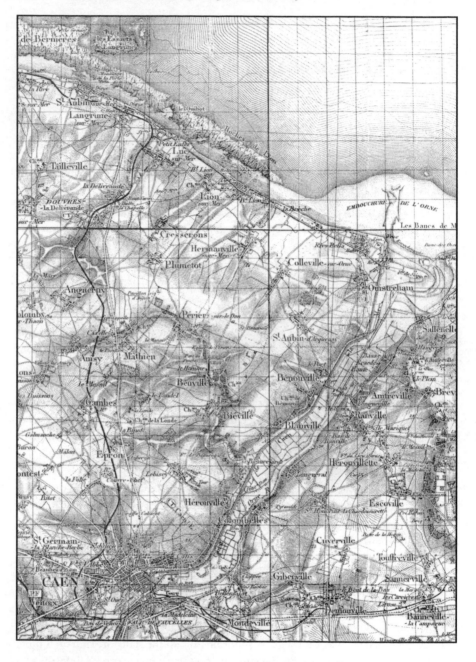

The area north of Caen

I SS Corps, to which the division had been subordinated since 2200 on 6 June, had ordered the 21st Panzer Division and the 12th SS Panzer Division to continue their attacks on 7 June with the objective of throwing the enemy into the sea. This attack was never launched, as only one regiment of the 12th SS succeeded in establishing connections with the 21st Panzer Division on 7 June, and that only at 1600 hours. For the attack the two divisions had planned that the 12th SS Division should advance along the Caen–Gazelle railroad with its right wing, and that the attack on Douvres and the coast should be carried out jointly, as soon as the right wing of the 12th met the left wing of the 21st. The moving up of the 12th was considerably delayed by enemy air activity.

By 7 June it had only succeeded in committing one Panzer Grenadier regiment and one Panzer battalion, which, when attempting to reach the left wing of the 21st Panzer Division via St-Contest–Buron, had already had to break through strong enemy resistance and were thus not in a position to launch another attack once they had reached the 21st Panzer Division's left wing north of Épron at 1600 hours. Quite apart from this, the artillery forces, let alone the air support necessary to an attack on such a scale, were lacking.

The divisional artillery of the 21st was in position. But on the previous day I Battalion of the 155 Panzer Artillery Regiment had lost two batteries while subordinated to the static division. Thus the division disposed only seven batteries for a 25-kilometer side sector of large-scale fighting. The batteries of the assault gun battalion with Combat Team 125 were, however, mainly used as replacements of artillery, just as the infantry heavy weapons companies, with six self-propelled heavy field howitzers apiece, were subordinated to the artillery. These moves proved valuable in later fighting. At that time there was as yet no artillery from the 12th SS Division in position.

On 7 June it was possible to shape the main line of resistance running through the Division into one line, to consolidate it, make adjustments and to put it in a state in which it would be able to repel large-scale energy attacks.

On 8 June the High Command issued orders to the effect that the division was to defend the now established main line of resistance. It was stressed repeatedly that Caen with its important road net must on no account fall into enemy hands.

The division held this position and remained there until 5 July. On 5 July the division was relieved by the 16th Air Forces Field Division.

The fighting until then was divided in four main phases:

8 until approximately 13 June: Strong enemy attacks against the western wing of the Division (Orne region south of Cambes) by the British 3rd Infantry Division, Canadian 3rd Division, one British armored division and one British armored brigade;

14 to 27 June: Throwing back of attacks east of the Orne and preventing enemy bridgehead from spreading. Support of counter-attacks in the Bavent Wood;

20 June to 3 July: supporting the divisions adjoining on the left (12th SS and Panzer
   Lehr Divisions) by handing over Panzer and Panzer Grenadier company;
2 to 5 July: building up of defenses east of Carpiget.

This list is only an approximate picture of how the center of gravity shifted from time
to time. In the remaining sector of the division heavy fighting continued without
interruption.

On 8 June, and during the period following, the armored group was attacked by
armored forces with air support after heavy artillery fire, with the main weight of the
attack at Lebuesy-Épron. Statements made by British prisoners and captured orders
revealed that the enemy was attempting to take Caen. The attacks were supported by
British special-purpose tanks. These had large-caliber guns capable of destroying
concrete to a depth of 1.5 meters—only at a short distance (approximately 100 meters),
however. About eighteen of these tanks were shot up and a fairly large number of their
crew were taken prisoner.

To judge by statements from the prisoners, the enemy had expected a fortified
defense system in this sector of the Atlantic Wall . . . [but the] defense system had not
been built in this area, excepting for defenses at the mouth of the Orne and a few
command-post bunkers. On the beaches it consisted of linear trenches with but a few
light turrets. There were no other defense fortifications; the other defensive weapons
and artillery were also in open field positions. The crews of these concrete-smashing
tanks had vainly endeavored to locate the Atlantic Wall and were shot up by the defensive
fire of the armored group. Due to the heavy artillery fire and the bombing, our own losses
were considerable during these defensive battles; they amounted to 50 percent of the
infantry forces and 25 percent of the tanks. To these losses must be added those incurred
on 6 June.

The supply problem was particularly difficult for the defense in this sector as British
heavy naval artillery kept the supply routes under fire far into the hinterland. The heavy
consumption of ammunition during the defensive fighting necessitated draining supplies to the utmost. After 12 June the ammunition dumps within reach of the supply
columns no longer had the most important types of ammunition in stock and these had
now to be collected in trips of several days' duration. Thus, in addition to the loss of
valuable transportation space due to fighter-bomber attacks, any regulated supply
stopped also, with the result that the artillery defense forces suffered many losses.

The division received no reinforcements of any kind. The air support which had been
promised by the High Command at the beginning of the invasion was lacking
completely. The division did not see any German planes whatsoever. In the I SS Corps
sector an antiaircraft brigade was committed to fight the enemy's strong air activity, but
it did not ease the situation much either. It only fired during large-scale enemy air attacks,
whereas the numerous fighter-bombers and enemy liaison planes, which could direct
their own artillery fire unmolested, were not fired at.

. . . The Combat Team 192nd Panzer Grenadier Regiment, together with II Battalion 192nd Panzer Grenadier Regiment, had to take over the area on both sides of the Orne as far as and including Hérouville, while I Battalion 192nd Panzer Grenadier Regiment took over the Bernsay area which had so far been occupied by I Battalion 125th Grenadier Regiment. . . . On 15 June the 22nd Panzer Regiment handed over one company to I Battalion 192nd Panzer Grenadier Regiment and two companies to Combat Team 125; with this move the defensive strength in tanks diminished still more. The loss was equalized by the addition of approximately eight 88mm antitank guns which had been reconditioned and were now deployed in the sector of the armored group . . .

711th Infantry Division Counterattack, 7 June

by Generalmajor Joseph Reichert

On the morning of 7 June the 744th Infantry Regiment reported that an enemy reconnaissance patrol had felt its way forward along the Varaville–Périers-en-Auge causeway through the flooded sector of the Dives as far as the Dives bridge near Périers-en-Auge. This was only possible if, in the meantime, the Varaville strongpoint of the 716th Infantry Division had been taken by the enemy.

As the carrying out of the attack, as ordered, against the Orne bridge depended on the possession of Varaville, the commander of the 744th Infantry Regiment was ordered to recapture Varaville with the Reserve Battalion of the regiment, which was once more placed under his command for this purpose. Thereupon a strong assault detachment was committed by the regiment to attack Varaville from Périers-en-Auge and advanced with two companies along the Cabourg–Varaville road. After a short fight the enemy, about one platoon strong, evacuated the Varaville strongpoint and withdrew in a westerly direction.

After the report had come in that Varaville had been cleared again of the enemy, I drove there with the regimental commander of the 346th Infantry Division and gave him detailed information about the assembly area. In the strongpoint, Varaville, a terrible confusion prevailed. There were parts of uniforms lying about, steel helmets, cooking utensils, ammunition and the like, but not one corpse of the former strongpoint garrison (a Russian platoon)—which very likely had been suddenly attacked while sleeping and had been taken prisoner or had gone over the enemy.

At about 1400 hours the first portions of the regiment of the 346th Infantry Division arrived. It might have been 1600 hours until the artillery had been emplaced and the moving into the assembly area had been concluded. Then the advance was made without encountering any enemy resistance at first. Slight resistance east of Bréville could be overcome in a relatively short time. In spite of strong enemy resistance, we also succeeded in penetrating into Bréville and in crossing the road leading from Bréville to the south. There, however, the attack bogged down in the enemy defensive fire. Likewise we did not succeed in approaching Amfreville under the fire of its garrison, which had very skillfully barricaded itself in the place, and the excellently directed artillery fire of the enemy. Moreover, our forces, which had penetrated into Bréville, were soon driven out of the village by a counterattack launched by British troops.

Simultaneously with the regiment of the 346th Infantry Division, the Reserve Battalion of the 744th Infantry Regiment had also advanced from the region west of

Cabourg, but was soon taken under fire from Franceville-Plage, where in the meantime British forces had pushed forward in order to take the coastal strongpoints located there from land. They did not succeed, however, in penetrating into any of these strongpoints; only one battery position near Merville had been taken by them. However, the artillerymen had barricaded themselves in the adjoining chambers of the gun pillboxes, taking with them the sighting devices and breeches of the gun barrels; apparently the enemy had no explosives available, because the guns were still intact when they fell into our hands once more during our present attack against Franceville-Plage and Merville. Later on, this battery was the only one, apart from parts of the Army coastal artillery, which was able to harass enemy operations near Ouistreham and west of it.

However, during these actions by the battalion much time was lost. By the evening, the attack carried only as far as Sallenelles, which soon after was recaptured by the enemy in a counterattack.

Although we succeeded on 7 June in penetrating deeply into the enemy bridgehead east of the Orne, the objective of our mission had not been achieved. On the other hand, the attack of the two battalions of the 346th Infantry Division had caused us heavy losses. A continuation of the attack on the following day without bringing up new forces, especially artillery, was out of the question. For the time being we could be glad to hold the lines gained.

This estimate was also reported to Corps, whereupon the bringing-up of an additional battalion and one artillery battalion of the 346th Infantry Division was promised.

In the meantime the Reserve Battalion of the 731st Infantry Regiment had combed the area searching for airborne troops and approximately an additional one hundred men were taken prisoner.

Commitment of Kampfgruppe Hartmann: 346th Infantry Division

by Oberst Paul Frank

During the evening of 6 June the division received orders from Corps to send a reinforced Kampfgruppe of regimental size to the 711th Infantry Division to clear up the situation east of the Orne. Under the command of Oberst Hartmann (857th Infantry Regiment) were collected a Fahrradbewegliches (composite) battalion from each regiment, a battalion of light artillery and a company of engineers. The Kampfgruppe was ferried across the Seine without the slightest opposition from French civilians or from the enemy air force. The crossings were effected at Quillebeuf, Caudebec, and Mailleraye.

At about noon on 7 June the Kampfgruppe was able to launch a counterattack in the vicinity of Varaville. The attack successfully cleared the area northwest of the town, to the mouth of the Orne, of British airborne troops. This eliminated the threat of an attack from the rear on the coastal defenses east of the Orne, which sector had as yet received no seaborne attacks.

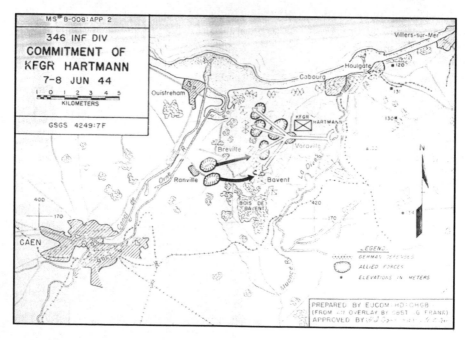

In the evening of 7 June, to facilitate the clearing of the rest of the territory east of the Orne (Bréville-Ranville area), Corps ordered the 346th Infantry Division to dispatch to Kampfgruppe Hartmann one additional infantry battalion and one artillery battalion. Division itself recommended the use of all its forces to guarantee the successful completion of the mission. Corps, however, overruled this plan as it considered such a massing of strength unnecessary in view of the enemy's apparent weakness east of the Orne. Also, still expecting the main enemy effort north of the Seine, Corps could not risk denuding the area east of Le Havre.

Kampfgruppe Hartmann's attack in the direction of Ranville did not succeed. It was able only to strengthen its own line of defense in the Bavent area.

Panzer Gruppe West Moves into Action

by General der Panzer Leo, Freiherr Geyr von Schweppenburg

On the morning of 7 June I was ordered to take over, with my staff, the sector on both sides of the Orne river up to Tilly-sur-Seulles. I moved out immediately. After reaching Argentan, two conditions became evident, both of primary importance to the movement of Panzer forces. Enemy air action had thoroughly and skillfully destroyed those points along the main arteries where the roads narrowed within the defiles of villages and towns. Owing to the road net and the terrain, it was difficult even in daylight to find a bypass, and then only with considerable delay. Furthermore, because of the increasing manpower shortage, military police or traffic regulation units were not attached to the higher staffs in sufficient numbers. The Ortskommendanturen (town or garrison headquarters) failed completely in the employment of similar units—a situation which seriously handicapped us.

The chain of command from Panzer Gruppe West up was most unfortunate. Panzer Gruppe West was still under Seventh Army. The decision to interpose another staff between Rommel and von Geyr may have been made by OB West because it was aware of the friendly relation between Panzer Gruppe West and the staff of Seventh Army—the latter acting as a "buffer state." At a moment when everything depended on rapid action, orders were issued to just two and three-quarters Panzer divisions by the following headquarters: I SS Panzer Corps, Panzer Gruppe West, Seventh Army at Le Mans, Army Group B, OB West, and OKW.

I SS Panzer Corps Concentrates for a Counterattack, 7 June

by Generalmajor Fritz Krämer

During the night of 6/7 June, we had not succeeded in clarifying the situation in the combat area of the 716th Infantry Division and that of its adjacent units on the right and left. Telephonic communication with Army was poor, we were not able to contact the adjacent Corps by phone. Some of the telephone lines had been interrupted by the bombing attacks. That night Corps dispatched liaison officers to adjacent Corps. Radio encoding and decoding charts were not delivered by Corps Signal Officer before afternoon on 7 June. A radio blackout was maintained by Corps to avoid detection by the enemy.

No contact had been established with the Panzer Lehr Division. Immediately upon arrival at the command post of the 21st Panzer Division, Corps dispatched an officer of the signal battalion with encoding and decoding charts for the Panzer Lehr Division to the bridge at Thury-Harcourt, where it was supposed elements of the division would pass. On 7 June, at about 0500 hours, the Chief of Staff found this officer dead on the road. The driver of a truck, passing in the darkness, had failed to see the officer or his motorcycle and had hit him. The intended speedy exchange of code charts had not taken place. The commander of the Panzer Lehr Division did not report to the corps command post until late in the afternoon of 7 June.

False reports spread rapidly during the march to the new command post and during the following day. According to these reports, Caen had been taken by the enemy, enemy tank spearheads were driving toward Falaise, etc. Individual soldiers and members of rear services of divisions committed at the coast, including railwaymen, Organization Todt, and ration supply workers, were caught while "retiring from the zone of danger." (Faint-hearted rabble who had grown unaccustomed to war during their stay in the west.) Corps immediately ordered that all approaches to Falaise be sealed off along the northern outskirts of the town and the so-called stragglers be detained there.

Although these were all "fright reports" and had been so evaluated, during the forenoon the Commanding General went to the command post of the 716th Infantry Division at the western outskirts of Caen to get information about the situation and to examine the terrain.

Even ignoring these false reports, Corps expected an attack of enemy motorized troops in conjunction with his air forces and airborne troops, at least as far as the Falaise–Argentan area. With the help of careful air observation the enemy was bound to notice that no considerable German forces were committed at the front and that the spearheads of German motorized troops were only approaching the combat area. Countless numbers of enemy airplanes were in the air during the night of 6/7 June and also early in the morning on 7 June. German military agencies could not judge whether or not they delivered correct and adequate reports on the situation. It may be that they were having more fun chasing German vehicles along the roads. This could be observed everywhere and it seemed the fighters were not the only ones which shared the sport.

It probably was extreme nervousness that caused the German High Command to let slip its opportunity for retaining for a few days the Panzer forces in the west, then committing them, together with all the air forces that could be made available, in an open battlefield after it had obtained an exact picture of the entire situation. By premature commitments in driblets, the Germans missed their opportunity to stake everything on one card—to lose or win all.

But the Allied High Command also failed to make the most of the situation. After their easy landing operations they should have followed up their advantage by driving ahead with all available manpower and material. The way to Paris and a chance to break apart and split the German formations in the west lay open to them. Of course, it is difficult to surpass objectives in a large-scale landing operation and to go beyond prepared timetables. But here it would have been worthwhile, and a surprise assault would have proved successful.

The "tactics of orders" (Befehlstaktik), outlined in the French General Staff precepts, proved a drawback here as they repeatedly did during the subsequent course of the war. Events proved that the German "tactics of military tasks" (Auftragstaktik) were decidedly superior.

In the forenoon of 7 June enemy attempts to widen the beachhead were repelled. Early in the afternoon the Commanding General returned from the 716th Infantry Division command post. His visit had confirmed his previous impression that this division no longer possessed any combat power. Those elements which had been committed in the advanced concrete shelters had been enveloped by the enemy; it was impossible for the division to relieve them with its own forces. The majority of the troops which had been hastily assembled and subordinated to the Battle Commandant and the Commandant of Caen Military Post were without substantial combat efficiency and lacked heavy weapons.

Except for the reconnaissance battalion and the tank-destroying battalion, all component parts of the 21st Panzer Division were committed on the left bank of the Orne. Thus the division was tied up and could not be employed as a compact divisional formation.

When the commander of the Panzer Lehr Division reported late in the afternoon, he brought word that his division still was on the approach march. Bombs had damaged the bridge at Thury-Harcourt and it had to be repaired and reinforced for tanks. It became apparent that the divisions could not complete their assembly before early on 8 June. The 12th SS Panzer Division reported that its formations without tanks would presumably reach the assembly area as ordered, during 7 June. The tanks of both of these divisions had to cover very long distances—for the most part on paved roads—and needed to halt for repairs and refuelling before being committed.

Contact had not been established with the corps to the left. We did not know the extent of the gap on our left or what forces were committed there.

Since the reconnaissance battalion of the 21st Panzer Division was still on the right bank of the Orne, Corps ordered the reconnaissance battalion of the 12th SS Panzer Division to reconnoiter this gap on the left and guard against a flanking attack from the direction of Bayeux. Intercepted enemy radio messages had informed us that there was a British beachhead near Caen and an American one near Bayeux.

During the afternoon of 7 June increased enemy pressure was perceptible on the front of the 21st Panzer Division. The enemy artillery fire became heavier and the effect of enemy naval gun fire of heavy calibers became noticeable. Reports from our artillery—particularly from the observation battery—indicated that the enemy naval guns were developing a drumfire barrage. Enemy air forces were active with a great number of fliers in the air, and their harassing made all movement in daylight hours extremely difficult.

We occasionally saw groups of the German Luftwaffe, comprising at most three airplanes. We could get no air reconnaissance report before late on 7 June. On that evening it became evident that there was a gap of from seven to ten kilometers between the 21st Panzer Division and the adjoining corps through which the enemy could push forward at any time.

The Commanding General decided to order an attack on the forenoon of 8 June, if necessary without the Panzer Lehr Division. The reasons which resulted in this decision were: strengthening of the enemy forces ahead of our front, the danger of an enemy drive through the gap separating the 21st Panzer Division from the adjacent corps, and the danger of enemy air attack on the 12th SS Panzer Division and the Panzer Lehr Division in their assembly areas. The choice of terrain was important. The maps showed that the coastal area was intersected by streams, some with high, steep banks. The terrain was covered with hedgerows which denied visibility to tanks. An attack on the enemy's flank, possibly from the area between Bretteville and Douvres, probably would have been most appropriate. The entire 21st Panzer Division was needed for such an attack but it was tied up at the front. The Panzer Lehr Division probably would not complete its approach march by early on 8 June. Only the 12th SS Panzer Division was available, and it did not seem to be an adequate force for a penetration. There was no other choice but to resort to an emergency solution.

This solution was presented in the following attack order, first given to the commanders verbally and later delivered in writing:

"The attack will be conducted with the 21st Panzer Division (on the right) and the 12th SS Panzer Division (on the left) along the Caen–Lion-sur-Mer road. The point of gravity to be on the left, where the bulk of the artillery will be employed. The Panzer Lehr Division will follow the attack echeloned rearward to the left in order to be able, depending on the situation, to bypass the 12th SS Panzer Division, swing to the left and attack the enemy flank, or, in the case of an enemy thrust through the known gap, to prevent a possible flanking attack against the 12th SS Panzer Division."

Operations of I SS Panzer Corps

by General der Panzer Leo, Freiherr Geyr von Schweppenburg

To the left rear of the 21st Panzer Division, I SS Panzer Corps and the 12th SS Panzer Division were advancing from the area south and southeast of Évreux, respectively, to the sector west of Caen. On 7 June the 12th SS Panzer Division, which had approached by way of Évrecy, was deployed between Caen and Brouay, west of Bretteville-l'Orgueilleuse. Behind this screen, the Panzer Lehr Division was assembling in the vicinity of Aunay-sur-Odon and by noon of 8 June had occupied the ground northeast and northwest of Tilly-sur-Seulles as a line of departure. At this time the Panzer Lehr Division was ready to carry out an attack in the direction of Brouay, near which the enemy was reported to be in force. For this operation it was necessary to pass through the lines of the 12th SS Panzer Division. Pending the arrival of Panzer Gruppe West, the staff of I SS Panzer Corps had, as of 0400 on 7 June, assumed command of the three Panzer divisions east of the boundary line of the 352nd Infantry Division. This boundary extended along the line Asnelles-sur-Mer–Fontenay-le-Pesnel–Aunay-sur-Odon.

The first action of the staff of I SS Panzer Corps should have been to ignore the confusion of contradictory orders, especially since no one in higher headquarters had the slightest conception of tank tactics, except perhaps Rommel and his chief of staff. However, Rommel had a knowledge based only on his experiences in desert fighting, but Normandy was not Africa. Moreover, because the enemy had acquired complete superiority in the air, Rommel had lost faith in the possibilities of mobile tank warfare.

The way was open to push to the coast, disregarding the flanks, with the combined 12th SS Panzer and Panzer Lehr Divisions. This attack was ordered by I SS Panzer Corps with Courseulles-sur-Mer as the common objective. It would have been sensible also to shift the 12th SS Panzer Division nearer to Caen and to strike north immediately with the 12th SS Panzer Division and elements of the 21st Panzer Division, assigning definite objectives to this group as well as to the Panzer Lehr Division. What actually happened was that Corps halted the Panzer Lehr Division, already prepared to attack abreast of the 12th SS Panzer Division, and began to maneuver in order to regain Bayeux. Meanwhile the 12th SS Panzer Division began to drift more to the northwest of Caen. This meant splitting the Corps and unclenching the fist ready to strike. It also meant further delay and the opening of a gap in the Bretteville-l'Orgueilleuse area, which the enemy was not slow to exploit on 10 June.

It it not known why I SS Panzer Corps wavered, but probably the divergent influence of higher staffs must share in the blame. If one has to pass final judgment on the conduct of this Corps, it should be stated that it had missed the psychological moment—and the bus. It was still possible in the morning of 8 June to deal the British a severe blow in the vicinity of Courseulles-sur-Mer. On 10 June enemy concentration along the entire beachhead had progressed so rapidly that the German forces were no longer permitted the same freedom of action as existed 48 hours earlier.

7 June: III Flak Corps
Moving up to Normandy

by General der Flak Wolfgang Pickert

The unit arrived in the area of Paris during the night of 6/7 June and on the morning of 7 June tanked up (with gasoline) and moved on again immediately. The regimental commanders, ordered out to the Commanding General in the region of Dreux, were here informed, on the morning of 7 June, of the next place to which they were to move— the area east of Falaise, in the camouflaged assembly areas of the wooded terrain there.

Immediately afterwards the Commanding General hurried on ahead, to take up contact with Panzer Gruppe West. This journey was repeatedly interrupted by attacks from low-flying planes. However, what made it (the journey) most difficult were several villages he had to pass through, which were completely wrecked by bombing, and entirely devoid of human life. Roads buried under piles of rubble, missing detours (alternative roads) etc. . . .

In Vimoutiers the Commanding General met Field Marshal Rommel, who informed him in more detail regarding the landing that had taken place and the intended German counterattack from the Caen area towards east of Bayeux, and urged the Corps to still greater hurry. Despite the heavy enemy air activity, it was to continue moving throughout the day, so as not to lose any time.

A few days previously, when I reported to him, Field Marshal Rommel had summarized to me his conception of the repulse of the invasion. He had said: "Unless we succeed in throwing the enemy back into the sea in 24 or, at the latest, in 48 hours, then the entire West will be lost to us." This statement made by the responsible OB West decided me to spur my men to the utmost dispatch, despite the continuous danger from low-flying planes.

Since the bridges over the Seine, downstream from Paris, were all known to be destroyed, the march had to be routed via Paris. Soon after leaving Paris we were forced to make the first detour owing to the fact that the road through the western part of Versailles had been closed after an air raid. The further journey of the Corps was extremely difficult and costly. On the way to Normandy, III AA Corps lost around 100 dead and 200 wounded, and about 100 vehicles. However, the first 35 enemy planes were also reported to have been shot down.

PART TWO

8 June, D+2

The Germans were still trying to follow through on the objectives of the previous day, but the Allied position was becoming stronger.

The advance of the US VII Corps towards cutting off the Contentin peninsula, moving from Utah Beach, was slowed, with the 4th Infantry Division checked in its advance on Montebourg. The advance of the US V Corps, from Omaha Beach, was also slow, but, with the help of elements of the newly arrived 2nd Armored Division, the planned D-Day objectives were finally occupied. As a result, both wings of the 352nd Infantry Division had to withdraw, despite Hitler's "stand fast" order.

The British and Canadians were able to make limited gains towards Caen, their own elusive D-Day objective. Despite German counterattacks, enough terrain was gained to give the British hope that as soon as the 7th Armored Division was ashore and ready to move, it could exploit the situation. However, while the German counterattacks against the British and Canadians on 8 June were limited in scope, they allowed I SS Panzer Corps, making skillful use of terrain, to set up a defensive position north of Caen that would not only defeat attempts at exploitation but endure for over a month.

D.C.I.

OKW War Diary: 8 June

by Major Percy E. Schramm

The third day (8 June) was again marked by the uninterrupted employment of the enemy's air force. It covered the combat area as far as the hinterland and thus neutralized our own Panzer attacks, put the staffs out of action and disrupted radio communications. The enemy thereby succeeded in reestablishing contact with the forces cut off to the east of the Orne and in merging the existing bridgeheads west of the mouth of the river into one single bridgehead, 60 kilometers long and 10–12 kilometers wide, leaving Bayeux in Allied and Caen in German hands.

LXXXIV Corps—Pushed Back on 8 June

by Oberstleutnant Friedrich von Criegern

On 8 June the enemy succeeded, as expected, in widening his beachheads and in landing new troops without being harassed at all. Enemy forces with tanks advanced from Bayeux along the Bayeux–St-Lô road toward the southwest and rolled up the coastal front until they were north of Isigny and in the rear of the islands of resistance still holding out. Thus a continuous beachhead developed from the Orne river to the mouth of the Vire river. Enemy forces pushed forward from the Colleville area to Trévières. The resistance by the 352nd Infantry Division could only be weak since a majority of the heavy weapons and the artillery had been built into the coastal positions and because the division had suffered severe losses during the engagements along the coast. Opposite the beachhead of Ste-Mère-Église, the troops which had been forced on the defensive more or less succeeded in preventing an extension of the beachhead. Only the 6th FS Regiment was thrown back on Carentan. The cessation of the battle and the withdrawal southward across the canal was carried out by the enemy with comparatively little interruption.

An operational order of the US V Army Corps captured on 7 June disclosed the enemy's intention. According to this order, the US VII Army Corps had landed on the east coast of Cotentin with two divisions of airborne troops ahead and two divisions from the sea. Its mission was to prevent, with the air-landed forces, the commitment of German reserves at the isthmus of the Cotentin peninsula and to protect the back of the division which landed afterwards and was attacking Cherbourg. In case the air-landed forces did not suffice, then an additional division, to be landed from the sea, was to pivot towards the south. For the capture of Cherbourg, newly landed forces were to be committed. V Army Corps, with two American and four British divisions, landed in the sector north of Bayeux with the mission to capture Bayeux and to establish and keep contact with VII Army Corps via Carentan.

As the first mission of the airborne forces and the US VII Army Corps had been prevented by the quick attack of the German reserves on the peninsula, it now could be assumed that enemy—in order to execute his mission—would break through the encirclement enveloping the beachhead at Ste-Mère-Église. The breakthrough was to take place towards the west and the north. It appeared possible for Corps to prevent this at least until the arrival of new forces. On the other hand, V Corps, which was only opposed by the badly battered 352nd Infantry Division, had almost accomplished its task without the German corps being able to make forces available for countermeasures.

54

8 June: 709th Infantry Division

by Generalleutant Karl Wilhelm von Schlieben

After an artillery and mortar preparation, the enemy renewed his attacks on the Ste-Mère-Église–Montebourg road. He was supported by tanks and air forces and threw back our forces on Émondeville. On this day, too, there was heavy fire from the enemy naval guns. That the enemy was prevented on this day from gaining considerable ground was due to the 456th and 457th Motorized Artillery Battalions under the command of Lieutenant Colonel Seidel and the 3rd Battalion of the 243rd Artillery Regiment under the command of Major Landgrebe.

On 8 June the large losses of officers were felt. Apart from many junior officers and non-commissioned officers, the machine gun commander of the 1058th Grenadier Regiment was missing. The commander of the 3rd Battalion 739th Grenadier Regiments, Major der Reserve Prof Dr Elbrecht, had been killed in action. The number of wounded and killed enlisted men was also increasing.

The lack of support on the right flank of the division could not be remedied by the means at the division's disposal. My intention to employ the 17th Machine Gun Battalion, a well-trained unit consisting of men from the younger age classes, could not be carried out because of orders given by higher headquarters. The corps commander did not wish to weaken the landward front of Cherbourg, which was insufficiently occupied, since another enemy air landing was thought possible in that area. In the evening of 8 June I learned from an operational order which had been found that the enemy planned to be in possession of Cherbourg six days after D-Day, i.e. 12 June. That was all the information given to me in connection with this order. The notes made by the Seventh Army in a record of telephone messages stated, as of 8 June, 0810 hours:

"Seventh Army High Command gives an abstract of the plan of operations of the American VII Corps. This shows the following commitments: Right: Amercan VII Corps with four divisions. Mission to attack northwards from the Carentan–Quineville beachhead and capture Cherbourg from inland."

8–10 June: Cotentin Coast Artillery

by Generalmajor Gerhard Triepel

Around 9 June two guns (Russian type, caliber 12.2cm) of the 6th Battery 1262nd Regiment, at Cateret, were employed in the region of Lestre, its front to the south. Simultaneously the 3rd Battery 1261st Regiment (French guns, caliber 15.5cm) was moved into position about 800 meters west of Bourg de Lestre with its front to the south. This battery acquitted itself well in the whole sector of Fresville as far as the coast.

The 5th Battery 1261st Regiment (French guns, caliber 10cm) removed its guns from the loopholes and emplaced them in its former firing position, with its front to the south cooperating with the defense against attacks in the sector of Montebourg–Quineville. The 6th Battery, too, changed its front line to the south and participated in the defensive fighting on the southern front.

Guns of the 4th, 5th and 9th Batteries were mounted on swivels before their loopholes. In these days, those guns had been removed from their swivels and mounted on gun carriages. Indeed, this was a difficult job, on which the weapon-training staff was working day and night while exposed to enemy fire.

The 4th and 9th Batteries were evacuated in order to reinforce the front line on the shore of Cherbourg, likewise the lighter type of guns allotted to the 7th Battery 1261st Regiment, with some of the men of the battery. Also evacuated to Cherbourg was the 4cm gun of the Naval Battery of Marcouf, which had been placed on a gun carriage near the castle of Fontenay.

Meanwhile, in the region of St-Martin-de-Varreville, the building of a landing bridge had just started. The 10th Battery 1261st Regiment (17cm guns, on mobile gun carriages) at Perbelle—with its long-range of fire (almost 30 kilometers)—was employed nearby against the landing bridge and transport ships. It could be perceived from the confusion which resulted that this battery had acquitted itself well. The observation for this fire had been given from the "Ginster Hill" regimental command post.

The 10th Battery 1261st Regiment met with great difficulties, caused by its prolonged firing; all anchorages of the gun carriage were pulled out from the earth and the guns thereafter could be moved into a new position only with the aid of prime movers. Only the two prime movers of the 456th and 457th Mobile Artillery Battalions were available. They were used by the 10th Battery every day. The change of position of the 3rd Battery 1261st Regiment had been accomplished with them also, as well as that of the 6th Battery 1262nd Regiment, from Cateret to Lestre.

8 June: 6th FS Regiment
Begins the Defense of Carentan

by Oberstleutnant Friedrich, Freiherr von der Heydte

In the early-morning hours of 8 June the positions of the 13th Company and the regimental command post were subjected to a heavy enemy barrage which lasted about thirty minutes and resulted in casualties.

At daybreak American assault detachments penetrated the sector of the Seventh Army reserve battalion and pressed forward as far as St-Côme-du-Mont. Again its defense line began to disintegrate. From the regimental command post it was possible to observe first individual soldiers and then whole groups retreating westward from St-Côme-du-Mont. The site of the battalion command post had also been changed and could not be located. Violent firing indicated that the elements of the 3rd Battalion committed east of St-Côme-du-Mont were engaged in heavy fighting.

In view of this situation, the regimental commander had no choice but to fall back behind the Douve Canal and conduct the defense of Carentan from there. He no longer had any reserves to close the gaps caused by the collapse of the Seventh Army reserve battalion, throw back the enemy troops who had broken through, or seal off the penetration. He issued the necessary orders to the regimental units fighting in the vicinity and to the two companies of the 3rd Battalion. Since radio contact with the 2nd Battalion had now also been disrupted, the order to withdraw was transmitted to the 1st Battalion as well as the 2nd Battalion but with no way of determining whether or not it was received. Neither battalion ever received this order. The 1st Battalion, as the regimental commander learned later, had been annihilated on 7 June, and the battalion commander had surrendered; only twenty-five men succeeded in making their way back to the regiment on 9 June through the marshy terrain along the Douve. The commander of the 2nd Battalion also tried in vain to establish contact with the regiment; when this failed, he decided on his own responsibility to break through to Carentan by piercing the lines of the Americans who were already in his rear.

It was not easy for the regimental elements committed at St-Côme-du-Mont to withdraw across the Douve. The majority of the men had to swim in order to reach the embankment of the Cherbourg–Carentan railroad line. The Americans apparently did not realize until later that this withdrawal was taking place; in any case, the widely scattered German paratroopers who were swimming across the Douve were subjected to but little fire, while the railroad embankment itself, which offered some cover, was not fired upon.

The regrouping of the elements which had crossed the Douve also took place without being affected by enemy action, so that it was possible for the 3rd Battalion to be moved into positions in broad daylight and in fairly good order on the southern bank of the Oure, a short distance from the northern edge of Carentan.

In the afternoon the 2nd Battalion, advancing over the railroad embankment, also reached Carentan without being subjected to serious enemy action. The regimental commander committed this battalion on the eastern edge of Carentan, the news having filtered through in the meantime that the Americans had entered Isigny (thirteen kilometers east of Carentan) and were advancing on Carentan from the east as well.

Up to the morning of 8 June, at least the regiment's non-commissioned officers and other enlisted men still hoped that it would be possible to drive back into the sea the Americans who had landed and to mop up the bridgehead north of the Vire estuary. After the withdrawal behind the Oure even the private soldier knew that the first battle of the invasion had been lost by the Germans. The morning of 8 June marked the beginning of the second catastrophic act of the drama in Normandy for the 6th FS Regiment—the battle for Carentan.

The Fighting on 8 June: 352nd Infantry Division

by Oberstleutant Fritz Ziegelmann

Progress of the Combat Day

At about 0200 hours the 726th Grenadier Regiment (right) reported that several enemy tanks had entered Bayeux on the Arromanches–Bayeux road, [that there was] street fighting in Bayeux, and that no communication was maintained with the security forces southeast of Bayeux. That meant that Sch. Brigade 30's counterattack in the direction of Vaux-sur-Aure could no longer be carried out. Orders were given to the 726th Grenadier Regiment (right) to throw the enemy out of Bayeux by using forces of Sch. Brigade 30 and then to form a defensive front eastern boundary–northeastern corner of Bayeux–course of the Aure up to Vaux-sur-Aure–Aunay–Asnelles. It was clear to the division that it was essential to withdraw the elements of Sch. Brigade 30 stationed east of Bayeux to Bayeux and north thereof in order to form a closed front.

At about 0500 hours the division learned through the radio message circuit [Rundspruchwelle] of the Commander-in-Chief West that the enemy planned to bombard the CP of the Supply Group of Staff Section [Qu. Abt.] of the 352nd Infantry Division near Cerisy. This bombardment, which took place at about 1100 hours, did not cause a loss in personnel, because the CP had been shifted and also because the French civilian population had been warned.

At about 0800 hours the picture was as follows. The 726th Grenadier Regiment (right) had not been successful in effecting an orderly withdrawal of the elements of Sch. Brigade 30 stationed east of Bayeux, in order to throw the originally weak enemy forces out of Bayeux. With elements of Sch. Brigade 30 which had been committed in the right wing sector, it was possible to occupy a new position south and southeast of Sully (CP of the 726th Grenadier Regiment) connecting with the defensive front west of Vaux-sur-Aure. Thereby, the enemy's attempt, which had to be anticipated, to make a thrust out of Bayeux toward the northwest and west, was to be prevented. In order to secure the roads leading from Bayeux toward the southwest, one antiaircraft combat unit [je 1 Flakkampftrupp] each, reinforced by one infantry combat platoon [je 1 Inf. Kampfzug] (remnants of the 352nd Replacement Training Battalion) [Felders Bn 352] was set in march to every Drôme crossing. However, owing to strong fighter-bomber activity, these elements reached their destinations only during the later afternoon hours. In the sector of the 916th Grenadier Regiment (center), after a brief, most powerful concentration fired by naval artillery against ground targets, and mortar formations, and supported by numerous tanks, the enemy had moved up for an attack directed from his beachhead simultaneously toward the east, the south, and the west. In the sector of the 914th Grenadier Regiment (left), a renewed attack east of Grandcamp had not yet materialized. However, this attack was anticipated. To be sure, during the fighting around Brévands about 80 parachutists had been taken prisoner so far. However, the enemy had succeeded in uniting both parachute groups just east of the bridge across the Carentan Canal and was holding this small bridgehead position with stubborn tenacity. Statements by prisoners showed that these parachutists, in their bridgehead position east of the Carentan Canal, had the mission to prevent an advance of the German forces across the canal into the beachhead of VII Army Corps [US VII Corps].

Until 1200 hours fighter-bomber activity of unheard-of intensity had developed, especially north of the line Bayeux–Trévières. There were no aircraft of our own in the air. The telephone network frequently could not be used for considerable periods of time. The division received its messages almost exclusively by radio. Later on, in the sector of the 726th Grenadier Regiment (right), southwest of Tracy, the enemy had broken through the flank main line of resistance and had entered Port-en-Bessin with tanks, withdrawn from the coast and disregarding the prepared positions [combat installations] there. A smaller enemy ranger group was repelled at the Longues strongpoint (2nd Battery 1260th Army Coast Artillery). In Port-en-Bessin there was heavy fighting during the noon hours. Another part of this ranger group had turned to the south at Port-en-Bessin. Just west of Bayeux smaller groups of parachutists and troop-carrying gliders had landed, which entered Bayeux from the west and advanced in force toward the north on Sully. Small groups of enemy armor were advancing from Bayeux in the direction of Port-en-Bessin. Weaker enemy groups held the roads leading south and southwest from Bayeux, occupied to about two kilometers from the city limits. Radio intercepts confirmed these reports. In the sector of the 916th Grenadier Regiment (center), enemy tanks had succeeded in breaking through the main line of resistance at the western boundary of Vierville and advancing on the Vierville–Grandcamp road. The prepared positions [combat installations] on the coast were not attacked. From the center of his beachhead the enemy had reached the northern limit of Formigny. Farther to the east the enemy had reached Surrain and was advancing southward. Other enemy forces succeeded in penetrating Ste-Honorine and pushing ahead with some elements farther to the east. In the sector of the 914th Grenadier Regiment (left) the enemy attacked the positions just east of Grandcamp but was repelled.

Based on these reports, an evaluation of the situation in the divisional CP showed that on D+2 the enemy had almost reached the objectives established for D+1 and that he would probably try to reach the objectives set for D+2 with his armored forces by the end of that day. Therefore, it was important to hold up the enemy throughout the day from positions held by German elements about noon, in order to make it possible to withdraw into a position more suitable for a weakened unit, south of the Aure and the Tortonne, at the beginning of darkness, while, furthermore, a bridgehead position east of Isigny was to be held. The division was aware of the fact that this decision, to withdraw before the enemy, was in contradiction with the Führer's order for the combat installations "Hold out to the last shot!" The Commanding General of LXXXIV Army Corps had given notice that he would be at the division CP at 1500 hours in order to accept the decision.

At about 1400 it was possible again . . . to communicate by telephone with the CP of the 726th Grenadier Regiment (right). The regimental commander reported that elements of the 30th Mobile Brigade [Sch. Brigade 30] had been pushed back out of Bayeux in a southwesterly direction. The mass of the 30th Mobile Brigade, including five assault guns, was fighting together with the regimental reserve for the regimental combat post, closed in from all sides. (Nearby combat noises could be heard clearly over the telephone.) The order was given to the regimental commander to resist doggedly with all forces, to break through toward the southwest at the beginning of darkness, and then to move into a "line of resistance" Agy–Ranchy–Hally (front toward the east)–south of Cottun–De Crousy–Blay. The order had to be transmitted in a sharp tone, because a weakening of this commander could clearly be discerned. In the sector of the 916th Grenadier Regiment (center) the enemy had crossed the Isigny–Bayeux highway to the south and was engaged in firefighting in Tessy, with the soldiers of the Artillery Regimental Staff [Artl. Rgt. Stab]. [There was] house-to-house fighting in the center of the village of Formigny. Elements of this Kampfgruppe were advancing west from Formigny (northwest corner) on Longueville. Consequently the sector of the 914th Grenadier Regiment (left) was given the order to reach Longueville with mobile elements and to hold that village. The mass of the 1st Battalion of the 914th Grenadier Regiment (reinforced by elements of the 621st Eastern Battalion) was speedily to reach the area around La Combe and to prevent, in a broad front, an enemy breakthrough which had to be anticipated.

When the Commanding General, General of Artillery Marcks, reached the divisional CP at about 1500 hours the situation was described to him. He was informed about the withdrawal order given to the sector of the 726th Grenadier Regiment (right) (radio and telephone communications with that sector were no longer possible) and the decision (see above) was submitted to him. It was especially pointed out to him that this decision was in contradiction with the Führer's order to hold all prepared positions and emplacements to the last shot. According to the division's opinion, this order by the Führer could no longer be enforced under the present circumstances. If it should be ordered, nevertheless, to hold out in the present emplacements "to the last shot," then on 9 June the enemy would have free passage to the south and the west in a very broad front. It even appears doubtful whether the 352d Infantry Division, in its very weakened condition as far as personnel and material were concerned, would be able to hold the proposed line of resistance (Aure–Tortonne), owing to the danger to its right flank on 9 June. After a long silence, the Commanding General agreed to the decision (proposal) of the division, with the additional instruction to continue to occupy the prepared positions on the beach (main line of resistance), and to interfere with enemy movements. Furthermore, he pointed out that this new position was to be held in order to ensure the success of our own armored attack on Bayeux from the south, planned for the morning of 9 June.

By about 1800 hours the sectors of the 916th Grenadier Regiment (center), the 914th Grenadier Regiment (left), the 1352nd Artillery Regiment, and all other troop units had received appropriate orders for 9 June.

At about 2200 hours the enemy had advanced in the sector of the 916th Grenadier Regiment (center) farther to the east, after reaching Mosles and bypassing Tour-en-Bessin. He had taken Tessy and had thrust ahead south from there. Our own forces had been pushed out of Formigny and, until nightfall, they were engaged in contact fighting with the advancing enemy on the Aure just north of Trévières and northwest thereof. These Aure bridges had been destroyed only slightly. In the sector of the 914th Grenadier Regiment (left) the enemy was stopped just east of La Combe. However, he achieved a breakthrough through the weak position south of La Combe, so that he could advance up to Osmanville. Renewed attacks just east of Grandcamp were repelled during the evening hours.

Final Survey for the Sector
of the 352nd Infantry Division on 8 June, 2200 hours

The enemy side: 8 June had resulted in considerable successes for the enemy. Besides taking possession of the city of Bayeux, he had succeeded in gaining control over almost one half of the sector of the 352nd Infantry Division (in breadth and depth). His objective for 9 June would be to cross the Aure valley, which was flooded but not deep. The advance for his 1st Infantry Division, committed in the left and following the Drôme creek, which flowed from north to south, would be easier than for his 2nd Infantry Division (center of the corps), which would be checked by the Aure and the Tortonne respectively. His 29th Infantry Division, committed in the right, might have succeeded, on 9 June, in capturing Isigny, which was situated in a valley, from the heights dominating the city on the east. It was not impossible that units of the 30th Infantry Division (XIX Army Corps) were already being moved up. It was not impossible, furthermore, that parts of the divisions committed in the area of the US V Army Corps would be assigned to mop up those prepared positions, which were still occupied, in the main line of resistance (beach).

Our own troops. Adjacent units: In the right sector (726th Grenadier Regiment) "confusion" had developed on both sides. Owing to the frequently prevailing numerical superiority of the enemy, it was impossible to count on combat units of this completely torn-up regiment on 9 June in the new "line of resistance." Unexpectedly, the commander of the 30th Mobile Brigade [Sch. Brigade 30] (Lieutenant Colonel von Aufcess) called by long-distance telephone at about 0000 hours and reported that he had pulled together about 500 stragglers near Ranchy. He was entrusted with the execution of the order given to the commander of the 726th Grenadier Regiment for 9 June and instructed to establish communication with the 4th Battalion of the 1352nd Artillery Regiment. Moreover, he was informed that, east of the Drôme, approximately along a line from St-Paul to the bridge just southeast of Agy, security forces (200 men—remnants of the 352nd Replacement Training Battalion [Felders Batallion 352]) were being committed, who were to establish communication with the armored forces which on 9 June would attack in a northerly direction toward Bayeux. Within the central sector (916th Grenadier Regiment) it had been possible to prevent the enemy from crossing the Aure. However, this day had caused the regiment heavy losses, that is to say, it was the first time that the number of our own missing men (prisoners) had to be defined as high. About 800 men were at the regiment's disposal for combat on 9 June. It was, however, reasonable to expect that an adroit grouping of these limited defense forces would make it very difficult for the enemy to cross the Aure. The realization was very unpleasant that the positions (front toward the north) which had been filled in months ago had to be built up again. In the left sector (914th Grenadier Regiment), the situation was definitely more serious.

Two points needed special attention. Firstly, it was imperative to succeed in leading the parts of the 1st Battalion 914th Grenadier Regiment as well as of the 1352nd Artillery Regiment, which were still fighting near Grandcamp, via Isigny to the south, whereby it was necessary to disable the guns of the immobile 3rd Battalion 1716th Artillery Regiment and to carry out all movements noiselessly and past the enemy, who was already standing east of Isigny. Secondly, the weakened 1st Battalion of the 914th Grenadier Regiment (including the 621st Eastern Battalion) had to prevent any enemy thrust and breakthrough on Isigny. The order was given to the 914th Grenadier Regiment to use the personnel unit [Personaleinheit] of the 3rd Battalion 1716th Artillery Regiment (about 300 men), which had lost its equipment, as reinforcement for the infantry forces of the 1st Battalion 914th Grenadier Regiment east of the Vire for this commitment, and the regiment was urged once more to hold the bridgehead east of Isigny by all means. In the final report of the day it was pointed out to the General Staff of LXXXIV Army Corps that the combat forces of the 352nd Infantry Division had considerably diminished during 8 June and that there existed the danger of an enemy breakthrough on both wings of the division on 9 June.

Synopsis of Evaluation of the Combat Day (8 June)

Obviously impressed by the operational order of the US V Army Corps, which had been captured on the previous day, and from which objectives and intentions could be deducted very clearly, by the evening of 8 June the conclusion had been reached that, beginning with that day, the 352nd Infantry Division could no longer be designated as a complete infantry division and that the enemy had been given the opportunity for "freedom of action." It was certain that the high number of casualties (about 2,000 men, including the crews of prepared positions) and the losses of material (among others 1½ light and one heavy battery disabled) would place the division in a situation on 9 June which cannot possibly be designated as "favorable." In the final analysis, it was due to the courage and the still prevailing endurance of the German infantry soldier that on 8 June it had been possible to prevent a breakthrough, especially to the south, despite the manifold superiority of the enemy in every respect. However, it was doubtful whether this same infantry soldier would hold up the more powerful enemy attack on 9 June.

As far as numbers were concerned, on 9 June there could be, in the right sector (30th Mobile Brigade [Sch. Brigade 30]), about 900 men (including Replacement Training Battalion [Felders Batallion] and eight heavy pieces of artillery [of the] Antiaircraft Combat Group [Flakkampftruppe]; in the central sector (916th Grenadier Regiment), about 800 men and six light pieces of artillery; in the left sector (914th Grenadier Regiment), about 1,000 men (including front to bridgehead Brévands) and twelve light pieces of artillery.

In a statement of this kind, which had to be repeated every night, any comparison with enemy numbers became superfluous.

As far as I can recall, enemy losses of material on 8 June amounted to approximately: ten tanks and 20 motor vehicles.

The command of the division was considerably aided by listening in to enemy radio traffic by means of the intercept unit.

The 711th Infantry Division on 8 June

by Generalleutnant Joseph Riechert

The night of 7 June passed without any special events. On 8 June, at about 1100 hours, I had reached the command post of the regiment of the 346th Infantry Division—Varaville—where the newly brought up infantry battalion, its vehicles still standing on the road, had arrived a short time ago, when four fighter-bombers attacked with bombs and aircraft armaments. At the time of the second air attack the necessary dispersal, which otherwise would have required a considerable effort of voice, had already been achieved by itself. The actual success of the air attack was not large. It caused a few being wounded, a few dead horses and two burned-out ammunition trucks, but for the inexperienced battalion this had been quite a shock. I can no longer remember where the battalion was employed at that time, whether for closing the gap near Gonneville or in the direction of Bavent, where parts of the Russian battalion of the 716th Division were said to be still holding their position. In any case, the battalion was not involved in any serious engagement on that day. The new artillery battalion arrived considerably later. At any rate, we had now at least sufficient forces for holding the line gained.

On the evening of 8 June the commander of the 346th Infantry Division arrived, and informed me that on the night of 8 June he was going to cross the Seine with all the remaining portions of his division and that he had been ordered to eliminate the enemy bridgehead east of the Orne, with his division and the subordinated portions of the 21st Panzer Division, which had tried to wipe out this bridgehead from the south.

Thus the portions of the 346 Infantry Division which had hitherto been subordinated to the division were placed again under the command of their own division, after having subordinated—according to the orders from Corps—the reserve battalion of the 744th Infantry Regiment, which together with an artillery battalion of the 346th Infantry Division had been employed to attack the enemy-held Orne bridgehead from Sallenelles from the north.

8 June: I SS Panzer Corps Counterattacks

by Generalmajor Fritz Krämer

The attack was launched on 8 June at about 1000 hours. Only about one Kampfgruppe of the Panzer Lehr Division started, as the remaining components of the division did not have sufficient fuel. Some of the elements of the 21st Panzer Division were engaged in defense and could not be withdrawn, and it attained only meagre success. The 12th SS Panzer Division advanced well in the beginning, but was pinned down by heavy enemy artillery fire—particularly fire from heavy naval guns. By evening it had reached the line Orne–Blainville–five kilometers south of Creully, a line which was held for many weeks in spite of the heaviest enemy attacks. As a result the roads leading from Caen to the north and northwest were in German hands and were blocked to the enemy.

On the first day of the attack the 21st Panzer Division and 12th SS Panzer Division suffered heavy losses of material and men. But by this attack we were able to clarify, in broad lines, the enemy situation before our front and define the extent of his beachhead. The depth of this beachhead was from 10 to 15 kilometers. The Panzer Lehr Division was ordered to establish and maintain under all circumstances a link with the left neighboring corps.

As had been expected, the Luftwaffe did not support the attack. The enemy air forces, particularly the fighter airplanes, were so numerous that they frequently intervened in ground combat and gave chase to individual German soldiers. If our men did not retreat under these attacks, it was due to the will to fight and excellent discipline still possessed by the German soldiers at that time.

Even late on 8 June telephonic communication had not been established with the Seventh Army and all reports were submitted by radio. OKH had directed that radio messages be encoded twice with different code charts, and this procedure made great demands on our time. Telephonic connection with divisions and Corps artillery was excellent. Therefore Corps was always able to exert influence on its divisions.

On the night of 8/9 June Corps received a mutilated radio message from Seventh Army, from which we gathered that I SS Panzer Corps was to carry out a large attack toward Bayeux. Obviously, the Army still counted on the infantry divisions at least being intact, as otherwise this radio message was incomprehensible. How could I SS Panzer Corps carry out an attack, when the divisions themselves were tied up along a broad front? Evidently, it was only possible to assemble armored combat groups within the framework of these divisions in order to conduct attacks with limited objectives.

8 June: 21st Panzer Division on the Defensive in the Orne Region South of Cambes

by Generalleutnant Edgar Feuchtinger

On 8 June and during the period following, the armored group was attacked by armored forces with air support after heavy artillery fire, with the main weight of the attack at Lebussy–Épron. Statements made by British prisoners and captured orders revealed that the enemy was attempting to take Caen.

The attacks were supported by British special-purpose tanks. These had large-caliber guns capable of destroying concrete to a depth of 1.5 meters, only at a short distance (approximately 100 meters) however. About eighteen of these tanks were shot up and a fairly large number of their crew were taken prisoner. To judge by statements from the prisoners, the enemy had expected a fortified defense system in this sector of the Atlantic Wall. Also, practically no coastal defences had yet been built in this area, except for defenses at the south of the Orne and a few command post bunkers. On the beaches it consisted of linear trenches with but a few light turrets. There were no other defense fortifications; the other defensive weapons and artillery were also in open field positions. The crews of these concrete-smashing tanks had vainly endeavored to locate the Atlantic Wall and were shot up by the defensive fire of the armored group.

Due to the heavy artillery fire and the bombing, our own losses were considerable during these defensive battles; they amounted to 50 percent of the infantry forces, and 25 percent of the tanks. To these losses must be added those incurred on 6 June. The supply problem was particularly difficult for the defense in this sector as British heavy naval artillery kept the supply routes under fire far into the hinterland. The heavy consumption of ammunition during the defensive fighting necessitated draining supplies to the utmost.

The Gap at Caumont

by General der Panzertruppen Heinrich, Freiherr von Lüttwitz

A comparison of the Allied movements along the boundary between the American and British ground forces on the one side and the German movements in this area on the other side reveals the surprising fact that here the Allies failed to make the most of an opportunity, the exploitation of which could have substantially influenced the entire course of operations in northern France—which could have been cut short, thus resulting in fewer casualties.

Without going into details about the first few days, it can nevertheless be stated that during the night of 7 June the British 50th Infantry Division took Bayeux, while during the course of 8 June the American 1st Infantry Division crossed the Aure and captured Tour-en-Bessin and Le Coudrai on the Bayeux–Isigny road. Our coast defense line was thereby broken and the way to the south was clear for the enemy. The mopping-up of the pockets of resistance, which had still remained here and there in the conquered territory, could not become the main task of these advance troops, but had to be left to the divisions which followed. Instead, the advance divisions had to exploit their victory and the American and British flanking divisions vigorously pushed southward in a joint operation. Enemy air superiority made sufficient aid possible and, above all, permitted reconnaissance operations in the area south of Bayeux, which had ascertained that hardly any of our troops were left there. Actually, they were only small, isolated pockets of resistance whose troops had built up some local supply dumps.

Although the German High Command soon recognized the danger which was developing here, no reserves worth mentioning were available with which this danger could effectively be met. Motorized divisions which could have been inserted in this area were stationed at the Somme, in central France, in southern France and in the Bretagne. The bringing up of these reserves would have taken days, and due to heavy enemy air activities it was extremely uncertain when they would arrive. Likewise, it was indefinite what their fighting strength would be.

In any event, these divisions were immediately alerted and started off. The first division (Panzer Lehr Division), during its advance, suffered very heavy casualties through all sorts of enemy air forces. After its arrival, it had to be employed for the securing of the left wing of the Army employed at Caen and was, therefore, no longer available for service at the actual gap. The remaining divisions were not expected to arrive before 12 to 14 June. In this emergency, the High Command sent a reconnaissance battalion of the 17th SS Panzer Division into the area south of Bayeux, which seemingly did succeed in completely deceiving the enemy as to the actual situation.

How easily the gap at Caumont could have become a bridge into the depth of our rear area! Instead, the British at Caen and, later, the Americans at St-Lô dug in in positions which were favourable for our defense.

Instead of diverting those forces of the British or American army groups located on the inside wing, either to the west or to the east, they could quite easily have moved straight ahead to the south under a combined command, either that of the British 30th or that of the American 5th Corps. It would have been quite easy to immediately overcome the resistance at this point, which consisted of practically nothing but one reconnaissance battalion stationed in the area between Tilly and Bérigny (about 25 kilometers). On 8 or 9 June, and without having to meet any resistance worth mentioning, the Allied forces would have been able to cross the road from Tilly to Balleroy; they could have captured Commont [sic] during the night of 9 June, and on 10 or 11 June could have occupied the heights at the Bois du Homme; on 12 June at the earliest, and perhaps even not before Le Bény Bocage, they would have encountered the first fit portions of the 2nd Panzer Division. The Allies could thereby have established a pivot from which they could have substantially speeded up the course of events and influenced same entirely in their favor. With the exception of the above-mentioned reconnaissance battalion, only weak portions of the Panzer Lehr Division would have been able, in case of emergency, to resist this push. However, at the most, they would have had to confine themselves to blocking the eastward advance of the enemy, while at the western flank and in the south there would have been—up to 12 June—no German forces worth mentioning.

If, instead of remaining in the area of Caen or St-Lô, the Allied forces could have been brought up to the resulting wedge, it would later have been impossible for any German command to crush same. However, because of the unequal proportion of forces, it could have been widened by the Allies without any trouble. This was later proven by a similar case in Holland.

Even the bringing up of our motorized reserves (2nd Panzer Division, 3rd Fallschirmjäger Division and 17th SS Panzer Division) could not have affected this outcome in any way, because:

1. A unified employment of these divisions would never have taken place. The German Command had been compelled to employ these troops—in some cases even precipitately—as soon as they arrived, for the immediate strengthening of front lines which were already shaky. These commitments took place at various sectors, each of which was located quite far from the other.

2. The heights of the hills and their wooded nature made unified employment of our armored forces impossible.

3. Allied air superiority would have quickly crushed any concentrated employment of German forces (see counterattack at Avranches).

Such a thrust into the depth and widening of this wedge would have given the Allies every chance. From there, they could later have advanced eastward, in order to cut off our troops stationed at Caen from their lines of communication, and then could have annihilated those coming from the south. A westward attack would have been still more effective and, I suppose one can say, would have been of decisive importance for the outcome of the campaign. First of all, it would have cut off the entire German forces still stationed west of the wedge from their lines of supply, then they could have been attacked from the rear, pushed towards the sea and encircled and annihilated to such a degree that it would have been impossible for our soldiers to escape in great numbers, as happened later at Falaise, where the pincer attack was launched from the west and, therefore, the weakest point was located at the eastern edge of the encircled area. Our troops would have been surrounded—in the west and in the north by the ocean and in the east and south by the Allies.

A decision to launch such a thrust along the boundary would have required the following:

1. Coordination of the British and American wing forces, which probably did not exist at that time. As examples have proven later, such cooperation was generally an exception on the battlefield.
2. A correct estimate of the German forces, their mobility and their reserves. Although circumstances were favorable and air reconnaissance and collaboration with the civil population were functioning, the active exploitation of these prerequisites was not sufficiently assured.

Comments by General der Panzer
Leo, Freiherr Geyr von Schweppenburg

General H. von Lüttwitz, who has a good record as a fighting soldier, has not had in his previous military career a special education to enable him to give an estimate on operations on a larger scale, especially of the amphibious type.

In passing a judgment on the merits of military leadership one has to keep clear of critics resulting from knowledge after the event.

Apparently the author has never had the opportunity for scientific studies of difficulties arising from fighting shoulder to shoulder with allies.

The Anglo-American leadership was fully entitled to suppose competent leadership on the German side and could never expect the actual situation in this regard. The German Panzer divisions might be expected to be fresh and thoroughly trained, as indeed they were.

If a combined force, consisting of V US and XXX British Army Corps, could have been rushed forward, containing not more than 1–2 Panzer divisions, and could have reached Le Bény Bocage on 12 June, Panzer Gruppe West would have welcomed such a situation. Supposing, of course, that this body was given a free hand.

Since the British could not be expected to pass to aggression on the whole extent of their front line at this date, the instantaneous reaction of Panzer Gruppe West, of which I happened to be in command, would have been to cover the right flank by the 21st Panzer Division less its tank regiment, the reconnaissance battalions of the 12th SS and the Panzer Lehr Divisions, supported by the bulk of their respesctive artillery regiments, and to strike by night attack outside the range of the enemy's shipborne artillery in the general direction of Balleroy, crossing the line La Bolle Épine–Caumont.

This is not ex-post wisecracking. When this sort of Anglo-Saxon notion and breakthrough seemed impending on the evening of 10 June, owing to erroneous messages coming in at HQ Panzer Gruppe West, this body at once decided to drop the orders for an attack towards the north. The British methodical way and slowness would have justified the risk of this sort of action, which, hitting the left flank of the breakthrough forces with two Panzer divisions and a third tank regiment, might have secured a temporary success and delay. This was the conception, when the staff of Panzer Gruppe West was annihilated by enemy air action.

The comparison of General Lüttwitz about situations at Avranches or later in Holland are far from being convincing. In either case the German Panzer divisions were entirely worn out in men and material.

The critic must therefore disagree with the proffered suggestions.

PART THREE

9 June, D+3

The fighting on 9 June was in many ways a continuation of that on the day before, but it also meant that the Germans' first potential chance for the long-planned massive counterattack passed. In the British sector, an initial attack by Panzer Gruppe West— Panzer Lehr Division leading—was repulsed in inconclusive fighting.

The fall of Isigny to troops advancing from Omaha Beach on 9 June prevented the 352nd Division from opening up the road to St-Lô, but US hopes that one more push from the leading divisions that had come ashore on D-Day would press on to hold were soon dashed by the German defeat of the lead battalion of the 29th Division's 115th Infantry Regiment.

West of Utah Beach the 82nd Airborne pushed aside the 91st Luftlande Division and seized a bridgehead over the Meredet river that allowed it to link up with some of its forces isolated since D-Day. The town of Carentan was also defended against US advances.

D.C.I.

OKW War Diary, 9 June

by Major Percy E. Schramm

On 9 June the battle surged back and forth without creating a new important factor. The British and American troops were still as yet separated; but the Americans enlarged their sector at the Vire, and pushed their front toward the west in the bridgehead at Carentan (at the bottom of the peninsula); the enemy employed tanks in the north, creating an obscure and possibly dangerous situation for Cherbourg. In order to intercept the Americans on their way to this area, the 77th Infantry Division was brought up in a race with the enemy.

In order to support our forces, reinforcements were brought up from the west and from Germany—especially, however, the Group of General der Flieger Meindl from the southwest. It became clear at this time that these forces would not suffice to throw the enemy into the sea. After having been informed by Chief West, the Führer issued an order on 9 June for the assignment of the following units, which previously had been employed in southern France, to assist in mopping-up operations: 2nd Panzer Division; 2nd SS Panzer Division; 1st Panzer Regiment 116th Panzer Division; two infantry divisions from the area of Army Group B; Werfer Brigade 8; and general headquarters troops, especially heavy artillery and Panzerjäger. In addition, a study was to be made to ascertain what further troops were available in case of a crisis. Since a report had been received stating that the enemy intended a landing in Belgium, the 1st SS Panzer Division was transferred behind the 48th Division as reserve since this area had been stripped as a result of the withdrawal of the 19th Lw Sturm Division.

During the late afternoon OB West was instructed to move all available supplies into the Cherbourg fortress, such as cattle and ammunition, for which a great need existed.

LXXXIV Corps Front
Threatened with Collapse, 9 June

by Oberstleutnant Friedrich von Criegern

The fighting on 9 June confirmed our fear that, without committing new forces, it was not possible to prevent a union of the enemy corps at the mouth of the Vire river.

At dawn the enemy penetrated into Isigny and advanced with armored reconnaissance troops towards the south beyond Lison. In the coastal position from Isigny to Carentan there were only weak elements of the 352nd Infantry Division as well as one Eastern battalion, whose fighting power was very doubtful. In addition we were threatened by the collapse of the front arc which was formed by remnants of the 352nd Infantry Division and the 30th Mobile Brigade between the road from Bayeux to St-Lô and Isigny.

In this situation, the commanding general stated his intentions at 1030 hours: withdrawal of all elements fighting east of the Vire river and reestablishment of a new front line behind the Vire river, with the mission to prevent an enemy crossing of the Vire river towards the west. Thus the mission of the corps would be to remove the beachhead of Ste-Mère-Église by concentrating all forces and by employing the 77th Infantry Division, which had to be brought forward to Corps. A gap east of St-Lô could have been accepted, provided the approaching II FS Corps together with I SS Panzer Corps went into action in a coordinated attack at a later juncture. The Commanding General saw no danger in this solution, as it was to be expected that the enemy would primarily carry out his tasks as known to us from the captured order before advancing with strong forces towards the south. He pointed out that it was only possible to remove the beachheads one by one, and that success near Ste-Mère-Église could yet be possible by bringing forward relatively small reinforcements.

General Marcks proposed that the command should be organized in such a manner that LXXXIV Infantry Corps would conduct only the battle on the peninsula. Thus II FS Corps was to be assigned to Panzer Army West. The Army agreed with the bringing forward of the 77th Infantry Division to Valognes but turned down the plan to withdraw the remnants of the 352nd Infantry Division to the Vire river.

During the day the enemy widened his beachhead at Ste-Mère-Église by attacking towards the north and the west, and succeeded in making a deep penetration in the direction of Montebourg and in the direction of Pont-l'Abbé. By evening he reached the Quineville–Montebourg road east of Montebourg and in a thrust towards the west he also reached the area directly east of Pont-l'Abbé. As expected, the troops fighting there had become too weak to be able to stop the continuously reinforced enemy after the failure of our own attacks. Therefore Corps asked for permission to transfer the two battalions (one regiment of the 243rd Infantry Division) which had been committed in the land front line of Cherbourg to the front line of Montebourg, since this would decide the fate of Cherbourg. If the enemy succeeded in breaking through near Montebourg, then one could not expect to hold Cherbourg for long period of time, considering the weak defensive state of the land front line.

In the evening Corps ordered that the commander of the 243rd Infantry Division assume command over the troops engaged around Ste-Mère-Église as Kampfgruppe Hellmich (709th Infantry Division, 243rd Infantry Division and elements of the 91st Infantry Division), because it was impossible to conduct the various tasks of the Corps—front line direction Bayeux and battles on the peninsula—from one single command post.

The Commanding General reported the tactical situation to the CG of Seventh Army, who was present at the Corps command post during the night of 9/10 June, and stated that he considered 10 June as the decisive day in the battle for Cherbourg. He urgently requested support by the Luftwaffe and the bringing forward of antitank weapons.

Comments by Generalleutnant Max Pemsel

Gen Marcks' suggestion to withdraw his right wing behind the Vire during the forenoon of 9 June came as a complete surprise to Seventh Army. The timely arrival of II SS Panzer Army Corps was an indispensable prerequisite for the execution of that plan.

Seventh Army opposed the plan emphatically because, fighting with its back to the sea, LXXXIV Army Corps' situation was bound to become hopeless very soon. The danger existed that a gap would be created in the center of Seventh Army's line.

9 June: 709th Infantry Division

by Generalleutnant Karl Wilhelm von Schlieben

On 9 June the enemy continued his attacks, supporting them with strong attacks from the air against batteries, positions, and communication routes. His naval artillery continued firing unopposed. As the Marcouf battery had already been silenced on 5 June, there were no German coastal batteries on the east coast with sufficient range to fight the enemy warships. Since the latter were not molested by the German Luftwaffe either, they were able to work undisturbed. Therefore, if the enemy was able to advance to Émondeville and Fontenay-sur-Mer, it was not because of his superior infantry and land-artillery forces, but because he employed tanks, air forces, and the navy—three elements in which the desperately struggling units of the 709th Infantry Division were totally lacking.

Late in the evening of 9 June, two battalions committed in the landward front of Cherbourg—the 2nd Battalion 921st Grenadier Regiment and the 1st Battalion 922nd Regiment of the 243rd Infantry Division—were detached from this front and moved in the direction of Montebourg. I had already filed an application for their release and employment at Montebourg a short time after the start of the invasion, but this was granted only later. The corps commander, General der Artillerie Marcks, who was later killed in action, said that Cherbourg was defended at Montebourg. This opinion and the early discernible pressure of the enemy in the direction of Montebourg prompted me to ask for a weakening of the landward front of Cherbourg in favor of the combat area around Montebourg. The restrictions imposed even on the higher command agencies in making independent decisions are shown through the fact that neither the corps commander nor the High Command of the Seventh Army could shift one of the two above-mentioned battalions. The first staff officer of the High Command of the Seventh Army made the following note about this:

"9 June, 1715 hours.
"... On account of this situation [the situation at Montebourg] General Marcks asks permission to commit the two battalions of the landward front of Cherbourg at the front south of Montebourg. The C-in-C grants the request."

Another note on a discussion with Feldmarschall Rommel on 9 June at 1730 hours at Army headquarters ran as follows. At this discussion the Chief of Staff of the High

Command of the Seventh Army expressed himself greatly concerned about further enemy air landings to capture Cherbourg. The following note was made on 9 June at 1730 hours:

"The Chief of Staff of Seventh Army explains that, owing to the increasing resistance of our troops south of Montebourg, the enemy may make further air landings in this area in order to accelerate the capture of Cherbourg. Feldmarschall Rommel does

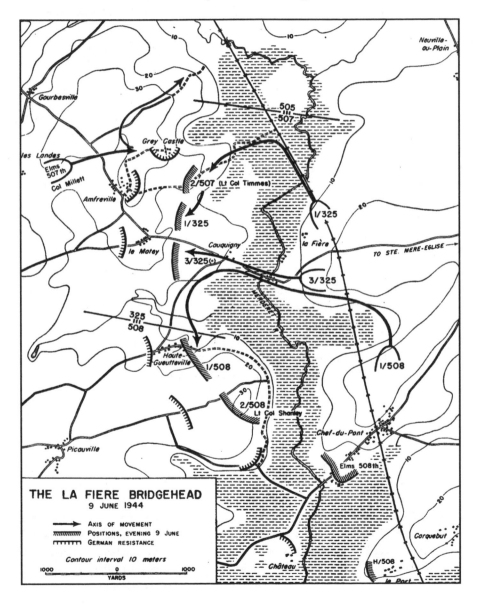

THE LA FIERE BRIDGEHEAD
9 JUNE 1944

AXIS OF MOVEMENT
POSITIONS, EVENING 9 JUNE
GERMAN RESISTANCE

Contour interval 10 meters

not share the opinion of the Chief of Staff. OKW, however, assumes that the enemy will make a major landing on the Channel coast shortly. The enemy would, therefore, have no air landing troops to spare for the Cotentin operation."

The fact that the higher headquarters expected a major enemy landing within the next few days at another place on the coast is proof of the complete failure of our air reconnaissance.

That Feldmarschall Rommel considered it vital to increase the defensive power of Cherbourg will be seen from the following note made on 9 June at 1730 hours: "Everything available must be used to defend Cherbourg." However, according to the English translation of the War Diary of the German Seventh Army, the Feldmarschall said at this discussion: "Apart from this, all power must be exercised for the defense of Cherbourg."

How different did matters appear on 17 June, when by order of higher headquarters three divisions and the heavy motorized artillery battalions were withdrawn to the south, leaving the 709th Division, which had been bled white already at Montebourg, alone in the final combat for Cherbourg. During the evening of 9 June the enemy succeeded in reaching the Montebourg–Quineville road at some places. Montebourg itself, for command of which I had appointed Captain (Res) Simoneit of the 919th Grenadier Regiment, remained in our hands.

The repeated requests I made on 9 June to silence the heavy enemy naval artillery by our own Luftwaffe were supported by Corps headquarters and the Seventh Army, as proved by the War Diary of that Army. But the German Luftwaffe remained absent. The requests of the division to send armor-piercing weapons were likewise supported by higher headquarters, but no help could be given.

How heavy the fighting was on 9 June in the area of Montebourg may be seen from the notes in the War Diary of the Seventh Army giving the opinion of General der Artillerie Marcks: "The Commanding General of LXXXIV Corps is conscious of the gravity of the situation and believes that 10 June will decide the fate of the fortress of Cherbourg."

The division also feared a breakthrough by the enemy and the capture of Montebourg, which was of the greatest importance as a road junction and on account of the dominating heights north of it. When in the evening twenty of our pseudo-tanks (with 37mm guns, which had no force of penetration) on captured French chassis were assigned to me from the west coast, I decided on a ruse. I knew from my experience in Russia that the noise made by tanks is audible at a great distance and generally causes the opponent to get uneasy. Therefore, I ordered the twenty tanks to proceed under cover of darkness to Montebourg and dig in on the town's outer border. Whether this ruse had the desired effect I do not know. Montebourg at any rate remained in our hands until 18 June. The noisy approach of the obsolete tanks under cover of darkness had the further result of reassuring our own infantry, who were exposed without any protection to the strong fire of the enemy naval guns, air forces, and tanks. I overheard exclamations like "Thank God, the tanks are coming!" The infantrymen did not know that these vehicles were merely toys.

How eager the High Command of the Seventh Army was to aid the 709th Infantry Division, which was fighting hard in the Montebourg area, is indicated by the entry in their War Diary, reading as follows:

"Because of the situation in the combat area south of Montebourg, the Army High Command requests the immediate aid of II Air Corps, since the outcome of the battle of the heavily engaged troops between Montebourg and Marcouf depends upon the elimination of the naval support from east of Quineville. Since the enemy drive from the Ste-Mère-Église area has developed into a decisive battle for fortress Cherbourg, the Army High Command reports that the 77th Infantry Division has been ordered to march to Valognes to reinforce the defensive front there. The Army High Command proposes anew the immediate destruction of Cherbourg harbour."

11 June again brought hard fighting along the line Montebourg–Quineville. The enemy succeeding in penetrating near Quineville, supported by concentrated artillery fire, tanks, and naval gunfire.

9–13 June: Cotentin Coast Artillery

by Generalmajor Gerhard Triepel

On 9 or 10 June the 2nd Battery 1261st Regiment—in a well-built concrete position—was attacked from all sides by enemy tanks and flamethrowers and finally was lost after heavy fighting. Meanwhile an enormous amount of artillery had been disembarked; it was furnished with an astonishing quantity of ammunition. Concentration of fire, with its large consumption of ammunition, brought about an effect much more unpleasant than the fire delivered by heavy naval artillery. In spite of strong and heavy fire by land-based—and naval—artillery, all telephone connections held fast without exception so that the control of artillery was always sure until 12 June.

Next to the battery position, built of concrete, of the 1261st Naval Artillery Regiment on "Ginster Hill", west of Quineville, there was also the one of the infantry regiments (Commander Oberst Müller), which was defending the sector east of Montebourg as far as to the coast, making possible good cooperation between infantry and artillery.

The naval guns were able to fire away merrily—more or less as they pleased—being beyond the range of the German guns and assisted as they were by their own spotter planes. For hours, airplanes were maneuvering in circles above German batteries and so neutralizing their activity. A strong feeling of insecurity, caused by American parachutists, appeared behind the front. Only large-scale mopping-up operations of the infantry restored order. As a result of these operations, a considerable number of prisoners were brought in.

During the night of 12 June, the 3rd Battery 1261st Regiment changed its position from Lestre to the region north of Videcosville. Again, it was difficult to make available prime movers from the 456th and 457th Motorized Artillery Battalions.

About 13 June, as an emergency, guns of the 1st, 2nd and 10th Batteries of the 1709th Regiment were teamed with horses, and batteries employed under the HQ of the 3rd Battalion 1709th Regiment in the region of St-Germain-de-Tournebut.

On 13 June the regimental staff of the 1261st Coastal Artillery Regiment was withdrawn and took over the duties of the artillery commander at the 709th Infantry Division. The command post on "Ginster Hill" was taken over by the headquarters of a battalion of the Infantry Regiment (Commander Oberst Müller).

The front-line—facing the south—which the 709th Infantry Division had established, ran, on 13 June, from about Montebourg as far as Quineville. Until 17 June, this front had gradually been pressed back to the north.

9 June: 6th FS Regiment Defends Carentan

by Oberstleutnant Friedrich, Freiherr von der Heydte

During the night of 8 June elements of the 2nd Battalion were, for security reasons, moved eastward as far as the Carentan–Isigny/Carentan–St-Lô road fork, 3.5 kilometers east of Carentan. These elements were not withdrawn to the eastern edge of Carentan until the evening of 9 June. On 9 June reconnaissance patrols of the regiment pressed forward on a wide front as far as the Vire. The reconnaissance patrols of the regiment did not come across any German troops in position in the reconnoitered area. During 9 June elements of the 2nd Battalion of the 709th or 710th Infantry Regiment, which were committed at the Canal du Port de Carentan, moved back toward Carentan. Other troops, including an "Eastern battalion" [a battalion consisting of personnel from non-German territories in the East] under the command of a Major Becker, withdrew to Carentan from the Isigny area. On 9 June a reconnaissance patrol of the regiment blasted the railroad bridge across the Vire, four kilometers southwest of Isigny.

For the defense of Carentan, which separated the two Allied bridgeheads south and north of the Vire estuary, the corps attached to the regiment (which still remained under its direct control) two Eastern battalions composed of Russians and the remnants of the Seventh Army reserve units from the Isigny area. The combat efficiency of these units was limited. In view of the fact that the main attack on Carentan was to be expected from the north, these units, which did not belong to the regiment, were for the most part committed on the eastern edge of Carentan, while the 2nd and 3rd Battalions established themselves in defensive positions at the two likely points of main effort—the demolished Douve bridges north of the city and at Pommenauque, where the railroad embankment reached the southern bank of the Douve.

Progress of the Combat Day, 9 June: 352nd Infantry Division

by Oberstleutnant Fritz Ziegelmann

At about 0400 hours the 914th Grenadier Regtiment (on the left) reported that the enemy had entered Isigny with tanks—slight resistance still continued there—and that the bridges in Isigny had not been blown up by the 621st Eastern Battalion. Several tanks with weak infantry protection were standing at the southern exit of the city. Other tanks had driven ahead toward the west in the direction of the Vire. Immediately thereafter the Commander of the 1st Battalion 1352nd Artillery Regiment (Major van dem Bergh) reported from the 914th Grenadier Regiment CP that, when he and his battalion were about to drive across the emergency bridge just north of Isigny, the enemy had already advanced with tanks and motor vehicles on the main street of the city in direction toward the west. He had to leave his guns behind and had just arrived, as a personnel unit (about 400 men), at the 914th Grenadier Regiment CP.

Consequently, it was a matter of fact that the 352nd Infantry Division on 9 June had only fourteen pieces of artillery left for its sector of approximately 40 kilometers' width, and that the enemy would try, on one hand, to thrust through from Isigny in the direction of Carentan and, on the other hand, to advance from Isigny toward the south, bypassing the Aure valley. Therefore the order was given to the 914th Grenadier Regiment (left) to occupy and hold a position on the Isigny–Vouilly road in the neighborhood of Hill 35 (east of La Madelaine). The 1st Battalion 1352nd Artillery Regiment was placed under its [914th Grenadier Regiment's] command for infantry committment. Furthermore, the 914th Grenadier Regiment (left) was given the order to reinforce the Vire crossing near Auville with elements of the 2nd Battalion 914th Grenadier Regiment (including the 621st Eastern Battalion) in order to prevent an enemy breakthrough toward Carentan.

At about 0900 hours fighter-bomber activity over the Aure valley and over the area around Bayeux started again. The security posts east of Balleroy reported strong battle noises east and northeast of St-Paul respectively. (Signal communication with the Panzer Lehr Division attacking in that locality could not be established.) Enemy tanks with infantry had passed to the defense on the Bayeux–St-Lô Road at the destroyed Drôme crossing near Agy. In the sector of the 30th Mobile Brigade (right) everything was quiet otherwise. About 100 men, with five assault guns, had assembled again in this sector, coming from Sully, including the commander of the 726th Grenadier Regiment, who was again placed in charge of this sector. In the sector of the 916th Grenadier Regiment (center), attacks near Rubercy and south of Trévières on the Aure were repelled. In the sector of the 914th Grenadier Regiment (left) the enemy, who was advancing, about two companies strong, on the partially destroyed causeway across the Aure north of Monfréville, was stopped and forced to withdraw. The enemy standing near Auville and on the southern limits of Isigny did not advance an further. Considerable battle noise could be heard from the area just north of Carentan. Telephone communication with the 91st Airborne Division [91st LL Division] could not be established.

At about 1200 hours the 726th Grenadier Regiment (right) reported that a light attack east of Cottun could be intercepted. In the sector of the 916th Grenadier Regiment (center), near Blay and west thereof, the enemy had advanced as far as close to the Tortonne. Enemy artillery fire on the back country was intensifying. It was noted that the naval artillery fire had ceased. In the sector of the 914th Grenadier Regiment (left) the enemy had succeeded in crossing the Aure valley east of Monfréville, unnoticed, with forces which, as was learned later, were outfitted with special equipment. By their flanking attack, parts of them forced the German units, which were stationed near Monfréville, to withdraw toward the south. Almost at the same time the enemy had effected a breakthrough with considerable armored forces from Isigny through the positions northeast of La Madelaine and had reached the road intersection two kilometers west of Vouilly.

At 1400 hours, after lighter attacks in the sector of the 726th Grenadier Regiment (right) and in the sector of the 916th Grenadier Regiment (center) had been repelled, whereby in the latter case strong artillery activity could again be noted, the enemy had further advanced toward the east with tanks and artillery within the sector of the 914th Grenadier Regiment (left), after brief but severe fighting at the road bifurcation one kilometer west of Vouilly. These and other Kampfgruppen, which had crossed the Aure valley, were standing just this side of Colombières, which was only weakly occupied by German troops. Approximately at this time a strong bombing attack on the "Forêt de Cerisy" took place. According to the statements made over the radio broadcasting circuit of the Commander-in-Chief West, the enemy must have assumed that stronger German forces were being concentrated in this forest. It is possible that the enemy was misled by the transfer of the 352nd Signal Battalion (8 June at night) from Vaubadon to this forest. Owing to the forewarning there were no losses.

At about 1700 hours, in the right sector (726th Grenadier Regiment), the enemy had broken through with infantry, including also several tanks, from the north as far as the hills of Ranchy. The Commander of the 726th Grenadier Regiment (Colonel Korfess) was taken prisoner. The command in this sector was again assumed by the Commander of the 30th Mobile Brigade [Sch. Brigade 30], who succeeded in occupying a position somewhat south of the former main line of resistance and connecting with the firing positions of the 4th Battalion 1352nd Artillery Regiment. A thrust by enemy tanks on the Bayeux–Le Molay road was intercepted at a point in line with De Cronay by the Antiaircraft [Flakkampftrupp] Combat Group stationed there, and two tanks were knocked out.

In the central sector (916th Grenadier Regiment) further enemy attacks were unsuccessful. In the left portion of this sector (914th Grenadier Regiment) enemy elements coming from the west and after bypassing Colombières had succeeded in attacking the garrison of the bridge site northeast of Bricqueville from the rear, and had then joined up near Bernesq with the forces advancing from Colombières toward the east. Unexpectedly, these elements turned at Bernesq, headed southwest and stopped there. Our own reconnaissance patrols made the report, which at first sounded unbelievable, that the enemy was taking up quarters in St-Martin and in La Folie. However, these reports were confirmed by radio intercepts. Farther to the west enemy armored forces had advanced on the Isigny–St-Lô road up to the La Forêt supply base (V. St.). Men separated from their units and soldiers of the supply service had been used to form a weak "front" at this point, which was able to hold up even tanks, despite the prevailing lack of battle experience. It was possible to evacuate the largest part of this supply base.

At about 1800 hours the Commander of the Reconnaissance Battalion of SS Division "Götz von Berlichingen" reported and stated that he had to reconnoiter in preparation for the future commitment of his division in the area north and northeast of Balleroy. He was, however, equipped only with amphibious light army cars. After having been briefed on the situation, he was requested to carry out reconnaissance, especially in the directions of Tilly-sur-Seulles, Bayeux and Bernesq.

At about 1900 hours the division again described the situation to the General Staff of LXXXIV Army Corps, pointing out in particular that the remnants of the 352nd Infantry Division, in their present positions, would not be able to prevent further enemy advances on 10 June.

At about 2000 hours the order from the General Staff of LXXXIV Army Corps was received by telephone to withdraw toward the southwest at the beginning of darkness, in order to occupy, on 10 June in the morning, a new position with its right wing near Bérigny (inclusive), course of the Elle to Airel inclusive, western bank of the Vire, and with its right wing as until now on the Carentan Canal, and to ward off the expected future enemy attacks. Contact to the right (Bérigny, Cormolain, etc.) was to be maintained by Kampfgruppen of the 3rd Parachute Division, which were coming up. It was pointed out to the General Staff that the new defense front (35 kilometers) could not be sufficiently manned with the forces still available.

By 2300 hours the orders for the withdrawal and for the rearrangement on 10 June had reached the troops. It was requested that the troops were to be in the new position by 10 June at 0600 hours. Since explosives were no longer available, the order was given to damage all the bridges across the Elle and the Vire by means available to the troops or to block them by using mines. Furthermore, three antiaircraft combat squads [Flakkampftruppen] each were assigned to the 30th Mobile Brigade [Sch. Brigade 30] and the 916th Grenadier Regiment, and four antiaircraft combat squads to the 914th Grenadier Regiment for commitment in the vicinity of bridges.

Final Survey for the Sector of
the 352nd Infantry Division on 9 June, 2200 hours

The enemy side: It was noticeable that the enemy troops were inspired and felt to be superior. This was particularly true for the 29th Infantry Division, reinforced by one tank battalion. However, an exaggerated feeling of superiority was also apparent, as, for instance, the stubborn driving ahead of tanks on highways lacking security, the careless taking of quarters as soon as an objective was reached instead of making full use of the success achieved, etc.

On the German side the possibility had not been taken into consideration that the swampy Aure valley would be crossed. As a matter of fact, there were no German forces available to resist such action. Consequently the elements of the 29th Infantry Division which crossed over with the aid of their special equipment did not encounter great difficulties. It was, therefore, particularly strange that these forces, together with the armored units coming up from Isigny, terminated their advance at Bernesq and headed south. It seemed that the enemy divisions were lacking in cooperation and communication with one another. If the thrust of the 29th Infantry Division had been carried on toward the east, the entire, already weakened front of the 352nd Infantry Division would have been rolled up!

Probably, the enemy had reached his objective for D+3 on 9 June. It was to be expected, in accordance with the captured operational order of the US V Army Corps, that he would assemble on Balleroy and St-Lô on 10 June, and, furthermore, a thrust on Carentan had to be anticipated. That is to say, he continued to follow his operational plan despite the more favorable possibilities which presented themselves.

Our own troops—adjacent units: On the right of the 352nd Infantry Division the Panzer Lehr Division was supposed to have assembled for the attack on Bayeux. Except for battle noise which could be heard by the division CP coming rather from a southeasterly than a northeasterly direction, no news could be obtained from this division, not even through the General Staff of LXXXIV Army Corps. In the right regimental sector of the 30th Mobile Brigade, after the penetration west of Ranchy, the front had become stationary again. After the commander of the 726th Grenadier Regiment had been taken prisoner, the solid coordination within the sector deteriorated. In the central regimental sector (916th Grenadier Regiment), all attacks of the enemy, in order to cross the Aure, were repelled. Despite the enemy's considerable superiority in matériel, the troops started to feel more secure again. The antiaircraft combat squads [Flakkampftruppen] had by now gained experience, were able to stand their man, and were successful. In the left regimental sector (914th Grenadier Regiment), the second combat day had resulted in a failure for these troops. It had not been possible to blow up the very important Aure bridge near Isigny, because the Eastern soldiers had not held their positions there. In that sector, control of the battle was hardly possible because the forces were numerically too weak, and because there was not even one piece of artillery available.

Synopsis of the Evaluation of the Combat Day (9 June)

Despite the enemy's successes on the left wing of the 352nd Infantry Division, one could say for 9 June that the enemy had not correctly evaluated the division, otherwise he would have had to reach different conclusions and consequently had different successes. Continuing to be of inferior strength, both as far as personnel and matériel were concerned, on this day the weakened 352nd Infantry Division had held up the main body of the enemy (two infantry divisions) on a front 45 kilometers wide and without support on the right.

On 9 June at night, there were, approximately:

	On the German side	On the enemy's side
In the right sector	About 750 men infantry	2,000 men infantry
	8 guns heavy artillery	12 guns artillery (minimum)
	6 antiaircraft guns	
	5 tanks	20 tanks
	0 aircraft	12 aircraft (almost constantly)
In the central sector	About 800 men infantry	3,000 men infantry
	6 guns light artillery	36 guns artillery (minimum)
	6 antiaircraft guns	
	0 tanks	? tanks
	0 aircraft	12 aircraft (almost constantly)
In the left sector	About 700 men infantry	2,000 men infantry
	0 artillery guns	? artillery guns
	4 antiaircraft guns	
	0 tanks	40 tanks
	0 aircraft	12 aircraft (almost constantly)

For 10 June the picture looked different. It was essential to occupy a new defense front of 35 kilometers' width with about 2,500 men and to reinforce it with fourteen artillery guns.

It was imperative that the infantry reached this new front before daylight and could build it up at least to a certain extent. At least 20 kilometers had to be covered on foot and during the dark. The new front had to be occupied unnoticed by the enemy, that is to say, within seven hours after 2300 hours.

9 June: Advance Elements
of the 3rd FS Division Arrive

by Generalleutnant Richard Schimpf

Towards 1500 hours on 8 June I arrived at the south exit of Avranches, where I met my Ia, who had been sent ahead. He informed me that the enemy had captured Bayeux and had probed his way through the forest of Cerisy. Orders would be issued at 1800 hours by the Commanding General at Les Chéris (10 kilometers southeast of Avranches). After having ordered the Ordonnanzofficier to reconnoiter and establish a provisional Divisional Command Post in St-Georges (north-east of Avranches), I drove to II FS Corps.

There I received the order to push forward to the north edge of the Forest of Cerisy, after the arrival of the motorized group. Furthermore, I was to hold this forest against the enemy attacking from the north, and especially from Bayeux, until the bulk of my division was brought forward. After returning to my Divisional Staff HQ at St-Georges, I prepared my order, with appropriate details of execution, for the commander of the motorized advance troops, Major Becker.

On the morning of 9 June I drove to St-Lô, where I reported to the Commanding General of LXXXIV Infantry Corps, General der Infanterie Marcks, the local tactical commander, asking him for details concerning the tactical situation. The arrival of the motorized group directly north of St-Georges was reported to me after my return. This group received orders for the forenoon of 10 June to push forward via Dorigny–Rouxeville–Bérigny to the north edge of the Forest of Cerisy. I myself reconnoitered a divisional command post north of Torigni, which I finally established in a farmhouse in the little forest west of La Chapelle-du-Fest (three kilometers north of Torigni).

In the evening I transferred my staff there. After arrival of the motorized march group in the region north of Torigni, all motor transport vehicles were sent to meet the two groups marching on foot in order to facilitate and accelerate their transport.

Situation When Panzer Gruppe West Assumed Command

by General der Panzer Leo, Freiherr Geyr von Schweppenburg

In the evening of 8 June Panzer Gruppe West assumed command of the sector from east of the Orne to Tilly-sur-Seulles (excl.). I had been anxious not to interfere before. After visiting the combat divisions, I made a verbal report by telephone to the Commander Seventh Army. I informed him that I was prepared to attack at the earliest possible moment and requested a free hand as to the time and place. He agreed. This was the way leadership had been handled formerly in our army—to have confidence in a man and allow him freedom of action to draw up the details, holding him solely to his mission.

Panzer Gruppe West had a fundamental knowledge of British landing regulations and was familiar with the British orders for the Dieppe raid and the conclusions drawn from these experiments. There was no doubt that the enemy had succeeded in gaining a large foothold on the coast. Moreover, reinforcements and supplies had been building up for three days. Nevertheless, no counter measures were taken by the Luftwaffe during daylight. Minor activity at night was of little significance. The same was true of the activities of the German Navy, although the Goebbels propaganda emphasized its actions strongly.

Full credit must be given to the valor of the few survivors of the coastal forces of the 716th Infantry Division, who held out in bunkers and furnished information on the enemy for several more days. The remnants of these forces numbered about 300 men. The others were swept off the map by the torrent of fire.

A new front line was being formed. The enemy so far had refrained from showing an offensive spirit up to 9 June, except against the Panzer Gruppe in the vicinity of Bayeux and east thereof.

In our estimate of the enemy Supreme Command, we were not in doubt about the British. The British/Canadian High Command was not expected to launch a large-scale attack until thorough preparations had been made. We were uncertain as to the actions of the Americans. The exact boundary between the Allies was not known at that time. Panzer Gruppe West was in doubt as to the action the US Army would take on the American left flank, which was open. The more cavalry-like school of thought of the US Army, emanating from the Civil War, might prove rather different from the cautious, systematic strategy of the British. A more reckless strategy had to be considered— possibly a push into the gap between Panzer Gruppe West and the concentrating Seventh Army in order to separate the two forces.

The forces which Panzer Gruppe West was able to muster on 8 June consisted of only the 21st Panzer Division, the 12th SS (Hitlerjugend) Panzer Division, and the bulk of the Panzer Lehr Division. Although the 71th Infantry Division was mentioned in orders, it existed only in the imagination and on the maps of higher staffs. The corps troops of I SS Pz Corps, including the Tiger tank battalion, had just started a 700-kilometer march from western Belgium to Normandy, via Paris.

Purely theoretical considerations of strategy indicated that we should push against the British beachhead at once and, after delivering this blow, hold the British and turn with all availables forces against the American east flank. This would have been a classroom solution without hope of success. First of all, the forces at hand were not sufficient to attain this objective. Moreover, the basic idea of Hitler and the Wehrmacht-führungsstab (both equally inexperienced and incompetent in the control of large armored forces) was to use the strongest German force—at that time, the Panzer divisions—to block the enemy's direct route to Paris. This was the reason the staff made and adhered to the unfortunate decision to employ on the inner flank the most powerful and mobile force.

In this situation, according to the Schlieffen school, a practical and simple plan should have been selected—an immediate northward assault from Caen. This action was all the more necessary because the divisions were short of fuel and ammunition as early as 9 June. This shortage resulted from the outmoded ideas of the infantry staffs who handled supply. Moreover, enemy air action caused unpredictable delays in the movement and arrival of supply columns. For instance, fuel for the 21st Panzer Division was brought up from Le Mans and artillery ammunition from an area north of the Loire, or vice versa. The outcome of the extended controversy between Rommel and von Geyr was that the first attack had to take place within range of the tremendous mass of enemy naval artillery. Either it had to be carried out with little artillery ammunition and fuel on our side, or it had to be cancelled altogether. The forces available for the attack were half of the 21st Panzer Division and half of the 12th SS Panzer Division, combined. This was all, for the Wehrmachtführungsstab had given strict orders to "yield no ground, not even in mobile warfare." This policy restricted the Panzer force in the use of its most essential characteristics—mobility and concentrated surprise fire.

Proposed Attack of the 12th SS Panzer and 21st Panzer Divisions

The first thrust had to be made without the support of the Luftwaffe. However, some excellent assistance could be rendered by independent flak units. Because of the lack of air support, an attack could be launched only at night. Both divisions had been thoroughly trained in night fighting and were quite equal to this difficult mission.

After talking over the impending attack with the Commander of I SS Panzer Corps, we decided to jump off from the high ground north of Caen with the vicinity of Anisy–Anguerny as the objective. The artillery was to support the attack by fire on the landing areas. The logical question of the commander of I SS Pz Corps was, "What next?" I was unable to answer this question except to say that the first objective was but a platform for further action. The main idea was to avoid the worst decision—namely, to do nothing at all. It was not a question of making a perfect decision, but of doing the least objectionable thing. Moreover, I put my trust in a supposed British tendency which had impressed me in peacetime—when attacked, "wait and see," that is to say, stop when the enemy takes offensive action and see what happens.

Therefore, the objections of Ogruf Dietrich were overruled. He and the commander of the 21st Panzer Division, whom I saw next at his command post (St-André-sur-Orne), were ordered to be ready to attack from the area north of Caen as of nightfall 10 June. I told them that I was going to reconnoiter the ground in person the next day at dawn. I made the reconnaissance early on 10 June from the steeple of the abbey at Caen, the command post of the 25th SS Panzer Grenadier Regiment. The decision was made to thrust forward with the combined Panzer divisions astride the narrow-gauge railroad which runs due north from Caen. I knew this area very well, especially that part beyond ground observation. (In September 1940 I had trained the old XXIV Infantry Corps for weeks in the vicinity of Luc-sur-Mer, five kilometers northeast of Douvres-la-Delivrande, preparatory to an invasion of England.)

9 June: I SS Panzer Corps Holds the Line

by Generalmajor Fritz Krämer

Apart from a few German airplanes which allegedly were dropping mines into the Channel, enemy landing operations continued undisturbed. I SS Panzer Corps was not able to procure a photo showing the exact situation and the extent of the enemy fleet. Corps therefore resorted to selfhelp. The heavy artillery battalion stationed an advanced observer in a tower of a manor on the right bank of the Orne, close to the coast. (Many of these towers can be found in the coastal area of Normandy and the local inhabitants say that in former times they served as lighthouses.) This observer could see almost the entire enemy fleet and he prepared a sketch which was reproduced. This enabled us, beginning 9 June, to fire on the landing fleet with two 175mm gun batteries. This at least caused a disturbance and perhaps some delay in landing operations. An observable result, however, was an immediate smokescreen. It can be assumed that the fire of these two batteries was the only action carried out against the landing fleet by German weapons. Unfortunately Corps had at its disposal only 400 rounds of 175mm ammunition. It required eight days to obtain additional ammunition, which had to be brought from the Worms or Mainz area by Corps supply columns.

The line which had been reached on the evening of 8 June was reinforced the following day. During that day the three divisions employed most of their tanks in the front lines, usually in company strength of from five to nine tanks, to help local assaults by Panzer Grenadiers and to create a force able to deal with anticipated enemy attacks.

This action stood up under the test of 9 June when infantry attacks, supported by heavy artillery fire, were absorbed and repelled almost everywhere. An enemy air attack on the Panzer regiment of the 21st Panzer Division put it out of action for almost one and a half days and a critical situation developed in this sector. Direct damage from the bombing attack was slight, but at least 50 percent of the 60 tanks were rendered inoperative, in most cases by mechanical damage arising from the tanks being buried in mud.

By the evening of 9 June the remaining elements of the 716th Infantry Division were no longer capable of combat and they were withdrawn from the action. The division then consisted at the most of 200 men and it had entirely disintegrated. The men who had been in the advanced shelters or armored command posts had been given up altogether; probably all were taken prisoner. There had been radio contact with some of them until 9 June, but no communication by telephone. It was not known whether they offered resistance until the very last moment, but it was assumed that further resistance became impossible. The lack of visibility, of telephone and radio contact with neighbors and with the rear services, brings a feeling of helplessness to a man in such a fortress, particularly if fighting is going on in his rear and there is no possibility for him to force his way out. Under such conditions he may become alarmed and give up. Usually the enemy inched ahead to the entrances and exits of shelters, making escape impossible. Even a tiger, difficult to chase in its natural freedom, is helpless when it is caged. Fortifications (in the style of former fortresses) are expensive installations in the modern era of air forces and artillery. They cannot be held for long in spite of the best intentions and will on the part of the defender. This became obvious to the commands of corps and divisions, both in the West (Maginot Line) and in the East (Stalin Line). Subsequent fighting in the West Wall confirmed these experiences. The dug-in infantry can offer better defense of a MLR if the trenches are well adapted to the terrain and the MLR is built with adequate depth and reinforced, with mines for instance.

Generally the line reached by Corps was held. Sporadic engagements took place during the night of 9/10 June.

First Counterattack
by the 346th Infantry Division

by Oberst Paul Frank

At 1200 on 8 June Corps ordered that all combat elements of the division cross the Seine that night to continue the attack on 9 June. The division was to eliminate the enemy bridgehead east of the Orne. The river crossing was made without incident at the ferry points at Quillebeuf, Caudebec, Mailleraye, Berville, and Declair. A rainstorm, which began during the night, made it possible to continue the crossing into the next day. At about 1200 the weather cleared and the crossing had to be stopped. Certain elements, in particular the artillery, were thus delayed in entering the battle area.

The enemy had consolidated the beachhead. Enemy forces strengthened the bridgehead east of the Orne by bringing up forces across the Bénouville bridge (which had been seized intact). This bridgehead had been defended in the first few days only by airborne troops. Pressure began to bear on the German units near Bavent and Bois de Bavent.

The divisional view was that, under the circumstances of the enemy's increasing strength, an immediate attack by the individual units of division as they arrived in the battle area could no longer succeed. The suggestion was therefore offered to Corps that the division should first assemble and prepare, and not launch its attack before 10 June. Corps approved the proposal and in addition attached Kampfgruppe Luck, located west of the Bois de Bavent, to the division to insure a unified command for the attack. This Kampfgruppe had been operating on the division's left flank and had already unsuccessfully attacked the town of Hérouvillette. This failure on the afternoon of 9 June was most unfortunate as it demonstrated a weakness and succeeded in alerting the enemy. Kampfgruppe Luck was composed of elements of the 21st Panzer Division, with the commander and staff of the 125th Panzer Regiment, two understrength battalions, and approximately one Sturmgeschutz company and one Aufklärung company. In addition to Kampfgruppe Luck, division had attached an infantry battalion and an artillery battalion from the 711th Infantry Division. The battles of the previous days had considerably weakened three battalions of the 346th Infantry Division.

The attack was to proceed in the form of pincers closing on the Orne river bridge. The 346th Infantry Division, forming the right spearhead, was to attack from the area southwest of Varaville via Amfreville–Bréville to the Orne bridge. Its primary objective was the high ground Amfreville–Bréville which overlooked the river and the bridge. On the left, Kampfgruppe Luck would attack from Ste-Honorine to the heights west of Ranville at more or less the same time and push off simultaneously for the bridge.

9 June: 2nd Panzer Division Ordered to Move to Normandy

by General der Panzertruppen Heinrich, Freiherr von Lüttwitz

Toward 0300 hours, 9 June, the division received orders to march through Paris, and on into the Argentan–Sees sector. It was ordered that the march movement was to become effective with darkness on 9 June, and was was be carried out only under the protection of darkness. The reason for the movement route through Paris was because all other bridges between Paris and the river estuary had been bombed out. Bridges in the heart of Paris were the only passages still intact. Immediately road reconnaissance patrols were dispatched, and field gendarme patrols, which with the aid of the town commander of Paris organized the division's movement through the city.

Rainy weather prevented the enemy's air activities. For this reason, the division was able to begin at 1400 hours the movement with its first elements.

The division's movement took place in two march groups, as follows:

March Group A: Via Amiens–Claimont–Creil–Paris–Rambouillet–south of Dreux, to Sees.

March Group B: Poix–Beauvais–Paris–Versailles–Dreux–Laigle–Argentan.

On the roads, ahead of both march groups, was the reconnaissance battalion. Nearly all tracked vehicles were marked to be transported by rail, which was aimed to preserve the condition of all tracked vehicles.

The division realized clearly that its entire march movement would be endangered at the moment the enemy's air activity was renewed, that losses would be caused as soon as the air raids were renewed. For this reason, the division intentionally renounced its hitherto adhered SOP—standard operational procedure—for closed-up march formation. Thus the division gave unit commanders a free hand concerning the march and gave orders concerning only the roads to be used during the march movement, assembly areas, and a certain time by which the destination had to be reached by such units. Those unit commanders ordered on days when air activity was especially active that their vehicles travel in small groups or even individually. This way, the division reached its destination as a group of "individually moving travelers." By this measure were losses kept to a minimum; however, on the other hand it brought great responsibilities upon the individual drivers and vehicle commanders. The division's confidence in taking such a step was fully justified: even in the huge city of Paris, not one of the division's vehicles was reported to have broken down.

Because of the numerous detours, caused by destroyed bridges between Amiens and Paris, the first elements of the division arrived in Paris only after dusk. At first the movement through Paris went smoothly and undisturbed until midnight, when on account of an air raid the entire traffic control system began to collapse. This traffic control consisted largely of men from the City Police of Paris. As the policemen sought shelter in air raid shelters, the march movement through Paris became so confused that an entire group from the left march group column came on the wrong road, which later on required hours before it finally found its way back again onto the right road.

At first the Division Staff went to Lusarches, north of Paris, then into Paris, where later also the commander of the division arrived. Up to now he had supervised the Division's movement.

PART FOUR

10 June, D+4

On 10 June the 346th Infantry Division and Kampfgruppe Luck launched a spoiling attack against the 51st Highland Division and 4th Armored Brigade that had come over the Orne at Pegasus Bridge to support the 6th Airborne Division, which had been holding its ground against these units since D-Day. All the Allied bridgeheads were now linked. These attacks gained little ground, and a counterattack by the British 5th Parachute Brigade pushed them back. In another spoiling attack, the Panzer Lehr Division again tried to strike at British armor. It too gained little ground, encountering heavy naval gunfire. Also on the British front, the headquarters of Panzer Gruppe West, brought up to prepare a decisive counterstroke, was destroyed by Allied medium bombers (targeted by 'Ultra' decrypts), and its commander, General von Geyr, was wounded. Seventh Army thus assumed control of the entire invasion front again.

On the US front, V Corps, advancing from Omaha, and VII Corps, advancing from Utah Beach, linked up at Auville-sur-le-Vey. V Corps' 2nd Infantry Division joined the offensive towards the Cerisy Forest. The first elements of the German 77th Infantry Division came up from Brittany and went into action along the Merderet river, defending the flank of Montebourg against the US VII Corps' advance. To the north, the 243rd Infantry Division came into action against the US 82nd Airborne and 90th Infantry Divisions, pushing towards Cherbourg. The 90th Division encountered strong resistance, though slow advances continued for several days.

D.C.I.

OKW War Diary, 10 June

by Major Percy E. Schramm

On 10 June the enemy succeeded in uniting the British and American bridgeheads. A critical situation was created due to the fact that the staff of Panzer Gruppe West had been almost completely annihilated through air attacks and had to be replaced by I SS Panzer Corps. The attacks on the Cotentin peninsula could be blocked in the north and in the west.

10–13 June: 91st Luftlande Division

by Generalmajor Eugen König

On 7 June 1944 I had just arrived in Bitburg (Eifel) from the East in order to visit my family. There I received an order by telephone from the acting commander of XII Infantry Corps to proceed immediately to the invasion front. On the way I was to report to Army Group in Paris. I was ordered to take over the command of the 91st LL Division, the former commander, Generalleutnant Falley, having been killed on the first day of the invasion.

At about 1700 on 10 June I arrived at the division command post in Rauville, one and a half kilometers east of St-Sauveur-le-Vicomte. From the orientation given me by the Ia, Oberstleutnant iG Bickel, I learned that the division (normal T/O) had been disposed over a large area on the Cotentin peninsula before the invasion. The division mission had been as follows:

a. Improvement of the passive air defense.

b. Defense against enemy airborne landings.

c. Alertness to repel enemy seaborne landings.

During the night of the invasion, the division commander had been at a conference in Rennes. It had not been possible for the Ia to contact him. The report of invasion had been received: Ste-Mère-Église was in enemy hands. Therefore, the Ia had decided to assemble the division and prepare to counterattack at Ste-Mère-Église. This proposed action had been prevented by the jump of the bulk of the 82nd and 101st Airborne Divisions (US) into the quartering area and the proposed divisional assembly area. The ensuing minor engagements, in which even the supply troops had participated, had been terminated by 9 June. Elements of the 1058th Grenadier Regiment had advanced as far as the northern outskirts of Ste-Mère-Église, but the forces from the west had succeeded in reaching only the Merderet river. In the meantime, the enemy had been strongly reinforced, so that further attacks with the forces available appeared to be hopeless. The division had been forced to revert to the defensive.

When I assumed command, the division was in position with the right flank at Carentan (incl.) and the left flank at Le Ham (excl.), sixteen kilometers northeast of St-Sauveur-le-Vicomte. In the first few days of combat, the division had lost approximately 3,000 men and was not capable of occupying the sector with the existing forces. Moreover, elements of the 1058th Grenadier Regiment had been attached to the 709th Infantry Division. In addition to the 6th FS Regiment (Major von der Heydte), which was under divisional control at the beginning of the invasion, the division received the 941st Grenadier Regiment [sic] from the 243rd Infantry Division. With these forces, the division had to defend an exceedingly broad sector in which observation was limited. In conformity with our mission, we were not to conduct a passive defense but to counterattack frequently and in force. By these attacks as well as other measures, we were to prevent the advance of the enemy.

The enemy artillery superiority increased from day to day and from hour to hour, while our ammunition shortage became more and more acute. A few days after D-Day, one-third of the guns of our artillery regiment had to be withdrawn from the front because of the lack of ammunition. The division had been equipped according to the T/O with Geb H 40s (105 mm mountain howitzers—Ed.), but these had only one basic load of ammunition. In spite of the efforts of division, Corps, and Army, it had been impossible to get supplies until mid July. Therefore, it was ordered that all local defense guns be withdrawn from the positions on the west coast of the Cotentin; the regiment was equipped with these guns as an expedient. Through this measure the divisional artillery regiment, instead of a single type of gun, was equipped with guns from all countries. Coordination of the fire of the artillery was rendered impossible.

In spite of all these difficulties, we succeeded on the whole in halting temporarily the advance of the enemy. Minor penetrations were eliminated. However, the fighting continued unceasingly; our failures as a result of the strong enemy artillery superiority made an active defense less possible. Here and there we had to give up local terrain in order to prevent a penetration on a larger scale. There were growing indications that the enemy would launch a concentric attack from west of Ste-Mère-Église in order to gain possession of the important road junction at St-Sauveur-le-Vicomte. To counter such an attack, we contemplated moving a grenadier regiment to the vicinity of Orglandes for a thrust from north to south in the direction of Pont-l'Abbé. This thrust was to be directed at the flank of the expected enemy attack. In spite of the acknowledged urgency of the situation, these plans were not carried out because of the lack of reserves.

Comments by General der Panzer
Leo, Freiherr Geyr von Schweppenburg

The assembly and coordinated attack of the 91st LL Division was prevented by the jump of the 82nd and 101st Airborne Division (US) during the first, decisive days of the invasion. The newly organized division, which had not yet been fully trained and equipped, performed well owing to the energetic leadership of Generalmajor König. From an historical viewpoint, the report has little value. The actions are not described in detail; accuracy is lacking.

10 June: 709th Infantry Division

by Generalleutnant Karl Wilhelm von Schlieben

On 10 June the enemy renewed his efforts to carry his attack across the line Quineville–Montebourg in the direction of Cherbourg. The daily report of Army Group B for 10 June stated that one of the points of main effort of the enemy was in that area. However, as the enemy was also exercising heavy pressure in a westerly direction from his beachhead, there was a growing threat to the right of the 709th Infantry Division. The 77th Infantry Division, which had been withdrawn and assigned to LXXXIV Corps to counter this threat to the flank, was still on its way from Coutances to Valognes on the evening on 10 June.

Group Hellmich, to which the 709th Infantry Division belonged, thinly held the line Carentan–Abbeville–Beuxsville–Pont l'Abbé–Gourbesville–Montebourg–Quineville. The enemy did not perceive and profit by this weakness. Thus, a day full of anxiety had come to an end. In this respect, the War Diary of the Seventh Army stated: "The line blocking the enemy in the area Montebourg–Quineville was maintained and thus the necessary basis for a successful countering of the enemy's push of Cherbourg was created".

10 June: 6th FS Positions at Carentan under Pressure

by Oberstleutnant Friedrich, Freiherr von der Heydte

On 10 June the commander of the American 101st Airborne Division [Major General Maxwell D. Taylor] called upon the regiment to surrender; the regimental commander refused.

It was not so much the steadily increasing enemy pressure which made the defense of Carentan difficult as three unfavorable factors on the German side. The first of these was the lack of any artillery, except for one 88mm antitank/antiaircraft battery which was attached to the regiment. The second was the slow but steady giving way of the units adjacent to the regiment. On the right, east of Carentan, the regiment was compelled to turn its front more and more southward, until finally there was a southern front as well as an eastern front, while the actions of the units on the left, west of Carentan, forced the regiment to keep on extending its front until in the end it became necessary to maintain strong reconnaissance patrols to keep watch—not to occupy or to hold—over the area as far as the bridge at Baupte. The third factor was the shortage of ammunition, especially for the heavy infantry weapons which were the mainstay of the defense. Originally, the regiment had been instructed to obtain its ammunition from an ammunition distributing point where no ammunition had as yet been stored; then it was assigned one which, it turned out, had been destroyed in an enemy air raid; and finally it had to depend on an ammunition point which, because the bridges leading to it had become impassable, could be reached only by making long detours.

The Fighting on 10 June: 352nd Infantry Division

by Oberstleutnant Fritz Ziegelmann

The Course of the Fighting During the Day

The Commanding General rang up at about 2 o'clock pointing out the great importance of strengthening the left wing of the 352nd Infantry Division on the Vire to the west of Isigny. The enemy must not be permitted to unite with his own bridgehead north of Carentan. The actual fighting strength of the 352nd Infantry Division was pointed out to the Commanding General, and he was informed that the combat groups of the division would only be able to reach the Elle sector by 6 o'clock. It is questionable whether these forces (approx. 2,500 men) would suffice to halt an enemy thrust across the Elle toward St-Lô, which was expected on 10 June. If the other anticipated enemy thrust across the Vire toward Carentan was to be halted, the division could renew its request that its forces west of the Vire be reinforced by the 91st Airborne Division. The heavy artillery battalion of the division was then to take up a position west of St-Jean-de-Day, where it would be effective over the greater part of the Elle area in front of the Vire (west of Isigny). The artillery battalion had to be brought south of St-Lô and was only able to take up its firing position a little before noon, because the Vire bridges north of St-Lô had been destroyed.

There was an impression that the Commanding General's demand for a strengthened divisional left wing was the result of a lengthy, long-range discussion with the higher authorities, who themselves were not in the picture. Shortly afterwards, the Chief of Staff of LXXXIV Corps, Lieutenant Colonel von Criegern (General Staff), informed us by long-distance telephone that a combat group of the 275th Infantry Division was to be subordinated to the 352nd Infantry Division for the strengthening of the Vire font on 10 June.

The Divisional CP at Littry was given up at about 3 o'clock, and the new divisional CP at Le Mesnil-Rouxelin (north of St-Lô) was occupied by 5 o'clock. At 6 o'clock contact was sought with the divisional combat groups. Telephone communication had proved to be impossible. Radio detachments answered only with the "change of position." Special-missions staff officers were dispatched to establish contact with all regiments and the 2nd Battalion 914th Grenadier Regiment, to which was attached the 621st Eastern Battalion. The divisional commander himself drove to the 916th Grenadier Regiment (centre). The divisional staff engineer officer was given the task of blowing up the Vire crossing west of Reuilly with a dynamite detachment. There were

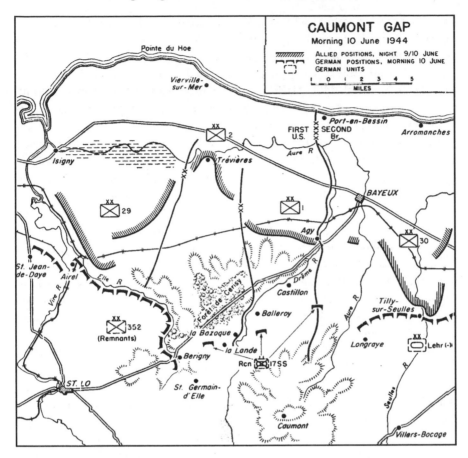

none of the familiar sounds of battle during the entire morning. The listening detachment reported enemy radio silence.

The first messages started coming through at noon. The "Götz von Berlichingen" Artillery Battalion reported that fairly strong enemy forces, including tanks, had entered the Forêt de Cerisy from the north and had occupied the village of Balleroy. A patrol from St-Paul reported sounds of extensive fighting from the region of the Panzer Lehr Division which was fighting to the north of Tilly-sur-Seulles. A message was received from the 30th Mobile Brigade (Schnelle Brigade 30) (right) to the effect that the six-kilometer long front line was occupied in strongpoints by 900 men (mixed units with hardly any heavy weapons), that the Elle bridge at Bérigny had been destroyed, and that enemy movements in the southwestern part of the Forêt de Cerisy had been observed. The Combat Group of the 3rd Parachute Division, which was to establish contact at Bérigny, had not yet arrived. The 916th Grenadier Regiment (centre) reported that it had occupied the seven-kilometer long sector with about 1,000 men, many of whom were stragglers. The enemy had crossed the Elle with infantry west of St-Jean toward noon.

At first he had been pushed back, but he had renewed the attack. Orders had been given to eliminate this bridgehead. The 914th Grenadier Regiment reported that it was occupying the four-kilometer long Elle sector with about 500 men (the bulk of the 1st Battalion 1352nd Artillery Regiment), and had halted a fairly weak thrust by the enemy from Moon across the Elle. There was no contact with the 2nd Battalion 914th Grenadier Regiment (west of Isigny). All the regiments reported that the antiaircraft combat detachments had not arrived yet.

At about 1500 hours the 1352nd Artillery Regiment reported that the 4th Battalion 1352nd Artillery Regiment had found a ford across the Vire just south of Pont-Hébert, made use of it, and had occupied the firing positions west of St-Jean since about 1400 hours. The enemy, who had been advancing from his bridgehead at Auville in the direction of Carentan since 1400 hours, was being engaged by the battalion. The Isigny–Moon road, upon which north–south movements were observed, was under harassing fire. The ammunition situation had considerably improved since the morning. The 2nd Battalion 1352nd Artillery Regiment supported the counterthrust on the bridgehead west of St-Jean on the Elle, and attacked troop movements from Cerisy toward Le Bois. For attacks on the ground targets, a heavy (8.8) antiaircraft battalion, which had not been previously used for this task, was to cover the effective area of the 2nd Battalion 1352nd Artillery Regiment.

In the course of the afternoon, the commander of the combat group of the 275th Division, Colonel Reinz, reported that his 275th Infantry Battalion (cyclists) would be able to reach the area of St-Jean by 11 June. The remaining elements of his combat group, (1st and 2nd Battalions 984th Grenadier Regiment, 275th Engineer Battalion, 3rd Battalion 275th Artillery Regiment, two radio detachments and elements of the supply troops) would reach the area west of St-Lô on foot, unit by unit, from 12 June on. In addition, the special-missions staff officer who had been sent to the 2nd Battalion 914th Grenadier Regiment reported himself back during the course of the morning. Meanwhile the enemy had advanced from Euville to Catz with infantry and armored formations. Coming from the north, the American 101st Airborne Division, which had been fighting in the bridgehead west of Brévands until then, had joined up with the enemy advancing from Euville. Their advance had been delayed by the well-directed fire of the 4th Battalion 1352nd Artillery Regiment. An AA combat detachment was in position on the road bridge two kilometers south of Catz. During the return journey, the divisional engineer officer had reported that the Elle bridge west of Neuilly was damaged and the Vire bridge destroyed. The enemy was weakest to the west of Neuilly. Intercepted elements of the 914th Grenadier Regiment were being used to secure the crossing at the destroyed Vire bridge (west of Neuilly).

At about 1900 hours a liaison officer from II Parachute Corps and the 3rd Parachute Division reported himself. Of the latter, a combat group had established contact with the right wing of the 352nd Infantry Division in the late afternoon. The "Götz von Berlichingen" Artillery Battalion was attached to the 3rd Parachute Division.

Summary of the Picture of the
352nd Infantry Division at 2200 hours on 10 June

The enemy: While still under the impression of the captured operational order of V Army Corps (American), it was easy to assume that the enemy would endeavor to surround Caen from his deep bridgehead, and on the other hand would try to unite with his bridgehead north of Carentan (US VII Army Corps). Failing this, an insertion of the US XIX Army Corps between the US VII and V Army Corps had to be reckoned with— this in order to carry out a decisive thrust in the direction of St-Lô with the US XIX and V Army Corps, after XIX had advanced west of the Vire as far as the mouth of the Elle.

Contradictory radio messages were intercepted on that day, so that it could be assumed that the enemy (US V Army Corps) was deviating from his objectives of the day in his D-Day plan for reasons of supply in men and materials. There was no other explanation for the inactivity of V Army Corps. Preceded by fighter-bomber activity, the enemy actually commenced his concentration on the line of the Elle late in the morning; thereby the left wing on the Vire was left open, and it had been possible for him to form a small bridgehead to the west of St-Jean on the Elle. The successful thrust along the Isigny–Carentan road and the contact established with the paratroops of the 101st Airborne Division from the bridgehead west of Brévands at Catz proved that the enemy intended to thrust toward the eastern edge of Carentan on 11 June at the very latest, and that he would then succeed in joining up with the US VII Army Corps.

Own forces, neighbours: 10 June proved that the unprepared withdrawal from one main line of resistance and the occupation of a new one along the Elle required time. It should be remembered in this connection that the weaker combat teams were not comprised of [*sic*] close-knit units, but of improvised ones whose men were of poor physical quality, and the equipment of which could only be described as inadequate. If— in spite of this—it had proved possible to build up a defensive front, and, with the exception of a small bridgehead to the west of St-Jean on the Elle, to hold it, such a thing could only be described as very fortunate indeed. Furthermore, it appeared that there was no reliance to be placed on the AA combat team of the 1st Antiaircraft Regiment, for they failed to occupy the positions to which they had been ordered before the evening.

The unpleasant position in the divisional sector was that on the left wing. A telephone conversation with the I General Staff officer of the 91st Airborne Division indicated that this division was not in a position to reinforce the front eastward of Carentan. It all depended, therefore, on the building of a defensive front to prevent the enemy from breaking through west of the Vire in the direction of St-Lô. For this, the small river sector parallel to the Carentan–Vire crossing appeared to be suitable. It was disappointing that the combat group of the 275th Infantry Division, which was scheduled for 10 June, had not arrived. The 1st Battalion 914th Grenadier Regiment (250 stragglers and two AA combat detachments) was therefore ordered to take and to hold the Vire crossing west and northwest of Neuilly, as well as the road bridge two kilometers south of Catz. A sort of security front from the Vire to Carentan and thus been created.

It was a concern that contact had been established on the right wing by means of a combat group of the 3rd Parachute Division. It was to be expected that the gap of the Panzer Lehr Division (at Tilly-sur-Seulles) would be closed, or at least reduced, by the next day. Without doubt, the enemy was deceived by the "Götz von Berlichingen" Artillery Battalion, which was put in between the Panzer Lehr Division and the right wing of the 352nd Infantry Division (Bérigny). In the evening the 2nd General Staff Officer reported that the enemy had marched into Balleroy at about noon, and that there were still about 200 German wounded at the main clearing station. American and German medical officers were engaged in the moving of these wounded until dark. The American holding forces (one infantry division) had come up to the southern limits of Balleroy, but did not advance beyond it.

Summarized Evaluation of Engagements up to 10 June

On the evening of 9 June the 332nd Infantry Division with its 2,500 fighting men was faced with a difficult problem. Should it scatter its weak combat teams along the 35-kilometer front line which had now to be taken up, or should it halt the immediate and threatened thrust of the enemy east of the Vire and in the direction of St-Lô with its strengthened right wing? It was clear to our division that in the latter case it would be possible for the enemy on our left wing to join the forces of the US V Army Corps at Carentan, thus attaining one of his objectives. On the other hand, it was also obvious to us that, in the first case, the enemy would be able to break through—even to walk through—taking St-Lô practically without fight to the south. On the evening of 9 June the evaluation of available time and space had also to be taken into consideration, from which it was deduced that it would be best to strengthen the right wing only of the divisional sector in order to be able to create a usable front as far to the north of St-Lô as possible after the bringing up of further combat groups (3rd Parachute Division, elements of the 275th Infantry Division, etc.).

It may be said without exaggeration that the 352nd Infantry Division forced the enemy to change his time schedule through its commitment along the coastal front at Bayeux, the enemy thinking this division to be in the area of St-Lô at that time, and describing it as an "offensive division." The enemy had intended to be on the line St-Lô–Balleroy by D+3, in order to be on the line Avranches–Domfront by D+17 (or D+19). It is true that the 352nd Infantry Division was no longer on the coast by D+4 (10 June), and that it could no longer be considered a full infantry division, but it had successfully fought with the old, soldierly virtues and given the US V Army Corps anxious moments, even making the success of the invasion itself seem in jeopardy—as was expressed in an American service newspaper which subsequently came into our possession. It received honourable mention as the premier division in the "deutsche Wehrmachtbericht" of 10 (or 11) June 1944.

It was doubtful whether the 352nd Infantry Division would be able to prevent an enemy breakthrough on the new front in the direction of St-Lô. It was far too sorely in need of rest and reinforcements. If the enemy failed to take advantage of a moment of weakness which, certainly, must have been known to him, this demonstrates but once again that he was working according to careful yet excessively long-term plans, and that his enemy reconnaissance displayed too many gaps.

10 June: I SS Panzer Corps Unable to Counterattack

by Generalmajor Fritz Krämer

Two or three fresh divisions were needed to enable Corps to launch a new attack as a Panzer corps. On 10 June, to the delight of everybody concerned, the Commander-in-Chief of Army Group B, Field Marshal Rommel, who had been made responsible for the entire invasion front, paid a visit to Corps. For the first time since 6 June we were in a position to report fully on the conduct of battle and the enemy situation.

As Panzer divisions could not be withdrawn from the front for an attack until we could expect infantry divisions which were to be committed for defense, it became apparent that a continuous and rectilinear front could never be established. Neither the terrain nor the enemy would allow it. As a result, manpower requirements increased to the extent that it appeared impossible to establish close contact with LXXXIV Corps, on the left. Corps reconnaissance assaults to the left disclosed no German formations or only very weak ones. The division, which appeared on map sketches of reports on the situation as adjacent to the 716th Infantry Division on the left, evidently had been smashed or had existed only on the sketches. Corps was compelled to throw forces of the Panzer Lehr Division further to the left. This strained the front like an inflated rubber ball; the time when it would burst was drawing nearer and nearer.

Corps decided to postpone its planned attack in the direction of Bayeux until further divisions arrived. The C-in-C of Army Group B agreed to this proposal, but demanded that strong attacks with tanks be carried out toward Bayeux.

It was still incomprehensible why the enemy exerted himself with assaults in the direction of Caen and did not make a powerful drive to exploit the open gap on either side south of Bayeux. There could be only one explanation: this place was approximately the boundary line between the British and American forces. As often happens in war, the forces of these two parties apparently were not overlapping each other and the famous line of contact existed only on the map. Fortunately for the German command, the line looked different on the terrain and there must have been a gap between the British and American troops, covered occasionally perhaps with liaison scouting parties.

The Commander-in-Chief Army Group B further informed Corps that:

  a. XLVII Panzer Corps with two Panzer divisions would be committed left of I SS Panzer Corps;

  b. The command agency General of Panzer Troops West would probably assume control between the Orne and the Vire;

c. Support from the Luftwaffe could not yet be expected.

Also at the top-level command, the opinion prevailed that the lack of the German Luftwaffe would render difficult or almost impossible every defensive operation, and was a greater bar to every large-scale offensive action.

On the evening of 10 June it became apparent that Corps had been forced to change over to defense and that an offensive operation would be conceivable only after Corps had been withdrawn from the defensive front which was incessantly sapping the power of its combat elements. Enemy attacks grew in violence; casualties and loss of material became conspicuous.

Panzer Gruppe West
Knocked Out by Air Attacks

by General der Panzer Leo, Freiherr Geyr von Schweppenburg

In the early morning hours I was able to observe, from the abbey, an attack by elements of the Panzer regiment of the 12th SS Panzer Division. They had scarcely left cover on the western outskirts of Caen when a very strong group of enemy bombers appeared and loosed a hell of fire on the Panzer formation. This was exactly what I was anticipating when I almost overdid night training prior to the invasion. At any rate, the incident strengthened my resolution to operate tactically only at night, dawn, or dusk.

I felt little concern about my right flank. The opposing forces were, and remained, closely engaged. No offensive action by the British was to be expected on the east flank for the time being. The situation on the west flank was different. The commander of the Panzer Lehr Division, whom I had seen on 8 June and whom I knew to be efficient and competent, had expressed some concern over the situation.

In the afternoon of 10 June Rommel came to see me at my command post near La Caine. I reported on the situation and informed him that the commander of Seventh Army had agreed with my decision to attack and had left the details to me. Rommel would have preferred an attack more to the northwest. I felt the same way, but this would have meant a delay of at least twenty-four hours for regrouping. What mattered now was not to maneuver, but to give evidence to the enemy of the aggressiveness of the German Panzer units—following the Napoleonic principle "s'engager, puis voir." Rommel agreed. When he left my command post, I warned him to watch out for the enemy low-flying aircraft. This discussion took place in the bus of my operation section, the operations staff being present. (Within an hour all of them had been killed in an enemy air attack.)

Only a short time after Rommel's departure, reports came in from the Panzer Lehr Division that the enemy was attacking in force. About 60 tanks had broken through the overextended front of the division and were reported pushing to the southeast from the vicinity of Bretteville-L'Orgueilleuse. With the exception of a few companies from the 21st Panzer Division and the 12th SS Panzer Division, no reserves were available; to organize a reserve was out of the question. Furthermore, we did not know when reinforcements were due to arrive. Under these circumstances, it would have been poor tactics to drive farther to the north and to enter a kind of sack, the formation of which had begun. Although with misgivings, I ordered the cancellation of the impending night attack.

About a half hour later the command post of Panzer Group West was subjected for several hours to severe bombing and strafing. All personnel of the operations section as well as most of the officers of the forward echelon were killed. The bulk of the vehicles and almost all the technical equipment of the Nachrichten (signal) battalion were destroyed, in spite of their thorough dispersion. Thus the staff could no longer function. Although I myself was slightly wounded, I was ordered to assemble and re-form the staff. Since this mission entailed working in Paris, I drove to Rommel and requested a new assignment at the front.

The experiences of these few but exceedingly strenuous and exhausting days were as follows:

a. Training and morale of the Panzer troops, including recruits, was adequate in every respect.

b. The action in Normandy demonstrated the limitations of a German *army* fighting the Allied *combined armed forces*.

c. The enemy naval artillery and low-flying aircraft caused excessive casualties and severely reduced the morale of the troops. Air observation was the decisive factor of both the ship-based and land-based artillery of the enemy. The German artillery depended entirely on ground observation. Because of the wooded terrain, this was a serious limitation.

d. The Panzer divisions were threatened with very rapid attrition. The close fighting in the hedgerows resulted in heavy casualties, and replacement battalions were not available in sufficient numbers.

e. Supply lines and conditions in rear areas required the use of battalions of military police. These troops were just as essential for traffic control as for combating numerous paratroopers, who were continually being dropped from the air. These paratroopers, who formed the backbone of sabotage and the intelligence service, seemed to melt away without any trace as soon as they reached the ground.

f. The current German tactics were bound to be unsuccessful. *Reinforcement of the enemy by sea was more rapid than our concentration on the ground.* Consequently, we renewed our request for a mobile central command characterized by the term "Jungle Tiger Tactics." Our intention was to concentrate the Panzer force beyond the range of naval guns, to disregard any temporary loss of ground, and to hit the enemy with the strongest possible concentration of tanks. These attacks were to be repeated after every gain in elbow-room produced by the strategic mobility of the Panzer forces.

10 June: III Flak Corps'
Initial Commitment in Normandy

by General der Flak Wolfgang Pickert

In the evening of 8 June the bulk of III AA Corps had reached the area west and southwest of Caen, despite the great difficulties on the way there. By the morning of 9 June, which, according to the opinion of OB West was actually already too late, they were in position for the intended counterattack. Due to strong enemy resistance, this counterattack was not initiated at the time. We went over on the defensive.

Enemy air activity was extraordinarily effective the whole of the time. Even at night, besides continuous harassing attacks, there were also concentrated air attacks. Thus I remember the nocturnal air raid on Évrecy, some eight kilometers south-west of Caen, in which a Panzer battalion resting in the area of Évrecy was heavily battered, in an air raid of half an hour's duration, without the possibility of nocturnal defense. During the day, besides continuous fighter-bomber attacks there were also concentrated raids by formations of Marauders, one of which smashed up the command post of Panzer Gruppe West—stationed, as far as I recall, in La Caine, 20 kilometers southwest of Caen—together with its command elements.

The forward command post of the Corps was at first immediately east of Évrecy, and then at Ste-Honorine-du-Fay (15 kilometers southwest of Caen).

III AA Corps immediately took up connections with the command in charge of the Caen area, i.e. that of I SS Panzer Corps, in Baron, 10 kilometers southwest of Caen, and with its artillery commander, so as to secure the support of this sector by concentrated AA fire above its centre of gravity, and by participation in ground combat with artillery fire [presumably meaning artillery fire on the part of the AA batteries]. The AA regimental commanders were ordered to cooperate with the divisions, and the artillery commanders of these divisions in their sectors.

Signals services: Beside the telephonic connections with the AA regiments and the various command headquarters of the Army, the maintenance of which connections was continually being worked at, radio communications were the most important means of communication. This was especially the case for the long-distance connections with the rear areas, with the Air Force Administrative Headquarters (Luftflotte) 3, and with the supply depots. There was often interference on the long-distance lines to the rear areas. Here the radio beam communications showed themselves to be an almost ideal means of communication, although their use was somewhat limited, owing to the alleged danger of enemy listening-in, by camouflage specifications, and other limitations. The small number of radio-beam implements was regrettable. The signal battalion of the Corps, and the signal platoons of the units, put up a remarkable performance under enemy fire and fighter-bomber attacks.

The organization of the supplies of the III AA Corps had been envisaged in the following manner:

The Air Force Administrative Command Headquarters (Luftgaukommando) West – France was responsible for supplying AA ammunition, equipment, vehicles and means of communication. The Army in whose sector the Corps was committed was responsible for messing, fuel, infantry ammunition, and close-combat equipment.

The supply routes for AA ammunition were initially very long, as AA ammunition stockpiles had not yet been laid down behind the Normandy sector. It had to be brought up from the Évreux region, or sent up. There were likewise at first no stores of fuel behind the Normandy front. It (i.e. the fuel) had to be brought up the whole long way from the Paris area.

For the repair of AA equipment the AA Corps received, at the beginning of the invasion, an AA maintenance shop and a motor vehicle maintenance shop. Both were insufficient, so that numerous repairs had to be carried out in the regions of Évreux and Versailles.

10 June: 346th Infantry Division Attacks

by Oberst Paul Frank

On 10 June the first impulse of the 346th Infantry Division attack captured Bréville and the heights just to the south of that town. The subsequent frontal attack on Amfreville could not get started. Before waiting for a second attack on Amfreville to get under way from the north, the division pushed a reserve battalion past the town in the south with the objective of seizing the bridge, and ordered Kampfgruppe Luck also to move out on its attack. Before its power was exhausted, this thrust took the forward elements to within 800 meters of the Ranville church. Considerable losses were suffered from incessant heavy naval artillery fire which covered the whole attack area. It was hoped that relief would come with the success of Kampfgruppe Luck's attack, but this attack was halted just 100 meters from its line of departure.

Toward noon, with powerful naval artillery and air support, British forces went on the offensive. Employing numerous tanks, they threw the forward elements of the division back onto the heights at, and south of, Bréville. As expected, evening brought another British attack. The enemy, determined to retake the important height (which

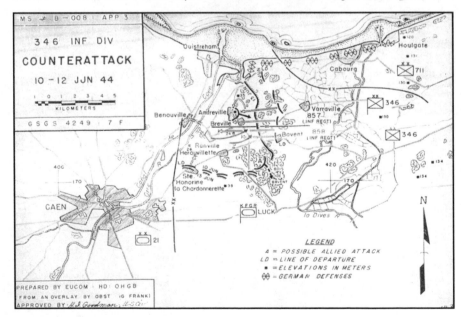

comanded the vital bridge), drove our forces northward out of Amfreville and onto the low-lying Sallenelles. Although Bréville itself (after a bitter struggle) remained in our hands, the enemy gained another foothold on the heights south of the town.

The attempt to eliminate the enemy bridgehead east of the Orne had failed. Complete air superiority added to naval artillery had given the enemy the deciding margin of power. He suffered a casualty rate of 30 percent in two battalions and 20 percent in two other battalions. [The author does not make clear to which regiments these battalions belonged.] From our narrow forward position at Bréville we were now able to move toward the Orne bridge only to a very limited degree. This Bréville position was, by itself, untenable. It had either to be given up or extended. Division decided to attack again on 12 June, southward out of Bréville, with the limited objective of seizing one and a half kilometers of high ground southeast of the town.

10 June: 2nd Panzer Division Moves to Normandy

by General der Panzertruppen Heinrich, Freiherr von Lüttwitz

The divisional commander went during the morning to XXXXVII Panzer Corps, at Gallion, where he received the following situation orientation. The enemy had taken Bayeux and launched attacks from there in the direction to the south. The Panzer Lehr Division fought north of Tilly. Four large gaps consisted [*sic*] to the west, toward Torigni, in which only reconnaissance patrols from the Panzer Lehr Division, 17th Panzer Grenadier Division, and I SS Panzer Corps were active. The Panzer Lehr Division left wing was held only, in its depth, by weak security elements. It was planned to rally the 2nd Panzer Division, 17th SS Panzer Grenadier Division, and 3rd Fallschirm Jäger Division, then to launch with all three divisions, together with the Panzer Lehr Division, an attack to recapture Bayeux.

Since the 2nd Panzer Division was nearest to the assembly area, the division was ordered to take its time, so that a coordinated arrival of all named divisions in the assembly area could be obtained. The other divisions were still farther in the rear areas.

By 1200 hours the following units had arrived at:

Reconnaissance Battalion:	The woods at Almenêches;
Right March Group:	The area of Nonant-le-Pin;
Left March Group:	Only the area north of Mortagne.

Both march groups were attacked during the morning by low-flying enemy planes. Losses occurred only to the left march group. Thunderstorms hindered repeatedly the enemy's air activity; usually it used to flare up again during the course of the afternoon.

Today all divisional tracked vehicles were supposed to be loaded onto railroad cars in the old garrison. The conditions of the railroads and tracks, which the division passed and saw during its march movement, created considerable concern about transportation by railroad.

PART FIVE

11 June, D+5

By 11 June Rommel realized that the invasion had succeeded and that the war would be lost. The issue was now how to get this information before the High Command and to Hitler himself. None of this answered the question: What to do then?

On the British front, the Panzer units joined the remaining infantry on the defensive. I SS Panzer Corps had already lost half the armored vehicles it had committed. The 17th SS Panzergrenadier Division started to arrive in its assembly areas as its commander went forward to contact the beleaguered German defenders of Carentan. The reconnaissance battalion had to be peeled away and sent to reinforce the buckling 352nd Infantry Division sector near Caen. The British started to resume the push to Caen with the newly landed 7th Armored Division, moving against Villers-Bocage through difficult, close terrain.

The US advance pushed north in the Contentin peninsula. The Marcouf battery, with its three 8-inch naval guns, finally had to be evacuated. The German 6th Fallschirmjäger Regiment could not longer hold on and was forced to retreat from Carentan, being put under the command of the 17th. On the V Corps front, the advance came up to German positions on high ground, including Hill 192, that blocked the advance on St-Lô and would continue to do so into July.

D.C.I.

OKW War Diary: 11 June

by Major Percy E. Schramm

On 11 June the Führer ordered the transfer of six antitank artillery battalions to the West, the strengthening of the front north of the town of Carentan, now in the hands of the enemy, by the Assault Gun Lehr Brigade and the 77th Infantry Division, and the provisioning of Cherbourg with supplies. He ordered further that the planned attack on Kowel [in Poland] be cancelled and that II SS Panzer Corps with the 9th and 10th SS Panzer Divisions to be transferred back to the West. The 353rd Infantry Division was moved up from Dunkirk. Besides, special units were transferred to the combat area. The combat group of the 6th FS Division was assigned to the Fifteenth Army as protection against air landings.

During an estimate of the situation which had been set for 2300 hours, Army Group B stated that it was obvious that the enemy had planned to gain a deep beachhead between the Orne and the Vire, and cut off the Cotentin peninsula. It was, however, entirely feasible that the enemy, in case the resistance was too strong in this area, would launch on early attack in a southerly direction. His operations had consumed considerably more time than had been expected and it seemed that the enemy was forced to employ more forces that he originally intended. He was now reinforcing his units continually. Due to his superiority in the air we had failed to bring up troops for a counterattack in the Orne–Vire area in good time; I SS Panzer Corps had been forced onto the defensive. For this reason the Army Group had to concentrate its efforts on the establishing of a cohesive front; the elements in the forward positions could therefore not be relieved. The Army Group intended now to replace the Panzer units with infantry divisions and transfer its focal point to the Carentan–Montebourg area in order to avert the danger to Cherbourg. According to this plan, the Army Group intended to attack the enemy between the Orne and the Vire. According to OB West, our own operations had become extremely aggravated or could partially not be carried out at all for the following reasons:

1. The enemy's superiority in the air (up to 27,000 sorties a day);
2. The effect of the enemy's ship artillery;
3. The equipment of the enemy;
4. The employment of parachutists and glider troops.

In conclusion, OB West reported: "The troops of all arms are fighting doggedly and with extreme tenacity despite the employment of enormous quantities of matériel by the enemy."

11 June: 709th Infantry Division

by Generalleutnant Karl Wilhelm von Schlieben

The enemy, too, had suffered severe losses, as could be gathered from intercepted radio messages. When it became apparent on 11 June that the enemy had not succeeded in his rapid push on Cherbourg, the Army deemed the following measures likely:

a) The employment of airborne troops at Valognes;
b) Minor landings at the Bay of Vauville situated in the northwestern part of Cotentin peninsula;
c) Air landings to capture the main defense installations at Cherbourg.

The division ordered the Commander of Cherbourg, Generalmajor Sattler, to keep all his forces in readiness to counter the above-mentioned measures.

Since the western part of the Cotentin peninsula was free of the enemy, and since the latter's intention to carry out a rapid push on Cherbourg had been frustrated, I expected that the German operational reserves, particularly the large Panzer formations, would be used to remove the danger threatening Cherbourg.

The advance battalion of the 77th Infantry Division did not reach the area south of Valognes until evening. On the Merderet river the battalion secured the approach of the bulk of the division.

The High Command of the Seventh Army proposed that its assault battalion, which was assigned to the 709th Division, be mentioned in the bulletin of the Army. Apart from the regiments of the 709th Division, elements of the 921st and 922nd Grenadier Regiments, of the 100th Smoke Battalion, the 709th AT Battalion, the Motorized 456th and 457th Artillery Battalions and of the 3rd Battalion of the 243rd Artillery Regiment also deserved a considerable share in the defensive success enjoyed so far. To them must be attributed the fact that the High Command of Seventh Army was able to submit the following estimate of the situation to Army Group B on 12 June: "The enemy was unable to carry out his intended rapid push on to Cherbourg from the landing area on the southeast coast of the Cotentin peninsula." It was, however, a defensive success which had cost us great losses in men and matériel. Already the lack of ammunition was being felt by the artillery, the smoke shell mortars, and the antitank artillery. On account of the enemy control of the air, it was difficult to get supplies.

11 June: 6th FS Regiment Retreats from Carentan, Links Up with 17th SS Panzer Grenadier Division

by Oberstleutnant Friedrich, Freiherr von der Heydte

By 11 June the ammunition situation in the regiment had become so critical that the commander requested the Parachute Army via radio to have Junkers 52s or Heinkel 111s supply ammunition by air. All the rifle ammunition of the rifle companies was collected and used for machine guns, with the result that the riflemen were reduced to fighting with nothing but hand weapons.

During the night of 11 June supply by air was actually carried out by the Parachute Army in an exemplary fashion. The ammunition was dropped south of Raids on a field, which had been marked off by lights, about fourteen kilometers behind the front line.

On the morning of 11 June, at Pommenauque, the Americans succeeded in forcing the first deep penetration through the regiment's main line of resistance. It was not possible to clear up this penetration, but it was halted and sealed off by assault detachments.

As a result of the steady extension of the front and the heavy casualties, the regiment's main line of resistance was thinned to such an extent that the regimental commander had no doubt that on 12 June the Americans would succeed in effecting additional breakthroughs and consequently in capturing the city. In view of these circumstances, he no longer felt able to take responsibility for sacrificing the remainder of the regiment in the battle for Carentan and decided to evacuate the town in the late afternoon of 11 June.

Contrary to expectations, he succeeded in evacuating Carentan in broad daylight without interference by the enemy, who seemed to be reorganizing his forces. There is no doubt that during this evacuation of Carentan, as during the crossing of the Douve on 8 June, a determined pursuit by the Americans would have led to the annihilation of the regiment.

The regiment, together with subordinate elements, occupied a new defensive position southwest of Carentan. Hill 30, at the southwestern edge of the city, constituted the most important point of the new position.

The regimental commander had advised LXXXIV Corps of his decision to surrender Carentan, and Corps had approved this step. The regimental commander was therefore all the more astonished when, on the afternoon of 11 June, just after the main body of the regiment had evacuated its former positions, the commander of the 17th SS Panzer Grenadier Division [commonly known as the "Götz von Berlichingen Division," after the historic German folk-hero] suddenly appeared and informed him that the division would arrive in the Carentan area the same night in order to take over the defense of Carentan. If the commander of the 6th FS Regiment had known only a few hours sooner that this division, whose foremost elements had already reached the Périers area early on the morning of 11 June, would be brought up, he would certainly never have made the decision to surrender Carentan. LXXXIV Corps, too, had apparently not been informed in time of the arrival of this division, for there is no doubt that the corps, which maintained constant radio communication with the regiment, would have immediately transmitted this information, which after all had considerable bearing on the regiment's decisions; besides, the corps would never have approved the regiment's decision to evacuate Carentan. Consequently it can only be assumed that the Army, the Army Group, or the Wehrmacht High Command, in this case going over the head of Corps, had ordered a division into the Carentan sector.

[The premature surrender of Carentan on the afternoon of 11 June, which the commander of the 6th FS Regiment decided on his own responsibility, was an incomprehensible and ill-advised step on his part, since he had been informed of the commitment of the 17th SS Panzer Grenadier Division at Carentan in advance and not afterward, as claimed by the author. According to the records of Seventh Army, they informed LXXXIV Corps by telephone as early as 1300 on 10 June and then again on 11 June at 1145 that "the 17th SS Panzer Grenadier Division was assembled for attack at Carentan." According to statements made by the Chief of Staff of LXXXIV Corps, he apprised the commander of the 6th FS Regiment in person of the commitment of this division not later than 10 June.

Neither the Army nor Corps were in accord with this independent decision of the commander of the 6th FS Regiment, because one of the most essential tasks of Seventh Army of necessity should have consisted in preventing, as long as possible, the Americans from establishing contact between their forces on the Cotentin peninsula and their forces stationed east of the Vire and with the British.

Afterwards, an attempt was made to justify the premature surrender of Carentan, which was a vital junction point, by pointing to the shortage of ammunition. It was at that time impossible to unequivocally fix the responsibility for this action. As a result of the previous severe and disastrous battles, the commander of the 6th FS Regiment had suffered a temporary physical and mental breakdown. This also explains his "misguided order," which, following the surrender of Carentan, he issued in connection with the occupation of the decisively important Hill 30 southwest of Carentan.

Only the fact that his command of the regiment had so far been outstanding and that he made a speedy recovery prevented the commander of the 6th FS Regiment from being punished or relieved of his command.—Pemsel.]

The 17th SS Panzer Grenadier Division was commanded by Brigadeführer Ostendorf, and Obersturmbannführer Konrad was Operations Officer. After the division arrived in the vicinity of Carentan, the division command post was located at St-Sébastien-de-

Raids, sixteen kilometers southwest of Carentan. The division was composed of two motorized infantry regiments, three battalions each, one reconnaissance battalion, one assault gun battalion, one artillery regiment, one engineer battalion, one signal battalion, and the supply services. After Brigadeführer Ostendorf was wounded at the end of June 1944, Brigadeführer Baum took over command of the division.

The 17th SS Panzer Grenadier Division had been activated during the first months of 1944 and as yet only a few of its elements had had contact with the enemy in the area extending from Caen to Bayeux. Although the division was well armed and well equipped, it was surprisingly poorly trained. The majority of the officers had had neither the training nor the combat experience to enable them to fill their positions adequately. In general, the commanders of the regiments, the artillery, and other battalions did not possess the elementary knowledge of tactics required of an officer candidate. The low standard of training of the officers of the division's artillery regiment was particularly noticeable. Like the Italian artillery, with which I had become acquainted in North Africa, the artillery of the 17th SS Panzer Grenadier Division was not able to concentrate its fire flexibly in brief bursts after observation or to fire ahead of attacking infantry from sector to sector (or, in Normandy, from hedge to hedge). The artillery of the 17th SS Panzer Grenadier Division usually fought a "private war" without paying any attention to the infantry.

Since the units of the 6th FS Regiment were already in the process of withdrawing when the commander of the 17th SS Panzer Grenadier Division arrived, and as the Seventh Army reserve units subordinated to the 6th FS Regiment had already occupied their new positions, it was no longer possible to revoke the regimental commander's decision to evacuate Carentan. The commander of the 17th SS Panzer Grenadier Division therefore decided to attack and recapture Carentan, and on the evening of 11 June he and the commander of the 6th FS Regiment reconnoitered the prospective terrain of attack.

352nd Infantry Division:
The Fighting North of St-Lô

by Oberstleutnant Fritz Ziegelmann

In the forenoon of 11 June the enemy had pushed forward from Balleroy to Cormolain to the right of the 352nd Infantry Division and had occupied that place. Our own reconnaissance forces and those of the enemy were in contact with each other south and southwest of Cormolain. Concentration of the enemy in the Forêt de Cerisy were observed again, and small-scale assaults from these woods to the Elle sector were repelled. Apart from that, everything remained quiet throughout the day in the right-hand sector (30th Mobile Infantry Brigade). The right border of the division (adjacent to the 3rd Fallschirm Division) had been changed so that the important Elle crossing near Bérigny had been given to the 3rd Fallschirm Division and was taken over by (a combat element of) this division at noon on 11 June. From his bridgehead west of St-Jean-de-Savigny the enemy started his attack south and southeastward. Round about noon this fighting had become particularly intense. The activity of the artillery increased and the air forces of the enemy (fighter-bombers) began to be active. In the hours of the evening the enemy succeeded in taking St-Jean-de-Savigny, although in this regimental sector (916th Grenadier Regiment) all reserves available had already been sent in as countermeasure. On the left regimental sector (914th Grenadier Regiment), weak forces of the enemy had crossed the river near Moon-sur-Elle during the afternoon. We did not succeed in repelling these forces until the evening. On that day it was quiet on the Vire front from Aire to Montmartin. Further northwest, from the area around Carentan, very loud noises of battle could be heard. We did not succeed in establishing telephonic communication with the 91st LL Division, nor with the 6th Fallschirm Regiment sent into Carentan to obtain information about the situation. Neither was the attempt successful to take up communication by motorcycle messenger from St-Jean-de-Daye (where the divisional commander had gone) with the weak elements of II/914th Grenadier Regiment fighting near Le Mesnil (east of Carentan)—among which there were elements of the 621st Eastern Battalion—as the enemy, coming from the west, had occupied the St-Jean-de-Daye–Le Mesnil road. It could be deduced from the noise of battle changing locally and via the artillery observation post telephone network of the IX/1352nd Artillery Regiment, which was supporting this defensive battle from the area west of St-Jean-de-Daye, that, on account of his superiority in men and material, the enemy had reached the eastern outskirts of Carentan in the late afternoon. The noise of battle from that region increased now, so that it was supposed that bitter fighting was taking place in that village. The endeavors of the 352nd Infantry Division to occupy as quickly as possible the area between the Vire and the Tante Canal on the level of the railroad line, with portions of the advancing combat element of the 275th Infantry Division, which it asked to have assigned to it, were frustrated on 11 June as not even portions of this combat element were yet available by the evening of 11 June. Thus on 12 June there was the danger that the enemy would start advancing from Le Mesnil to the south, along the main road running in the direction of St-Lô. His activity east of the Vire had been interpreted as a preparation for that.

The Battles East of St-Lô:
The Role of the 3rd FS Division

by Generalleutnant Richard Schimpf

When the advance group, on 10 June, under the command of Major Becker, had reached the region of Bérigny on both sides of the St-Lô–Bayeux road and probed into the forest of Cerisy, they encountered only weak enemy security detachments there. I was of the opinion that possessing the forest was of decisive importance for the further conduct of the battle, especially for the planned attack. Therefore I decided to thrust forward on the next forenoon to the Forest of Cerisy, together with the reconnaissance battalion of the 17th SS Panzer Grenadier Division, which already had arrived on my right.

Contact with the newly arrived elements of the 17th SS Panzer Grenadier Division existed. On the left, contact with the 352nd Infantry Division was maintained solely by liaison patrols. After having informed the Commanding General II FS Corps of my intention, I was forbidden to thrust into the Forest of Cerisy, because a considerable portion of the 352nd Infantry Division sector had to be assigned to me, due to the heavy losses this division had suffered during the first days of the invasion.

As a result, my front became a mere line of combat outposts. The bulk of the division was still on its march from the Bretagne. I set the point of main effort north of Bérigny, where the greatest danger of an enemy attack lay. If the Americans, at that time, had launched an energetic attack from the Forest of Cerisy, St-Lô would have fallen then and would not have been held for another whole month. The elements of the division already available (totalling the strength of a reinforced regiment) occupied the sector of St-Germain-d'Elle–Bérigny–Couvains. Due to the lack of artillery, the bulk of the flak battalion had to be committed as antitank defense (antiaircraft Kampftruppe combat), in some cases directly in rear of the front line. The situation was extremely critical, also because contact with the neighboring divisions was only a very loose one, maintained by liaison reconnaissance patrols. The attempt to tighten the contact to the right by advancing the right wing of the division further towards the northeast did not succeed on account of a heavy enemy counterattack against and out of La Vacquerie.

In the meantime, the enemy received such heavy reinforcements along the whole front line that a German counterattack could only be taken into consideration—if at all—when the necessary number of new troops could be made ready. Contrary to the former orders of attack, the division therefore received a defensive mission to hold by all means the former main line of resistance. At that juncture, the elements marching on foot had arrived in the divisional combat area, and the front line, occupied until then merely in form of outposts, could now be divided up into independently responsible defensive sectors.

Although the enemy attacked nearly all parts of the front line, it was never with more than one battalion, and, after having met considerable resistance, he retired to his line of departure. The strength and the manner of the enemy artillery fire and the fact that he confined himself to combat air reconnaissance also supported this impression. The defense against these continuous attacks, which were like combat patrols, was excellent training, and familiarized the German troops with the enemy's manner of fighting. The fact that a considerable number of tanks were put out of action, mostly by close-combat weapons, did away with the tank terror complex. On the other hand, the constant state of alert and the increased difficulty of each movement on the combat field brought about by excellently directed enemy artillery and mortar fire meant a heavy physical burden for the troops.

On 11 June the enemy began the long-expected attack, with the obvious objective of capturing St-Lô. During the night of 10/11 June there was heavy artillery fire which expanded over the whole front sector of the division, with the point of main effort first in the area of Bérigny–St-Quentin, which later was shifted to the region of Hill 192–St-André. The attacks, strongly supported by tanks, resulted in local penetrations near St-Georges-d'Elle and St-Quentin. However, it was possible to seal them off. Even a battalion of the 5th FS Regiment, already cut off, was able to beat its way through to the German lines, carrying with them all their wounded. Continuous enemy attacks, carried on further west with the heaviest support of artillery and tanks, succeeded toward evening in capturing Hill 192. However, a breakthrough on St-Lô was still prevented by a tenacious defense. The last and very limited reserves of the division were committed on Hill 147, which, because of its dominant position, had a decisive importance in the battle for St-Lô.

The self-sacrificing battles of the next three days were such a strain on each fighter, and the 9th FS Regiment suffered such severe losses of men and matériel, that the regiment had to be relieved. For lack of other available troops, the relief could only be made by the 8th FS Regiment, which was less occupied on the right wing of the division. As the division had no more reserves at its disposal, the relief was only possible by bringing forward a company formed out of the division signal battalion.

Attacks on I SS Panzer Corps (Now Commanding Panzer Gruppe West Forces)

by General der Panzer Leo, Geyr von Schweppenburg

In the morning of 11 June, southwest of Balleroy, the enemy took Cormolain, on the exposed flank of Panzer Gruppe West (now I SS Panzer Corps). The weak advance detachment of the 3rd FS Division stood fast in and around Bérigny. The principal idea of Seventh Army was to establish a solid front with I SS Panzer Corps and the right wing of LXXXIV Infantry Corps. In this respect the pondering of higher commanders played a major part. Schooled in the static warfare of 1918, they remained unfamiliar with the spirit and nature of mobile troops. They were not daring enough to tolerate gaps and to endure the enemy on the flanks and in the rear in order to effect a concentration of forces elsewhere. Because of their obsession for a compact front, they never waited for the complete assembly of a single Panzer division. Divisions were always committed piecemeal, and the effectivness of their mobility and concentrated firepower was lost. Anticipating the danger of piecemeal actions, Panzer Gruppe West, prior to the invasion, had gotten OB West to issue an order forbidding the splitting up of Panzer divisions and the removal of elements from the division commander's control. After the enemy had landed, this order was no longer obeyed.

11 June: I SS Panzer Corps Defense in the Caen–Bayeux Sector

by Generalmajor Fritz Krämer

During 11 June Corps issued an order for temporary defense. The boundary lines of divisions were fixed provisionally. We had to reckon with the necessity of an extension of our front to the east. It had become evident to Corps that the right division of the left neighboring corps (352nd Infantry Division) no longer possessed any combat power. We therefore requested Seventh Army to move up a division in full fighting trim to the right wing of the corps adjacent to our left. Ostensibly, the 2nd Panzer Division had been envisaged for this purpose, but we could not expect its arrival in the next few days. It was exceedingly difficult for Corps to maintain the necessary close contact with the corps adjacent to our left. For the time being we were still able to make available for this task the reconnaissance battalion of the Panzer Lehr Division.

The changeover from attack to defense was a very difficult task for Corps. Enemy air forces had upset computations of time during the approach march into the Caen combat sector, and now there were great difficulties in bringing up the materials for field-type improvements of the terrain. The division had only the engineer equipment belonging to the first issue of ammunition, but even this was not complete, as some vehicles had been destroyed by air attacks. We lacked particularly mines, wire, close-combat weapons (Panzerfaust, hand grenades, etc.) and spades. Except during lunch time, from 1200 to 1400 hours, the enemy air forces were in the air incessantly. Supplies could be transported only at night. The supply columns were highly efficient. Enemy air attacks had destroyed many ammunition dumps in the West and often it was necessary to bring ammunition and engineer equipment from depots east of the Rhine. In order to make full use of the few hours of darkness (from 2100 to 0500), vehicles moved with utmost speed. This resulted in a large number of serious accidents. The British had repeatedly claimed that the area around Caen had been transformed into a veritable fortress. This was by no means the case. The reasons that resistance could be offered for a comparatively long time were:

a. The troops committed there literally permitted themselves to be killed before they would give up ground;

b. The British High Command either decided to attack too late or made the attack with an inadequate number of troops.

By 11 June the three divisions controlled by Corps had been considerably weakened. At the time of writing this report, detailed strengths of men and material no longer could be given. In percentages the losses were as follows:

21st Panzer Division: Killed, wounded and missing in action—about 40 percent; put out of action—guns, about 30 percent; tanks, about 50 percent. The number of Type IV and V tanks fit for action, held by the division, was approximately 30 or 40. The tanks put out of action in the air attack a few days previously had not been repaired.

12th SS Panzer Division: Killed, wounded or missing in action—about 25 percent; put out of action—guns, about 10 percent; tanks, about 20 percent. About 60 Type IV and V tanks were fit for action.

Panzer Lehr Division: Killed, wounded or missing in action—about 25 percent; put out of action—guns, about 10 percent; tanks, about 20 percent. About 60 Type IV and V tanks were fit for action.

On 11 June the 101st SS Panzer Battalion, a heavy battalion, was attacked in a small wood by an enemy bomber wing and lost about 50 percent of its officers and men. The majority of its Tiger tanks were incapacitated for many days. Only fifteenTiger tanks were capable of commitment.

We could not expect a new supply of tanks or guns. The tank repair shops of division worked day and night in order to put the tanks in working order again. Continuous enemy attacks often prevented towing up or recovering tanks put out of action ahead of the MLR.

Losses of officers and men could be made good by our own resources as follows:

a. From the so-called officers' reserve (Führerreserve). About 20 percent of officers and NCOs were withdrawn from all units into the so-called March-baillone, or personnel replacement transfer battalion.

b. From the replacement battalions which, particularly for Panzer grenadiers, were quartered in the rear area.

Corps had ordered that the slightly injured and slightly sick be healed in the surgical hospitals of divisions or corps and then returned to the troops immediately.

During the whole day strong enemy forces attacked various points of our front and for the first time the British committed strong armored forces. These attacked the left wing of the Panzer Lehr Division toward Tilly-sur-Seulles, but were repelled in a counterattack by tanks of that division. Also the 12th SS Panzer Division was attacking the enemy, who skillfully exploited the terrain features. Individual points, such as sections of woods in the Bretteville area, changed hands repeatedly. During the night of 11/12 June this division threw in the last of its reserves for a counterthrust. In general we succeeded in holding the front, but Corps would not have been equal to an attack by massed enemy forces. All three divisions were in action and no reserves were available. Corps had ordered each division to keep a reinforced battalion in reserve, to be used only with Corps consent. The gap between us and LXXXIV Infantry Corps on our left, which had grown bigger and bigger and was no longer a baby, was our chief problem child (Sorgenkind). In order to have at least a small reserve group there, five Tiger tanks were moved to the northern outskirts of Villers-Bocage with the mission of annihilating enemy tanks that might attempt to break through there. Corps was unable to understand why the enemy did not make the most of this gap with a breakthrough.

After 10 June, upon orders of Corps, the firepower of the entire artillery was coordinated by being placed under the control of Arko I, and this fact was of great importance in our defense. We were able to direct the fire quickly and deftly to the most endangered sectors, and in addition to save ammunition. The flak artillery was included in this system of fire concentration. After 11 June two Luftwaffe flak regiments were ordered to cooperate with Corps. They were used for ground combat as well as antiaircraft defense.

Signal communications with Seventh Army still were very poor. Telephone calls could be made only through a relay station which was handled by an Army General Staff officer. On the afternoon of 11 June an enemy bomber attack smashed the headquarters of Panzer Gruppe West, which had assumed control on the previous day. Chief of Staff Generalmajor Ritter von Dawans and about 40 officers and men were killed. Corps was placed under the direct control of Seventh Army.

The troops still were fighting without support from the Luftwaffe. Representatives of the Luftwaffe who attended a conference at the command post of Panzer Gruppe West on the morning of 11 June to discuss the possibilities of a Panzer attack in the direction of Creully could not promise support from the air forces. Without such support any attack was deemed to failure. Continual attacks from the enemy air forces, in which the planes frequently were low enough for men on the ground to identify crew members, often had paralyzing affects on our troops.

Corps, in its report on 11 June, as it had done every day, particularly asked for air support, for infantry divisions, and for the sealing off of the gap on our left. We were promised that two Panzer divisions would be committed there, besides two projector brigades (8th and 9th) which were subordinate to Corps. Advance elements of these two brigades arrived in the combat area of Corps on about 15 June and thereafter efficiently supported our resistance. Apparently enemy forces, not accustomed to these kinds of weapons, were greatly impressed by them, just as the German soldiers were in the East by the so-called "Stalinorgel" (a projector with tubes mounted on trucks). Almost all enemy attacks were soon halted in the sectors where the projector brigades were used.

On the evening of 11 June our front extended along the following line: Orne–south of Elsinville–Bretteville–north of Tilly-sur-Seulles–10 kilometers northeast of Caumont. Strong enemy attacks were expected on the following day.

11 June: 2nd Panzer Division Moves to Normandy

by General der Panzertruppen Heinrich, Freiherr von Lüttwitz

Orders for 11 June were received which stated that the Athis–Briouze area must be occupied by the morning of 12 June. The division began to move with individually traveling vehicles during the course of the day, while the division's bulk was moved up in the evening. Other orders received made it necessary to dispatch the reconnaissance battalion to the left wing of the Panzer Gruppe West, where it was placed as reinforcement into the gap between the Panzer Lehr Division and the 3rd Fallschirm Jäger Division.

Simultaneously with that movement, the commander of the reconnaisance battalion had to be relieved on account of charges against him, which were of personal nature. However, this turned out later on to be very unfortunate, because his successor (the oldest company commander) was by no means able to cope nor to master the situation.

The division gave the reconnaisance battalion orders to reconnoiter in the existing gap between Tilly and Périgny while at the same time occupying quickly as much territory as possible, along a generally northern direction. Contact with the Panzer Lehr Division and 3rd Fallschirm Jäger Division was to be established and firmly held. (Time of the orders issued at 1900 hours.)

Faulty Tactics of the German Command

by General der Panzer Leo, Freiherr Geyr von Schweppenburg

Late in the evening of 10 June, when I SS Panzer Corps assumed command of the Panzer Gruppe West sector on both sides of the Orne up to Bayeux, the most endangered point was in the sector of the Panzer Lehr Division, southeast of Bayeux. Bayeux had been taken by the enemy on 7 June, and advance elements of the US Army were spearheading southwest toward the Drôme to drive a wedge between I SS Panzer Corps and LXXXIV Infantry Corps. Army and Army Group intended to rectify this situation by the coordinated attack of II FS Corps (on the approach march) and strong elements of I SS Panzer Corps. The left wing of I SS Panzer Corps was to remain on the defensive until strong forces of II FS Corps could arrive in the Balleroy area. Shortly thereafter, this proposed action was abandoned, and II FS Corps was rerouted toward Isigny.

To relate the fundamental mistakes of the German Command during this period is of greater importance than to describe in detail the local engagements over villages and hill masses. The initiative was on the side of the aggressor by reason of a large-scale landing. A few piecemeal tactical thrusts were not sufficient to enable us to regain the initiative. These tactics could not be avoided, perhaps, during the first days of the invasion; the first countermeasures were necessarily of an emergency nature. With the advent of German reserves, however, strategic measures were possible and should have been exploited. On or about 12 June, when decisions of a strategic nature were possible, it was time to establish a clearly defined succession of objectives. By examining the orders issued during the period 11–15 June, one comes to the conclusion that the German command simultaneously pursued four objectives. These measures, each *purely defensive*, were as follows:

   a. To prevent an enemy advance in the vicinity of Caen;
   b. To halt the enemy advance in the Bayeux area;
   c. To eliminate the beachheads which the enemy had established on both sides of the Vire river;
   d. To prevent the enemy from cutting off the Cotentin peninsula and to oppose his push to Cherbourg.

In accordance with the Schlieffen methods, our action should have been to attack Bayeux and the area north of it with elements of the 21st Panzer Division (Panzer regiment only), strong elements of the 12th SS Panzer Division and 3rd FS Division, the forward echelon of a Tiger tank battalion which had just arrived, the Panzer Lehr

Division, the 17th SS Panzer Grenadier Division, and the wheeled elements of the 2nd Panzer Division—action to take place on 13 June and all units to be under a single command. By concentration of forces and by aggressive action under a similar command, we had mopped up the Red armies in 1941–42. The quality and individual training of German Panzer divisions were better before the invasion than at the beginning of the Battle of the Bulge. It was necessary only to give them the opportunity to concentrate in order to make the most of their mobility and striking power. The armchair strategy of Berchtesgaden and Rommel's pessimism and lack of strategical schooling wore out the Panzer divisions in piecemeal engagements over trifling terrain features. Thus we were unable to oppose General Patton's later drive in open terrain with comparatively fresh troops of equal strength.

In the evening of 10 June Seventh Army had taken the surprising view that Panzer Gruppe West was probably strong enough to defeat the enemy between the Orne and Bayeux. This was proof that Army had not recognized the size and rapidity of the enemy landing. Seventh Army should not be blamed for this poor judgment. Army was unable to make a correct estimate of the situation because enemy air superiority had blindfolded the German defenses. By the morning of 11 June Seventh Army had altered its estimate. It was discovered that in the Panzer Gruppe West sector the enemy had landed five divisions—at least, strong elements of them. The strength of the Panzer Gruppe at that time was approximately three divisions.

PART SIX

12 June, D+6

The British attacks on the 12th—to the south by the 7th Armored Division to Villers-Bocage and to the east by the 51st Highland Division—both made limited gains with substantial loss in a foretaste of the hard pounding that would result in the weeks to come from the failure to take Caen on D-Day. In both, I SS Panzer Corps armored units provided the backbone to a mobile, hard-hitting defense. While Allied firepower superiority prevented a massive counterstroke, the German ability to take back most of the tactical gains made on the British front on the 12th showed their skill. A limited attack by the 6th Airborne Division had more success.

On the V Corps front, 12 June marked the reopening of the drive on St-Lô, which would be a major US objective into July. The remnants of the 352nd Infantry Division, reinforced by the 3rd Fallschirmjäger Division, held on and slowed the US advance. V Corps was at the entrance to the Caumont Gap—the space between the forces opposing the British and Canadians and those opposite V Corps—but there was no awareness of the German weakness.

The Germans continued to be pushed back in the Contentin peninsula. Near Carentan there was heavy fighting on Hill 30 while the Germans prepared for a counterattack the next day. General Marcks, commander of LXXXIV Corps, was killed in an air attack when trying to organize the situation.

D.C.I.

OKW War Diary, 12 June

by Major Percy E. Schramm

On 12 June the Führer issued on order to attack the enemy beachhead between the Orne and the Vire in sections and wipe it out. The enemy was to be annihilated first east of the Orne to free the 346th Infantry Division. OB West was informed at the same time that II SS Panzer Corps with the 9th and 10th SS Panzer Divisions would be assigned to him and that the 34 Infantry Division was not being transferred to Nineteenth Army but to OB Southwest.

OB West was further instructed, by order of the Führer, to move up especially heavy mortars as well as General HQ artillery for the attack on the bridgehead east of the Orne. Long-range artillery was to be employed on both sides of the mouth of the Vire. In addition, the Führer demanded that the 1st SS Panzer Division be merged with the 12th SS Panzer Division as soon as possible and subordinated to I SS Panzer Corps after the arrival of the 363rd Infantry Division.

A gap which occurred between I SS Panzer Corps and II FS Corps, and which was regarded as dangerous by OB West, could at first be temporarily closed and later completely sealed off. The danger of a breakthrough to the western coast of the Cotentin peninsula became more and more apparent.

Up to 12 June, seventeen units had been spotted, among then seven American. It could therefore be assumed that Group Montgomery would not attempt to launch a second landing; however, a second landing could nevertheless be considered east of the beachhead, either in the Calais–Le Havre area or between the mouth of the Schelde river and Dunkirk. In addition, the Führer again weighed the possibility of a landing in the Bretagne.

12–13 June: Decisions on the Defense of Cherbourg

by Generalleutnant Max Pemsel

It must be regarded as a decisive German success that the defenders of the Cotentin peninsula succeeded in keeping the entrance to the peninsula and thus to the fortress of Cherbourg open long enough to permit the German Supreme Command to move up strong reserves, just as Rommel originally suggested.

It was a grave decision for the Seventh Army to transfer the regiment of the 243rd Infantry Division, which was employed as a security detachment along the potential landing front of the fortress of Cherbourg, from the fortress to the battlefield around Montebourg. However, Seventh Army decided to take that risk because the fate of Cherbourg was being decided on the heights of Ste-Mère-Église–Montebourg. A long drawn-out defense of the landward side of the fortress was impossible, owing to a complete lack of tanks, adequate antitank weapons and air support.

The order to reinforce the land front of the fortress of Cherbourg came from the Wehrmacht High Command. It was clear to Seventh Army that the battle front could not be weakened at this time in favor of the useless reinforcement of that entirely undeveloped part of the fortress which was exposed to landings. Seventh Army, therefore, attached prime importance to the execution of the other missions—the holding of the important area around Montebourg and the keeping of the western part of the Cotentin peninsula open in order to move up reinforcements for the battle for the fortress.

The death, on 12 June, of Commanding General Marcks constituted an irreplaceable loss for the Seventh Army and for the entire German Army. Marcks' superior intellect had proved itself in the military as well as in the political sphere. Once General von Schleicher's right hand, he was temporarily retired by Hitler in 1933 and, though later reinstated, was always looked upon with distrust. In spite of all humiliations, Marcks never slackened in the performance of his duties as a soldier until his death, which he perhaps expected and even sought. The directive, regarded as a testament, which Marcks gave prior to his death—to the effect that, in case of an American breakthrough across the Cotentin peninsula toward the west, the bulk of the corps should withdraw into the fortress of Cherbourg—proves that he fully realized that the entire battle for the Cotentin peninsula was actually only a phase of the battle for Cherbourg. On the occasion of map exercises prior to the invasion, Marcks had always stressed this viewpoint.

During the invasion, however, the fate of Cherbourg was decided in the battle at Ste-Mère-Église–Montebourg, because, apart from the commitment of the 77th Infantry Division, the German Supreme Command failed to throw fresh reserves into the peninsula and, in addition, failed to order the withdrawal toward the fortress in time.

In my opinion, it would not have been possible for LXXXIV Army Corps to have accomplished its mission of defending the fortress of Cherbourg even if the entire corps had been withdrawn toward the fortress in accordance with Marcks' intention. The fall of Cherbourg would perhaps have been delayed by this but not prevented. To the south, the entire area from the Vire to the sea had been left unprotected because no reserves were available to the higher command for the conduct of mobile operations or the establishment of a new front.

A prerequisite for the other solution—namely the employment of LXXXIV Army Corps for the establishment of the southern front on the Cotentin peninsula instead of its withdrawal toward the fortress—was that the harbor installations in Cherbourg be very thoroughly destroyed beforehand. Prior to the invasion, the commander of the 709th Infantry Division, General von Schlieben, had made the interesting suggestion to destroy the harbor of Cherbourg before the start of the invasion so thoroughly that the principle motive for the Allies to invade the coast of Normandy would be removed. From the military point of view, this was a simple solution, which for political reasons, however, could not be resorted to as long as a state of collaboration existed between Germany and Pétain's France.

The Seventh Army was in a predicament. It had to split its forces in the peninsula in order to hold the fortress a little longer and thus to gain time for the establishment of the southern front on the Cotentin peninsula. The second task seemed to have priority, for, since the battle for the fortress of Cherbourg had been decided in the fighting around Ste-Mère-Église–Montebourg, it was of vital importance now to prevent an American advance into France proper. General Marcks' successor, General Fahrenbacher, shared this opinion.

There were sufficient food supplies in Cherbourg to sustain even stronger forces than those which were actually concentrated in the fortress.

12 June: 709th Infantry Division

by Generalleutnant Karl Wilhelm von Schlieben

The enemy exercised pressure west of the coast near Quineville, but without any success worth mentioning. For the rest, it was very calm. In the evening it was reported that the Commanding General of LXXXIV Corps, General der Artillerie Marcks, had been killed when his car came under fire from enemy planes. LXXXIV Corps was taken over by General Fahrenbacher

The line separating Group Hellmich, to which the 77th Division (less the 1050th Regiment) and II Parachute Corps had now been assigned, ran, according to the daily report of Army Group 5 of 12 June, as follows: Le Plessis (II Parachute Corps)–Baupte (Hellmich)–northern edge of reservoir area of Carentan–Carentan Canal–Moulin.

I am unable to recall the right boundary of the 709th Division and of the 77th Infantry Division stationed on the River Merderet.

The local commander of Montebourg, Captain Simoneit, was wounded by shell splinters and was no longer available for duty.

12 June: Kampfgruppe Keil Defends the Cotentin Peninsula

by Oberstleutnant Günther Keil

The days from 8 to 12 June were marked by hard defensive fights. The Azeville battery, lying in front of our MLR, was encircled and lost after brave resistance. During the days of holding out it greatly relieved our front. The 1st Battalion of Rocket Projector Regiment 100 (minus one company) was subordinated to the regiment. By its effective fire it contributed to the defense of enemy attacks. In addition one or two batteries of the GHQ Coast Artillery Regiment Triepel could effectively take part in the fighting, their guns being directed to the south. During one enemy tank attack—it was, I think on 12 June—seventeen tanks were disabled, partly by Panzerfaust charges. The infantry suffered severely from the fire of the enemy ship-based artillery, especially as it could entrench deep into the rocky ground. When the guns of the Marcouf naval battery had been destroyed, no artillery was available to fight the enemy ship-based artillery. An additional factor was the complete lack of our Luftwaffe. Enemy fighters made any movement by day practically impossible. Enemy bombardment planes could fly to their targets unhindered and release their bombs there. The front in the regimental sector— apart from the advanced battery of Azeville, which was lost—held out as on the first day of the invasion and was a good sign for the German infantry, especially if one considers the fact that the major part of the infantry was not battle-experienced and was now exposed to severe, crucial tests through the immense superiority of enemy material.

The adjacent front of the Rohrbach Combat Team had constantly been pushed back. On 12 June its connections with units were standing southeast of St-Floxel so that my right wing was hanging loose, jutting out almost a thousand meters. Only a thin security line established the connection to the 2nd Battalion of the 920th Regiment of the Rohrbach Combat Team, lying farther to the rear, and protected my open right flank. On the morning of 12 June General Marcks appeared and, having explained the situation, ordered that the Marcouf battery be given up and the front be withdrawn to the southern edge of the village of Fontenay-sur-Mer–southwestern edge of Dangueville. The line Montebourg–Quineville had already been ordered as the MLR that had to be held by all means; as far as possible, the enemy was to be stopped south of this line.

During the night of 12/13 June, unnoticed by the enemy, the 3rd Battalion of the 922nd Regiment and the 3rd Battalion of the 739th Regiment withdrew.

12 June: 6th FS Regiment Fights for Hill 30 while 17th SS Panzer Grenadiers Prepare to Counterattack

by Oberstleutnant Friedrich, Freiherr von der Heydte

During the occupation of the new position southwest of Carentan, the commander of the 6th FS Regiment made a fateful error. He had at first ordered this position to be occupied not by his own regiment but by the Eastern battalions and other Seventh Army units under his command, which he had withdrawn from the old position east and north of Carentan, where they had been distributed among the organic units of the regiment. He had intended to rehabilitate and reorganize on 12 June, immediately behind the new position, the regimental units and the two battalions of the regiment still under his command, and not to commit them again in the foremost line until the night of that day. On the basis of his previous, although very limited experience with the Americans, he did not expect them to attack until 13 June.

In fact, on 12 June the American 101st Airborne Division seemed to have had in mind nothing more than combat reconnaissance for the time being. However, during these operations an American reconnaissance patrol or assault detachment succeeded in capturing Hill 30, which was apparently halfheartedly defended by an Eastern battalion. This event also threatened seriously the new position of the regiment: the regimental commander believed it was out of the question to attack Carentan before recapturing Hill 30. Attacks on Hill 30 which were launched on 12 June by the engineer platoon under the personal leadership of the regimental commander were unsuccessful.

While the German paratroopers were fighting for Hill 30, one motorized infantry regiment, one assault gun battalion, and the main body of the artillery regiment of the 17th SS Panzer Grenadier Division moved into assembly positions in the area north of Meautis for the attack on Carentan. It was the aim of the commander of the 17th SS Panzer Grenadier Division to attack eastward on both sides of the Baupte–Carentan road, to capture Pommenauque, and to push on into Carentan from the northwest corner of the city. He expected that the Americans would of their own accord give up Hill 30 without a fight as soon as the divisional elements succeeded in penetrating the northwestern part of Carentan. Although the assault guns would be restricted to the Baupte–Carentan road and a few narrow side roads by the nature of the terrain, the divisional commander expected a great deal from them because he felt certain that the Americans would fall back in the bocage terrain to the right and left of the road, where observation was impossible, as soon as the assault guns succeeded in breaking through. The divisional commander did not wish to use any artillery preparation in order to maintain as far as possible the element of surprise. The 6th FS Regiment as such did not participate in the attack; only its 2nd Battalion was placed under the command of the attacking SS regiment and committed by the latter at the left of the above-mentioned road, on both sides of the railroad embankment extending from Baupte to Carentan, in very difficult terrain poorly suited for attack. The 3rd Battalion of the 6th FS Regiment was placed at the disposal of the division, but the regimental staff and units were not included in the framework of the plan of attack, nor in the order based on this plan.

The same reasoning which prompted the divisional commander to forego any artillery preparation also induced him to be totally opposed to battle reconnaissance operations on 12 June. As a result, the enemy situation was still completely obscure when the attack began. Reconnaissance reports on the foremost enemy positions and the strength of the enemy were not available. The attacking forces were consequently compelled to grope their way, while advancing in terrain quite unfavorable for offensive operations. Nevertheless, the divisional commander was confident of success. One of the questions he put to the commander of the 6th FS Regiment on 12 June when issuing instructions was as follows: "After Carentan has been captured, would you prefer to continue advancing towards Isigny or wheel to the left toward Ste-Mère-Église?"

12 June: 352nd Infantry Division Fighting North of St-Lô

by Oberstleutnant Fritz Ziegelmann

On 12 June, on the right side of the sector of the 352nd Infantry Division, it was possible for the enemy to penetrate into the area adjoining Caumont to the north, where at first the reconnaissance battalion of the 2nd Panzer Division succeeded in detaining him. Further reinforcements had arrived at the 3rd Fallschirm Division, among which there was an artillery battalion.

In the sector of the 352nd Infantry Division, the enemy continued his activity. In the right regimental sector (30th Mobile Brigade), fairly strong elements of the enemy units crossed the Elle southwest of Cerisy. In fighting, subject to frequent changes, he (the 2nd US Infantry Division) succeeded in taking this sector, Bois d'Elle, in the evening. In spite of the lack in fighting experience of the fortress engineers (elderly men) employed in this sector, the enemy did not succeed in taking complete possession of his bridgehead. At several spots, small supporting detachments near the Elle kept their position in spite of being enclosed, and so contained enemy forces.

In the central regimental sector (916th Grenadier Regiment), the attempts of the regiment to throw the enemy out of his bridgehead near St-Jean-de-Savigny, across the Elle by counterattack, were frustrated and caused considerable losses on our side. In the left regimental sector (914th Grenadier Regiment), the enemy succeeded during the fight in reinforcing his bridgehead near Moon-sur-Elle and in enlarging it during the day of 12 June toward the south. Rather heavy and continuous attacks in the Elle sector east of Aire made us suppose that the enemy, after having taken the locality of Aire, intended pushing further to the west across the Vire, in order to facilitate a penetration by assault to the south, for the forces of the US XIX Army Corps, which could probably be sent in west of the Vire from the north in the direction of St-Lô.

Therefore, the 352nd Infantry Division tried to accelerate the bringing-up of the combat element of the 275th Infantry Division subordinated to it, and already approaching, with the aid of its own trucks. By the evening of 12 June we succeeded in bringing up the 275th Fusilier Battalion (which had been reinforced by one engineer company) and the 2nd Battalion 984th Grenadier Regiment. By the morning of 13 June the last battalion occupied positions on the western bank of the Vire, its right wing being near Aire, and the reinforced 275th Fusilier Battalion on either side of the Le Mesnil–St-Jean-de-Daye road, adjoining the railroad line running across south of it. The northern wing of this newly formed regimental sector could further be reinforced by the former personnel of the Army Engineer School (consisting of 250 men) sent in as infantrymen. Thus the left wing of the 352nd Infantry Division, which could formerly be qualified as "open," was more or less filled up, although our own artillery forces were very weak throughout the whole divisional sector.

During the night of 12 June the 352nd Infantry Division learned from a French deserter, who wanted to go further to the south, that the enemy was bringing up reinforcements via Isigny to the west and that a higher staff was stationed at La Cambe.

Piecemeal Panzer Attacks

by General der Panzer Leo, Geyr von Schweppenburg

By the evening of 11 June heavy enemy attacks on Caen from the north were anticipated. It was planned to join the forces of the 21st Panzer Division and the remnants of the 716th Infantry Division which still remained on the east bank of the Orne with those elements on the west bank. Command of the east bank was to remain under the 346th Infantry Division. This correct decision of Seventh Army was substantially influenced either by an order of OB West or of Hitler. OB West demanded that the gap between I SS Panzer Corps and LXXXIV Infantry Corps be closed with all available units; Berchtesgaden ordered the elimination of the beachheads, first east of the Orne, and then between the Orne and the Vire. The first objective of the I SS Panzer Corps attack was Bois de Bavent. By order of the Führer, the 7th Werf Brigade was to be transferred to the east bank of the Orne.

At 0900 on 12 June the enemy attacked west and northwest of Tilly-sur-Seulles with task forces of infantry and considerable armor. These attacks hit the Panzer Lehr Division and the left wing of the 12th SS Panzer Division. Furthermore, the enemy was pushing farther to the west, obviously toward the Balleroy area. The attacks in the vicinity of Tilly-sur-Seulles were repulsed and 32 tanks were destroyed. The enemy took Caumont. The forward elements of a Tiger tank battalion thrust from the left flank of the Panzer Lehr Division toward LXXXIV Infantry Corps with the mission of establishing contact. The battalion succeeded in contacting elements of the Panzer Aufklärungs (reconnaissance) battalion of the 2nd Panzer Division, which had reached the area south of Caumont–Biéville.

12 June: I SS Panzer Corps Defends, Battle of Villers-Bocage Opens

by Generalmajor Fritz Krämer

On 12 June the enemy repeatedly attacked with armored support. Both the 12th SS Panzer Division and the Panzer Lehr Division suffered extremely heavy losses. They were forced to give up ground, and the left wing of the Panzer Lehr Division had to be withdrawn and the area around Tilly was lost. Again, heavy fighting developed for individual terrain sections. In these actions the British for the first time committed tanks with flamethrowers. All enemy attacks were efficiently supported by his artillery and air forces.

Early in the morning the Panzer Lehr Division reported renewed tank attacks against Tilly.

As the Panzer Lehr Division was not able to establish a continuous front, we had to consider the possibility of enemy tanks breaking through along the Villers-Bocage–Caen road. The weak reconnaissance elements of this division's reconnaissance battalion committed in this gap on the flank of the adjacent LXXXIV Corps reported advancing United States forces, which, as it seemed, intended to capture the high ground west of Tilly.

Changes in the situation occurred almost every hour. Reports on successes and reports on disabled enemy tanks were mingled with cries for help and reports of losses. Again and again the troops requested air support.

On the whole it was an unprofitable day for Corps, but it brought about a favorable change in one minor combat sector. By 10 June the appearance of British tanks on the left wing of the Panzer Lehr Division and of United States forces within this gap made it appear probable that the enemy had discovered that few German troops were in the area of Tilly–south of Bayeux–Balleroy.

Early in the morning of 12 June the commander of the five tanks (Tiger) which had been placed in readiness north of Villers-Bocage sighted an enemy motorized column, including tanks, on the march from Tilly toward Villers-Bocage. Without hesitation he drove against this column and exterminated with his tanks about 30 enemy tanks and a like number of motor vehicles. Thus, by the personal courage of this officer, the enemy's intention to break through by way of Villers-Bocage was frustrated.

The idea of placing in readiness the five Tiger tanks which had been left intact during the enemy air attack had produced good results, preventing an enemy attack and a probable rolling up of the entire Corps front at least on 12 June or the day following.

151

12 June: 346th Infantry Division Attacks

by Oberst Paul Frank

On 12 June, led by two battalions of infantry and elements of Panzer Jäger Abteilung 346, the division attacked out of Bréville. The limited objectives set by the division were achieved and held in spite of an entire day of intense British counterattacks. The heaviest kinds of concentrations of fire were placed on certain of our units, which suffered continuous heavy losses. The commander of the Sturmgeschütz Kampfgruppe personally disabled eleven enemy tanks.

In the late evening, after a very heavy half-hour bombardment, the enemy in great force attacked to the east and south of Amfreville, threatening the rear of our forces in and south of Bréville. The only two roads across the flooded Dives lowland passed through Varaville and Bavent, and an extension of the enemy drive to these places would have cut the division in two. Having no forces immediately available for a counterattack, division HQ decided to abandon the forward position at Bréville, and to establish a new MLR west of the Dive lowland, which could insure flank support for the coastal defenses east of the Orne and could be used to launch further attacks. Thus the first counterattack had come to an unsuccessful conclusion.

12 June: 2nd Panzer Division Prepares to Attack from the March

by General der Panzertruppen Heinrich, Freiherr von Lüttwitz

The nightly road march movement, on the basis of experiences of the first days, was connected with a considerable amount of difficulty. Crossroad intersections in towns had been bombed out so severely that unforeseen detours became necessary. On account of this the troops were moved before dawn, and covered the longest distances before low-flying planes began their attacks. At that time, the bulk of the troops then went under cover, or continued to march with individually, separately [sic] traveling vehicles. The bulk of the troops resumed their movement only after 1700 hours, for, as a rule, the enemy air force began to cease its activity at that time.

The morning of 12 June saw the arrival of the 2nd Panzer Division, with its advance elements of the right march group, in the Athis–Carneille area, and with elements of the left march group in the area south of Blione–Louley le Terron. The bulk of the march groups arrived toward evening.

Throughout the day the division staff remained at the old command post (Cornière), from where it directed troops to the new area; they transferred their command post during the evening to Lignou, south of Briouze.

By noon the slowly forward-moving reconnaissance battalion arrived in the woods at Le Mesnil-Auzouf (11 kilometers southwest of Aunay-sur-Odon.) Now the effects were felt, which resulted from the change in command of this battalion. From this point on the battalion was reconnoitering in a northern, northeastern, and northwestern direction. In spite of its orders to occupy as much terrain as quickly as possible, in a general northern direction, the battalion remained hesitatingly inactive and awaited first reports and results from its reconnaissance patrols. For this reason the division commander ordered, by radio, a speedier forward movement of the battalion. Nevertheless, it was not until the divisional commander had dispatched a special-mission staff officer who had orders to move the battalion forward that they began to move on during the same afternoon, and by evening occupied Caumont, and contacted the 3rd Fallschirm Jäger Division units near St-Germain-d'Elle.

For 13 June, the division was slated to remain in its present area; during this time some of the units were closed up further, or the time was used to repair defects on weapons and vehicles, which became faulty during the course of the movement. The division made every effort possible to obtain contact with its tracked vehicles. It requested repeatedly at Corps headquarters to unload its tanks again from railroad cars, which were still standing on account of the enemy air situation in the same railroad yard, and to bring them up to the division via a road march. The division discounted the belief that its tanks would be on hand by the time of commitment. The division would much rather have taken the risk that not too many losses might result as a matter of the road march. In any case, the bulk of the tanks would have been on hand earlier and all losses that might have occurred on the road could have been easily repaired again.

It was always the division's view that the invasion could only then be stopped and repulsed if all forces were committed quickly, in their whole strength. Each additional day of delay would thus aid the enemy in receiving fresh reinforcements, and cause on our side a decrease in the commitment capacity, as well as in the supply situation, which were all due to the enemy's unlimited air superiority.

The rest period which had been ordered for 13 June became ineffective. Toward 1700 hours orders were received that the division should proceed with its march to the Aunay-sur-Odon area. This move was intended to get the 2nd Panzer Division in position in such a manner in the left wing of Panzer Group West that it would be able to attack simultaneously with the Panzer Lehr Division toward the northern and western directions in order to enable the division to strike against any enemy force in their flanks, which might penetrate between the still existing gap of the two armies. Nevertheless, reports received concerning reinforcements opposite the left wing from the Panzer Lehr Division caused an alteration to this decision. By now, the Höhere Führung (Higher Headquarters) was aware of the perils in case the enemy should succeed in occupying the hills of the Bois du Homme (south of Caumont), even that one at Le Bény Bocage, in the Corps' deep flank.

After the division was all set to march off in the direction to the north into the prescribed Aunay-sur-Odon area, orders were received at 2000 hours which instructed the division to move over the hilly terrain at Le Bény Bocage, and along both sides of the high terrain of the Bois du Homme, then to establish contact with the Panzer Lehr Division on the right and the 3rd Fallschirm Jäger Division on the left. Previously complete radio silence had been ordered. This made it difficult to alter the division's course in the complete darkness; nevertheless, it was done in a relatively short time. By now reports were received which stated that the reconnaissance battalion had completed its occupation of Caumont. Thus it became unnecessary to take the bulk of the division over these hills at Le Bény Bocage.

The march group on the right (2nd Panzer Grenadier Regiment with the 2nd Battalion 74th Panzer Artillery Regiment, with several light and heavy batteries of the Army Flak Battalion and one company of the 38th Panzer Pioneer Battalion) was slated to march via Athis, Condé, and St-Pierre-la-Vieille toward the north, but was turned off its course at Condé, from where it marched to Vassy, La Lamière, Le Mesnil-Auzouf and Jurques.

The march group on the left (304th Panzer Grenadier Regiment, 74th Panzer Artillery Regiment (less two battalions), 38th Panzer Pioneer Battalion (short of one company), one light and one heavy battery, and the 273rd Army Flak Battalion), marched beyond Briouze–Flers–Vassy–La Lamière toward the north but was turned off at Flers and marched from here on to Tinchebray–Le Boulay-aux-Chats (6 kilometers west of Vassy)–Estry–St-Charles-de-Percy–Brémoy (11 kilometers south of Caumont). The advanced elements of these march groups arrived in the high terrain in the morning of 13 June.

In the evening of 12 June the division staff transferred to St-Charles-de-Percy, where it arrived approximately around 2300 hours. The reconnaissance battalion reported that it had made contact with the enemy at La Vacquerie (3 kilometers west of Caumont). The Panzer Lehr Division was engaged in fighting at Tilly and protected with weak security units in the line St-Germain-d' Ectot (7 kilometers northeast of Caumont)–Anctoville–St-Louet-sur-Seulles.

The danger consisted that the enemy would break through between Caumont and Tilly, in the direction toward the south, and thus would encircle the Army's left wing. For this reason the division received orders around midnight to proceed at once over the high terrain, on both sides of the Bois du Homme, and to counterattack in a northern direction in the gap forward of the advancing enemy and to beat them back with the coordinated aid of the Panzer Lehr Division's left wing, a Panzer battalion (Tiger), and I SS Panzer Corps. The first objective of the attack was the road leading from Tilly to Balleroy.

PART SEVEN
13 June, D+7

June 13 showed much of the form the Normandy campaign would follow throughout June, July, and August. It was apparent that, despite the actions of Seventh Army, Cherbourg would soon be cut off. With its limited landward fortifications, it would fall on 27 June, though the Germans were to be dismayed how quickly, and astounded that, despite extensive demolitions, the port would be put back into operations in three weeks. In an attempt to prevent the Americans cutting across the peninsula, the Germans shifted more units—mainly from the 243rd Infantry Division that had been under 709th Infantry Division command—as a blocking force.

June 13 also showed that, although they took the town itself that day, the Allies would not be exploiting the "Caumont Gap." The Germans were able to bring up more units to plug the gap (by 15 June), hold the line and launch counterattacks. Once again, as with the road to Caen on D-Day and the road to St-Lô after the fall of Isigny, the planning, forces and drive for such deep exploitation were simply not present.

In the British sector, 13 June was the second day of the Battle of Villers-Bocage, in which counterattacks by the Panzer Lehr Division, 2nd PanzerDivision, 101st SS Heavy Panzer Battalion, and other units pushed back the British 7th Armored Division from their hard-won gains of the day before. The long and frustrating story of British armored operations in Normandy would see many comparable events over the following months.

The 17th SS Panzer Grenadier Division and 6th Fallschirmjäger Regiment's counterattack on Carentan never got far in the absence of artillery support. They were halted by the 101st and 82nd Airborne, supported by newly arrived elements of the 2nd Armored Division, carrying out the armored link-up with the paratroopers that was supposed to have happened in the evening of D-Day.

But these counterattacks were all limited and local assault. This was not the armored fist trying to sweep one beachhead into the sea and then roll up the remainder. There was no question of repelling the invasion any more.

D.C.I.

OKW War Diary, 13 June

by Major Percy E. Schramm

During an estimate of the situation on 13 June, OB West discussed the development of the battle in retrospect. He stated that the enemy had failed to reach his objectives as far as localities and the time schedule were concerned but had succeeded in forcing our own troops onto the defensive. Our efforts should now be concentrated on the protection of Cherbourg.

A second landing should be expected by 20–30 large and four airborne units. It was impossible to predict if this landing would occur in the Somme area or in Belgium. The tension had become considerably stronger at the southern French front: 70 transports had been reported in North Africa on 24 May.

Acts of sabotage had increased in the interior, but not to the extent that had been expected. In the areas earlier occupied, in France as well as in Belgium and Holland, no incidents of importance had occurred. The activation of guerrilla bands had increased around Limoges, at Tulle and Cantal, and also to the west of the Rhône river, near Bourg and in the Basses Alpes (Lower Alps). Forces have been committed to cope with the situation. The population had been informed that those bands were being regarded as guerrillas.

During a briefing, [OB] West was greatly concerned with the Supreme Command in the West. It was proposed to strengthen the Normandy front, disregarding all risks which the withdrawal of troops from other coastal areas would entail, including partial transfers from OB Southwest.

13 June: 709th Infantry Division

by Generalleutnant Karl Wilhelm von Schlieben

The naval gunfire against Montebourg during the night caused the Army commander again to try and eliminate the enemy naval artillery. At midnight I had ascertained that our nightly harassing fire was answered by concentrated army artillery fire. In order to give the battle-weary infantry a rest, I withdrew the order for harassing fire for the night of 12 June.

The division continued to hold an approximate line Merderet River–Montebourg–Quineville. It became apparent that the enemy intended to break out from his beachhead at Ste-Mère-Église to the southwest in the direction of the west coast of the Cotentin peninsula. During the evening of 13 June Seventh Army recorded the following: "13 June is especially noteworthy for strong enemy attempts to make a breakthrough with armor from the Ste-Mère-Église sector to the west coast of the Cotentin, and in that way to effect the isolation of the peninsula." At that time there was no immediate danger to the right flank of the 709th Infantry Division, as it was supported by the 77th Infantry Division which had in the meantime taken up defensive positions.

The daily bulletin of the Ia of Army Group B of 13 June reported an enemy penetration 10 kilometers deep, southwest of Ste-Mère-Église, and further stated (extract):

"In the zone of penetration near Ste-Mère-Église the enemy continued his attacks and captured Abbeville, Cretteville and Coigny, pushing further on the west to Prétot. For several days there has been heavy naval artillery fire off the east coast of Cotentin against the flanks and rear of the German forces holding the line Montebourg–Quineville, coupled with concentrated unchecked air attacks which, apart from the losses suffered, are unbearable, even by the best troops, unless countermeasures are taken. Demolition of the harbor of St-Vaast-la-Hougue has been ordered."

The War Diary of the Seventh Army reported on 13 June as follows:

"Forward thrusts undertaken at the same time between Quineville and Montebourg could be intercepted . . . While Montebourg could be held against the strongest pressure, the enemy succeeded in making armored penetration between Baupte and Étienville."

Above, left and right: Two views of
Generaloberst Heinz Guderian.

Right: Generalmajor Eugen König, who took
over command of the 91st Luftlande
Division on 10 June.

Above left: Luftwaffe General Eugen Meindl, commander of the airborne corps that started to come into the line on the St-Lô front after the first week of fighting.

Above right: Michael Wittmann, one of the great German tank aces of World War II. He commanded a Tiger heavy tank platoon that played a major role in the defeat of the Desert Rats at Villers-Bocage on 12 June.

Below: Waffen SS troops waiting for the enemy.

Above: A wartime painting by Hermann of a German sniper, armed with a modified 98K Mauser and a Zf42 telescopic sight. Such snipers played a key role by slowing down the Allied advance inland.

Below: A Waffen SS BMW motorcycle. In Normandy these were used more often for courier duties than for scouting.

Above: German infantry advance with a Tiger heavy tank in support. In the initial fighting Tigers were employed exclusively against the British, where the better tank country threatened a potential breakthrough.

Right: Waffen SS troops rest in a weapons tractor under cover. Such vehicles spent many of the daylight hours pulled off the road and camouflaged.

Above: Waffen SS troops on the march. The time taken by German infantry units to move into position was an important factor in preventing successful counterattacks against the beachheads.

Below: A wartime German sketch of an infantryman in action in wooded terrain of a type frequently encountered in Normandy.

Right: A German paratroop NCO.

Below: German paratroopers attack in a town. This reflects the nature of the fighting in Carentan by von der Heydte's 6th FS Regiment. (A wartime drawing by Gross.)

Above: A wartime sketch of a German 80mm medium mortar. Mortars inflicted many of the Allied casualties in Normandy.

Below: A camouflaged German antitank gun in action. These would often engage Allied armour from close range in Normandy.

Above: A wartime German artist's impression of an 88mm flak gun in the long-range direct-fire role. III Flak Korps was called upon to provide such support against the British and Canadians throughout the Normandy campaign.

Left: Another sketch, this time of a 100mm M18 field gun.

Above: A 150mm K18 heavy gun in action.

Right: Directing traffic on the Normandy roads.

Above: A German 50mm antitank gun and its prime mover. Even though it had been supplanted by later, heavier weapons, the 50mm—and even the earlier 37mm—was still widely used in Normandy.

Below: A sketch of a 150mm SFH 36 howitzer moving through a destroyed town and pulled by an understrength horse team. In Normandy such movement was normally carried out under cover of darkness.

Above: Armed with a long 75mm gun, the Jagdpanzer IV was highly effective in Normandy but relatively rare on the ground.

Below: A knocked-out StuG III German assault gun near Ste-Mère-Église on 10 June. These were extensively used in Normandy, often as self-propelled antitank guns or in direct support of infantry units, but sometimes as substitutes for tanks.

Right: A destroyed German 88mm flak gun. The peeled-back barrel suggests a premature detonation, possibly done before capture but also possibly reflecting the poor quality of late-war German munitions.

Below: The PzKpfw V Panther tank was the most powerful medium tank in Normandy, although its long 75mm gun could limit its usefulness on narrow roads and tracks. This Panther is being inspected by a group of US Army Air Forces fighter-bomber pilots.

Above: Continued air attacks against German lines of communications meant that it was increasingly difficult to bring infantry formations that relied on rail transport to Normandy. In the crucial opening battles, Panzer units had to hold the line rather than counterattack.

Below: A captured rocket launcher. Rocket launchers, and the more common Nebelwerfer, were a major element of German artillery in World War II.

Left: A captured Panzerschreck, the reloadable antitank rocket launcher that saw heavy use in Normandy, often substituting for the heavier weapons that were not available.

Below: US infantry attack with armored support in the Cotentin peninsula.

Right, upper: A column of German prisoners is led across the invasion beaches to be loaded onto landing craft for the trip to captivity in England.

Right, lower: The developing situation, 8 June.

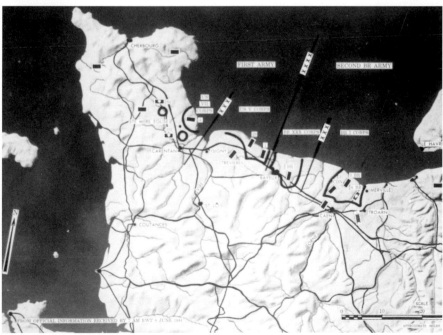

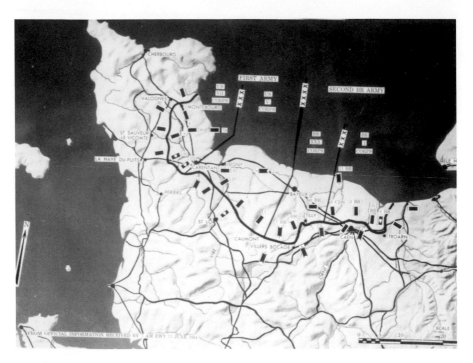

Above: The developing situation, 15 June.

Below: The developing situation, 22 June.

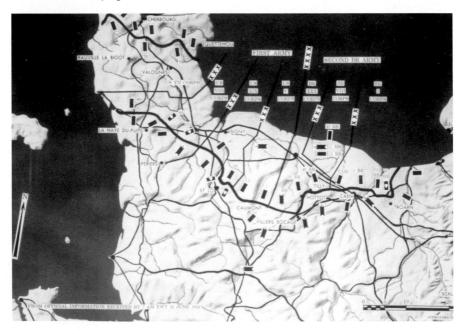

13 June: 6th FS Regiment and 17th SS Panzer Grenadier Division Fail in Their Counterattack

by Oberstleutnant Friedrich, Freiherr von der Heydte

On the morning of 13 June, at about 0700, the attack was launched from the assembly positions. On 12 June the Americans had apparently only employed patrols in order to reconnoiter the new German position. In any event, during the first two hours of the attack the attacking forces did not come into contact with the enemy. About 800 meters west of the northwestern edge of Carentan the assault gun units encountered antitank elements which prevented them from advancing any further. At about 0900 the SS troops and paratroopers made contact with strong American elements; it was my impression that these were not organized for defense but were in the process of advancing.

Severe fighting raged from hedge to hedge, at close quarters and hand to hand. The paratroop forces nevertheless succeeded in gaining several hundred meters of terrain north of the railroad embankment, while the SS Panzer Grenadier units were stopped cold in unfamiliar terrain where observation was obstructed.

The exercise of command in such terrain is extremely difficult. During combat, the SS units became disorganized and commanders, no longer masters of the situation, lost control of their units to an increasing degree; communications were disrupted, sometimes at one and sometimes at another point; and gaps developed through which the enemy skillfully infiltrated. At one farm the division commander himself was for several minutes engaged in close combat with enemy troops who had broken through. In short, by about 1200 it was obvious that for this day the attack on Carentan had failed.

The casualties among the SS forces were unusually high; the fighting spirit of the inexperienced troops was weakened; and an ever-increasing number of individual SS soldiers as well as whole groups straggled to the rear, so that the commander of the 6th FS Regiment had to instruct his adjutant to check the fleeing SS forces and assemble them in the vicinity of his regimental command post. In some instances the adjutant was compelled to enforce this order at the point of a gun.

While the attack on Carentan launched by the SS troops was thus hopelessly bogged down, the commander of the 6th FS Regiment received about noon alarming reports from Baupte. The 100th Panzer Battalion of the Seventh Army reserve had been committed at the Douve river in the area of Baupte, at first facing eastward. For unknown reasons the commander of this battalion evacuated these positions on the Douve on the morning of 12 June and dug in in Baupte proper, after which he and a few other officers left his battalion. In the meantime, the Americans had apparently crossed the Douve without encountering resistance and had cautiously approached Baupte. There utter chaos apparently prevailed among the German forces: some of the troops who had been forsaken by their commander surrendered, while others still tried to fight. There was no doubt, however, that it would be only a matter of hours before the Americans were in undisputed possession of Baupte and thereby threatening the flank and the rear of the 17th SS Panzer Grenadier Division. In view of this situation, the commander of the 6th FS Regiment sent one company of the 2nd Battalion, which was engaged in combat west of Carentan, to protect the bridge east of Baupte against forces advancing from Baupte to attack the rear of the division. Anxious hours passed until this company arrived at Baupte, for there was a distinct possibility that the American commander in Baupte would recognize his opportunity and make a quick decision to push across the bridge. The danger was not over until about 1600.

In the meantime the situation west of Carentan continued to deteriorate. The commander of the 6th FS Regiment was under the impression that a single energetic thrust by the Americans would be sufficient to induce large portions of the SS regiment to take to headlong flight, which would result in a deep breach at a decisive point in the German lines—a breach which might make possible a breakthrough during the night. He therefore employed his 3rd Battalion and the regimental units to form a rear line along the road leading from Raids southeastward to the Carentan–Périers road. He placed the dazed commander of the SS regiment under his command, and ordered the SS and paratroop forces to fall back to a position which had been reconnoitered and in part improved prior to the invasion. This extended from Le Varimesnil, southwest of Meautis (which was to be given up), and along the southern edge of a marshy valley, to a point north of Raffoville (about three kilometers northeast of Bléhou) at the eastern edge of the big "swamp" (Prairie des Gorges). In relation to the jump-off point for the attack on Carentan, the withdrawal to this position amounted to retiring generally about four kilometers. The regimental commander considered it absolutely essential to get beyond the range of the American heavy infantry weapons, which would require the Americans to shift the position of these weapons and especially to advance their artillery to the south side of the Oure.

The cover provided by the wooded terrain, which rendered the daytime attack so difficult, facilitated disengagement from the enemy and withdrawal even in daylight. Without marked interference by the enemy, the SS regiment and the 2nd Battalion of the 6th FS Regiment, crossing the rear line formed by the 3rd Battalion of the 6th FS Regiment, moved into the new position in which, by verbal agreement between the two regimental commanders, the SS regiment was committed on the right, to about 300 meters northwest of the main road from Carentan to Périers, with the point of main effort at the road. The FS regiment was committed on the left.

While the commander of the FS regiment was supervising the withdrawal of the retreating elements of his regiment along the road leading southeastward from Baupte

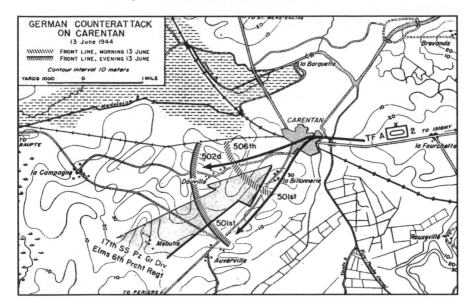

to the Carentan–Périers road, he was suddenly called for personally by the operations officer of the SS division and escorted to the divisional command post. There he was reproached by the divisional commander for his arbitrary actions and his "cowardice in the face of the enemy," as indicated by his order to withdraw. The divisional commander informed him that he was under arrest and that very night had him questioned by an SS military judge.

However, the next morning, when the Commanding General of II FS Corps, who was temporarily in charge of LXXXIV Corps, approved the conduct of the commander of the 6th FS Regiment, the commander of the 17th SS Panzer Grenadier Division released the regimental commander, and allowed him to return to his regiment.

The reader may wonder at the strange lack of activity on the part of LXXXIV Corps during the second phase of the battle for Carentan. The initiative was taken exclusively by the division and the regiments. The reason for this inactivity by the Corps can be found in the fact that during this period the Corps commanders were being continuously changed. On 12 June, the day on which the evacuation of Carentan took place, General Marcks, then Commanding General of LXXXIV Corps, was killed in an attack by fighter-bombers on the Carentan–St Lô road. General Fahrmbacher, the Commanding General of XXV Corps, was first appointed to succeed him, but as early as 12 or 13 June General Meindl, the Commanding General of II FS Corps, was assigned to act as commander of LXXXIV Corps. Then, one or two days later, General von Choltitz arrived to take over LXXXIV Corps.

To complete the record, it should be noted that, during the night of 11 June, the 6th FS Regiment was, in accordance with its request, actually supplied by the Parachute Army with sufficient ammunition by air, by means of Junker 52s and Heinkel 111s. After

12 June the 17th SS Panzer Grenadier Division assumed responsibility for the regiment's supply.

With the conclusion of the battle for Carentan, the 6th FS Regiment broke off contact with the American 101st Airborne Division, which had been its first opponent during the invasion battles; the regiment was not to meet these forces again until September, when it encountered them at Schijndel, Holland.

During and after the war, the commander of the 6th FS Regiment was frequently asked for his opinion of the American paratroopers. The caliber of the American paratroopers who fought against the regiment was outstanding; they were excellently trained in combat techniques and their armament and equipment were first class. The regiment experienced similar stubborn fighting only against the Russian NKVD divisions [field divisions of the NKVD, the former GPU], the British 51st (Highland) Division, and the Canadian 1st Infantry Division.

However, as in the German parachute forces, the tactical ability of the American command, from the lower echelons up to and including division level, did not always appear to be on a par with the excellent combat efficiency of the units. During the first days of the invasion, the Americans could have saved a great deal of time and avoided many casualties if their troops had made their jumps and landings directly into the target to capture individual objectives of tactical importance, such as the Douve bridges north of Carentan. In Normandy, as later on at Arnhem, the Americans seem to have employed the same tactics of jumping and landing some distance away from the target and then attacking the tactically important individual objective on the ground—a method which did not always lead to immediate victory. In 1944 the Americans seemed to be unfamiliar with the procedure of capturing villages or small towns from the air by jumping into them. I am not in a position to offer any opinion concerning the technical aspects of night jumping, because I have no data indicating the speed with which these units were able to assemble nor the percentage of those who made false landings. The Americans proved to be far superior to the Germans in the employment of troop-carrying gliders at night. It was odd that the Americans did not use Sturzlastensegler [dive-gliders], even where their commitment would have been advantageous.

In the opinion of the German parachute troops, the American 101st Airborne Division, and particularly its 506th Regiment [commanded by Colonel Robert F. Sink], far surpassed the other American airborne units because its commander and staff were on a par with the outstanding combat efficiency of the troops themselves.

Comments by Generalleutnant Max Pemsel

The failure of the attack launched by the 17th SS Grenadier Division in the direction of Carentan was due not so much to the lack of air support as to the inadequate training of the young division, which ran into the simultaneously launched counterattack. The 100th Panzer Training Battalion had only a few obsolete and hardly maneuverable French tanks. It was intended to deceive the enemy by the name of this unit.

13 June: 352nd Infantry Division Fighting North of St-Lô

by Oberstleutnant Fritz Ziegelmann

By 13 June the enemy had taken Caumont and carried out some smaller, unsuccessful assaults toward Bérigny. In the sector of the 352nd Infantry Division, the activity of the enemy increased and was supported continuously by fighter-bombers. (Since 0000 hours on 13 June 1944, the 352nd Infantry Division had no longer denominated its subsectors with numbers, but with the names of its commanders.) On the right sector (Combat Element Von Aufsess), the enemy succeeded in enlarging his bridgehead toward the south and west. Portions of the US 2nd Infantry Division encountered portions of the left wing of the US 29th Infantry Division. During the afternoon the latter succeeded in taking Convains. On the right of the middle sector (Combat Element Goth) the enemy succeeded, after hard fighting at and around St-Clair-sur-l'Elle, in penetrating into this locality. Fighting here was still continuing on the evening of 13 June 1944. On the left of the middle sector (Combat Element Heyna), fighting took place only at the Elle crossing, east of Aire. In the left sector (Combat Element Heintz), rather weak enemy forces, consisting of no more than one or two companies, had crossed the Elle near La Ray. After a short battle, however, these forces withdrew again across the river. On the northern wing in this sector no fighting took place, but a reinforcement of the enemy units was reported.

On 14 June the 3rd Fallschirm Division on the right of the 352nd Infantry Division received more replacements so that it could separate some reserves. In the sector of the 352nd Infantry Division, the pressure of the enemy on the right wing was continuing. At Combat Element Von Aufsess (to the right), our own front became disjointed. This was the result of casualties and overexertion. The US 2nd Infantry Division succeeded in advancing to St-Georges-d'Elle and in taking it in the evening. In the sector of Combat Element Goth (to the right of the center), the enemy enlarged his bridgehead from St-Clair-sur-l'Elle toward the south and southwest. Also in the sector of the Combat Element Heyna (on the left of the center), the enemy was able to advance further south and southwest from his bridgehead south of Moon-sur-Elle. In the sector of Combat Element Heintz (on the left), the day was quiet. However, this combat element was not given any further reinforcements. Further west, in the sector of the left neighbor (17th SS Panzer Division), the enemy started advancing from Carentan along the road running in the direction of Périers and took Hill 30 (one kilometer southwest of Carentan) on 13 June.

On 14 June the ratio of subordination of the 352nd Infantry Division was changed. On account of the death of General der Artillerie Marcks (who was killed during an air raid), and due to the situation on the Cotentin peninsula becoming more serious, the 352nd Infantry Division was subordinated to II Fallschirm Corps (the Commander of which was General der Fallschirmtruppen Meindl).

Concluding Total Picture of the 352nd Infantry Division on 14 June

During the period from 11 until 14 June, the 352nd Infantry Division did not have the rest which it believed it had the right to expect, on the basis of the inactivity of the enemy on 10 June. Its intention of organizing its formations and giving them some rest could not be carried out. We succeeded in building up on the right wing of the 352nd Infantry Division a front becoming gradually stronger (3rd Fallschirm Division, 2nd Panzer Division) and thus in preventing the unhindered breakthrough of the enemy toward the south.

In the sector of the 352nd Infantry Division, however, the enemy was able to form a bridgehead on the right wing of the division, south of Elle, having a depth of about five kilometers and a width of about 12 kilometers. On the left wing of the 352nd Infantry Division, the danger of the enemy breaking through toward St-Lô was diminished by the slow insertion of Combat Element Heintz (275th Infantry Division), and a front to the adjacent 17th SS Panzer Grenadier Division was created, in which, however, there still existed gaps. The picture had changed with regard to forces. Instead of the very weak 352nd Infantry Division, there were now two numerically complete divisions (elements of the 2nd Panzer Division, the 352nd Infantry Division and the 275th Infantry Division), which continued to increase their numbers of men.

On the side of the enemy, there were three infantry divisions, the 29th, 2nd and 1st US Infantry Divisions, which were being filled up on account of casualties suffered, also the 30th Infantry Division and the 2nd Armored Division, which were being brought up, as well as some Army tank battalions. For the fighting during the next few days there were about three German divisions confronted by five American divisions. Considering this, it had to be taken into account that on the German side there were only combat elements, which had very little artillery at their disposal, and also that support from the German Air Force could not be expected.

On 15 June, between Caumont and Carentan (which is a distance of about 45 kilometers) there was the following German artillery with little ammunition:

12	7.5cm pieces (with the 3rd Fallschirm Division)
8	8.8cm pieces (available for assignment in a limited manner only)
18	10.5cm pieces (including some from 2 Panzer Division)
8	15.0cm pieces
46	pieces altogether

On 15 June 1944 there was the following American artillery at least:

96   pieces of medium caliber
48   pieces of heavy caliber
144   pieces altogether.

In addition, there were (most important!) artillery reconnaissance planes and a sufficient supply of ammunition! These figures show again the inferiority of the Germans and the impossibility for them of forming points of main effort with their artillery.

However, the German employment of six antiaircraft detachments (twelve 8.8cm pieces) could not be completely disregarded as they contributed to impeding the advance of enemy tanks. These antiaircraft detachments had only a limited view of the terrain crisscrossed with hedges, and thus a limited power of action. Besides, the camouflage of these weapons, owing to their high superstructure, was difficult!

During the period from 11 until 14 June, the German 352nd Infantry Division suffered losses in men, which, however, were still bearable! Our fighting power on 10 June, which was about 2,500 men, decreased to about 1,900 men due to casualties, i.e. about 200 men lost, and by the changed situation of the fighting near Carentan, to where the reinforced 2nd Battalion 914th Grenadier Regiment (consisting of about 400 men) had fought its way back.

Summarized Evaluation of the Fighting Period up to 14 July

At the command post of the 352nd Infantry Division, it was clearly recognized that the US V Army Corps intended taking St-Lô as quickly as possible. Therefore, the radio messages sent by the enemy and intercepted on 10 June, which indicated a holding of the position north of Elle, were actually rendered out of date by later events.

The enemy had apparently recognized how many gaps there were in the front north and northeast of St-Lô. The fact that he gained ground in the sector between Bérigny and Aire, but did not succeed in making the decisive breakthrough, was in the first place due to the difficulty of controlling the fighting in this elevated terrain.

Certainly the hedges offered the possibility of a camouflaged advance for his infantrymen. On the other hand, the defender remained unrecognized during a longer period than would otherwise have been possible. Besides, it was very difficult for the artillery, on each side, to find favorable observation posts.

About 14 June the employment of the artillery observation airplanes became advantageous to the enemy. All German movements were observed by these airplanes and attacked by the enemy artillery at once!

It struck us that the enemy, after taking only a few small sections of the Elle sector, employed a small number of tanks, some of which were put out of action by our Panzerfaust in the elevated terrain in spite of being covered by infantrymen. That happened mostly when these tanks got stuck when trying to cross the low but steep hedges. Therefore, the employment of tanks ceased in the next days.

The American infantryman was to prove himself in this terrain an agile and superior fighter. The decreasing of the impetus of the original attack was soon noticed and the cause of it was taken to be the terrain, which could not be surveyed clearly and had a visibility of about 100 meters at the furthest. The enemy got used to peppering every hedge with his machine guns during a longer and longer period and thus wasted much ammunition. We Germans thought that henceforth there would be a shortage of the enemy's machine-gun ammunition. On the whole, his expenditure of artillery and mortar ammunition could not be compared with the available quantities of German ammunition. It must also be taken into consideration that almost the whole of the German ammunition had to be collected from ammunition depots in Paris by truck. This was very difficult on account of the activity of fighter-bombers and the lack of gasoline, and took time in any case. (Because of the activity of the fighter-bombers, the trucks moved only at night and had to avoid the towns destroyed by air raids.)

The almost continuous activity of the fighter-bombers over the combat area had a very disagreeable effect! The continuous staying in foxholes, the filling up of the front lines with reserves during the light, only became more and more of an ordeal for the commanders and the soldiers. The inquiry about German fighter airplanes became a daily habit again and could not be answered! German bombardment airplanes and bombers did not appear at all over the sector of the 352nd Infantry Division even at night!

After the conclusion of this period of fighting it could be said that, contrary to expectations, we had succeeded in closing the great gap between Tilly-sur-Seulles and Carentan, occupied by only very weak forces. Although these German forces were inexperienced in fighting and incomplete in numbers, the enemy no longer had a chance of breaking through unhindered.

The obvious intention of the German High Command to throw the enemy back into the sea was declared to have been taken "too late" by the 352nd Infantry Division, which had had to do the fighting since 6 June. If it was to be carried out, then, in the first place, a German air force equivalent in number to that of the enemy's would have had to be sent in. That, however, did not happen and the units freshly arriving were gradually deprived of their belief of being able to reach the Atlantic coast by means of attack again!

Judging the situation on the evening of 14 June, it could be recognized that the enemy, after having taken Caumont, had enlarged his bridgehead to a great depth. There was the danger for him that new German forces could attack him on the narrowed point of this bridgehead (which was Isigny–Carentan), and that would be a danger to his further actions [sic]! Therefore, it had to be expected that within a short time the enemy would start an attack from the area north of the Vire-Carentan railroad line. The declarations of a deserter (French inhabitant), our own observations, and the information contained in a captured operational order indicated that the US XIX Army Corps, with the 30th Infantry Division, was preparing an attack there. The enemy did not recognize one highly awkward situation of the 352nd Infantry Division between 11 and14 June, or he certainly did not make use of it!

West of the Vire, from Aire to Montmartin, there were only security detachments on the German side. Forces which could have stopped a possible crossing of the Vire effected during the night were available there on 14 June only! (They were parts of the combat element of the 275th Infantry Division.) The enemy had apparently intended to take advantage of this, for about two companies of his started a thrust toward the west from Neuilly-la-Forêt on 13 June. These forces, however, withdrew again after reaching the Vire. This enemy act can only be explained by his inadequate reconnoitering or by his not changing an already elaborated plan (operational order).

13 June Situation

by General der Panzer Leo, Freiherr Geyr von Schweppenburg

On the night of 12 June the German front extended along the line St Louet-sur-Seulles–south of Livry–Caumont–Biéville–Lamberville. Heavy bombing and artillery fire during the night and the assembly of strong armored forces in the area of Cairon–Rots–Tilly-sur-Seulles were evidence of an imminent enemy tank attack. Under the direct command of Seventh Army, XLVII Panzer Corps, on the approach march, and its subordinate divisions, the 2nd Panzer and 2nd SS Panzer Divisions, were required to close the gap. On 13 June wheeled elements of the 2nd Panzer Division were able to reach Villers-Bocage, and the forward elements of the 2nd SS Panzer Division reached the area west of Caumont. Stronger elements were not due to arrive before 14 June.

While enemy activity on the west bank of the Orne opposite the 21st Panzer Division and 12th SS Panzer Division was limited to reconnaissance patrols and heavy artillery fire on 13 June, the 21st Panzer Division on the east bank was strongly attacked, but without result.

Near Tilly-sur-Seulles and Lingèvres, the Panzer Lehr Division was hit by severe enemy attacks, which continued until nightfall and ended with the annihilation of the enemy armored units in Villers-Bocage.

13 June: 21st Panzer
Division Remains on the Defensive

by Generalleutnant Edgar Feuchtinger

Apart from the 12th SS Panzer Division, the Panzer Lehr Division, once the invasion had taken place, was committed next to that division beginning about 8 June. These units had taken significant losses from air attacks and long-range artillery fire at that time. The first infantry division to be transferred to this sector and to arrive was the 346th Infantry Division.

In this time, the division supported the counterattacks on of the Panzer divisions to its left. On 8 June we reported that 70 of some 125 medium tanks in the division were operational after air attacks. That day British antitank guns and tanks knocked out a further thirteen. The activity of the enemy artillery liaison planes also assumed a form that influenced the morale of our troops very strongly. It was observed that one pair of enemy planes would fly over individual targets for hours on end and adjust the fire of their guns to a great pitch of accuracy; while, despite all requests, none of our fighters were sent up to counteract them.

In addition to the 6th Airborne Division, another British division (51st Highland) and some tank units moved into the sector east of the Orne prior to the attack on 10 June. Combat activity led us to believe that this was a prelude to what would be a large-scale attack from this area around the middle of June. The enemy was endeavoring, in stubborn fighting that neither gave nor asked quarter, to gain ground, inch by inch, in order to have the necessary jump-off positions for assembly areas and artillery observation posts required for future large-scale attacks.

The fighting in this sector increased in violence. The division experienced difficulties in not only holding a large sector with a small infantry force, but also taking advantageous positions by means of attack or, alternatively, equalizing similar breakthroughs on the part of the enemy through limited counterattacks.

Since the start of the invasion, the 21st Panzer Division had had orders every evening to forward a daily report that was to be submitted directly to Adolf Hitler via courier. The division took particular care not to embellish the situation but to describe it just as it had actually developed and openly to state future dangers.

13 June: I SS Panzer Corps' Defensive Fighting

by Generalmajor Fritz Krämer

On 13 June advance elements of the 2nd Panzer Division arrived in the area of Caumont, and removed much of our anxiety about the gap. A later attack by this division was not successful, but the enemy had let a favorable opportunity slip. On 13 June close contact was established between I SS Panzer Corps and LXXXIV Corps. Thus the gap which might have enabled the enemy to make an easy breakthrough almost without losses was sealed off. So far only the reconnaissance battalion of the 2nd Panzer Division had arrived, but other elements were to follow and could be expected in time for commitment.

After its own experience, it was evident to I SS Panzer Corps that the 2nd Panzer Division, which was coming from the Arras area, would become available in driblets and at a later date then had been computed because of enemy air attacks. But the fact that it was moving was a gain for Corps troops. But it was the fate of this division to be committed at a time and in a sector where, from the very beginning, it had to be on the defensive. Thus it shared the fate of almost all the Panzer and motorized divisions committed at the invasion front.

When heavy enemy air attacks prevented bringing up infantry divisions on foot, higher German headquarters should have made use of all motor vehicles in France so as to commit the Panzer divisions in accordance with their training and missions—as attack formations. Corps suggested such action, verbally and by teletype. It may be assumed that lack of fuel prevented such cross-country motorized transports. Corps assumed that Army considered the few available Panzer divisions a bird in the hand which was better than two in the bush. They had motor vehicles and fuel and could be brought up with comparative speed, in spite of the danger from the air, to close a gap; but by that their real task was denied to them. When the foot divisions finally arrived the Panzer divisions had been used up.

Infantry divisions, through no fault of their own, frequently speedily lost sections of terrain which long had been held by the Panzer divisions. Infantrymen were fighting with a courage which surpassed all expectations, but without tanks or air support it was a forlorn cause against any enemy with plenty of these weapons. The failure of the infantry can be traced to the failure, by no means deliberate, of higher headquarters to provide needed support.

As on the preceding days, strong enemy attacks in the sectors of the 12th SS Panzer Division and the Panzer Lehr Division were repelled. Very heavy fighting took place at some points of the front, the attacks being supported by lively British artillery fire. Particularly violent fighting developed for Bois de Bavent.

The enemy also resumed his attacks on the eastern bank of the Orne. Elements of the 21st Panzer Division still committed there had been formed into Combat Group Lück for technical reasons of control and they could not be given up by LXXXI [?]Infantry Corps. Corps proposed to Army to order LXXXI [?] Infantry Corps to recapture lost ground by attacks with limited objective, shortening its front or establishing a rectilinear front, and so commit its own forces with the object of relieving the elements of the 21st Panzer Division. We promised to support these limited attacks by Corps artillery and pointed out that it was absolutely necessary either to regain control of the bridge northeast of Blainville or to destroy it. Otherwise it would be easy for the enemy to move tanks or other motorized forces to the eastern bank of the Orne with the object of breaking through the German front.

As Army considered the situation south of Bayeux to be exceedingly dangerous, it was decided to commit the 2nd SS Panzer Division as well as the 2nd Panzer Division, but this was not done because another assignment had to be given to the 2nd SS Panzer Division.

III Flak Corps: The Defensive Battle— Battles in the Caen Area

by General der Flakartillerie Wolfgang Pickert

Mission

I. Supporting the Army in the sector of Panzer Gruppe West, soon renamed Fifth Panzer Army, against enemy air and ground attacks in the area close to the front, with emphasis laid on defense against enemy air attacks. Main basic principle: strict concentration of forces, no commitment in less than regimental strength. No fragmentation at Army request.

II. Commitment against the enemy in the air, for the protection of the supply routes of the Army, back as far as the line Falaise–Le Bény Bocage (anti-fighter-bomber commitment). Behind this line, this task was taken over by the forces of the Air Force Administrative Command (Luftgau), which were gradually brought up for this purpose. Emphasis was laid on the supply roads designated by the Army.

Commitment

The elements committed in the proximity of the front—i.e. the bulk of the forces—were committed by regiments at points of particular importance, in areas designated by whichever Army or Corps they were to cooperate with. Details can no longer be given from memory. Close cooperation with the artillery commanders for the purpose of superimposition on the artillery fire of the Army was very important. In this, the batteries of III AA Corps were commanded, for sudden concentrations of fire, by means of the so-called "Normandy" method, by radio. For this purpose the areas within reach were divided on the map into small squares and clearly marked. It was then possible, by broadcasting short, uncoded target indications, which were nevertheless in accordance with camouflage specifications, rapidly to direct the fire of numerous AA batteries for sudden concentrations of fire. The release of the surprise fire would also be ordered by radio, through the AA regimental commanders, by short, camouflaged signals giving the time it was to take place, and would generally be effected 10 to 15 minutes (or even less) after the target had been indicated. Thanks to the long range of the 88mm AA batteries and their unlimited extent of traverse, a large number of AA batteries could always be concentrated for these surprise fire concentrations.

The allocation of AA combat teams generally declined, as it would have caused an undesirable weakening of the firepower, with but little promise of success. As a rule, therefore, the combating of enemy tanks which had penetrated to some depth, by AA batteries was carried out from the normal firing positions, that is to say from the depth of the combat area.

Successes

In the first days of the Normandy battle, a considerable number of fighter-bombers and military aircraft (mostly Marauders) were shot down. Numbers are unfortunately no longer available. Soon the figure ran into more than a hundred. The enemy air forces were generally compelled to fly higher altitudes, and also became reluctant to attack in the face of AA fire. A lot of ammunition was expended lending a hand in ground fighting (by way of the "Normandy" method), for surprise-fire concentrations on whole battalions or regiments. Besides this, the heavy AA batteries had forward observers, mostly with radio communications, and, whenever the situation in the air and the ammunition situation permitted it, attacked ground targets by observed fire. An undesired limitation was the fact that only impact fuzes were allowed to be used for attacking ground targets, so as to save up the valuable clockwork fuzes for aerial targets. This was disadvantageous in that the extraordinary effect of the points of burst could not be used to sufficient advantage against living targets. Participation by the AA batteries in the harassing fire of the remaining artillery of the Army had to be refused. Some enemy tanks were put out of action.

A new type of task was the combating of the overwhelming numbers of fighter-bombers over the routes of supply. The so-called "fighter-bomber traps," initially envisaged, did not prove to be of much use. These were medium and heavy AA guns, camouflaged to resemble motor vehicles, moving or stationary. They became direct targets of the fighter-bomber attacks, without sufficient promise of success [to compensate for their losses]. However, concealed commitment in the vicinity of the roads, in hedges etc., not under battery strength, proved its worth. By frequent changes of position, surprises were effected, and many successes scored. The enemy was gradually driven to fly higher altitudes. Prerequisite for success was: not too early an opening of fire, but then with as many guns as possible simultaneously. The close-range fire of heavy AA batteries against low-flying aircraft attacking these batteries also proved successful. Aircraft were even shot down, which was hardly to be expected from this type of firing. By close-range firing is meant the rapid fire of several groups, with fuzes set for this purpose, as a rule to 700 meters. Thus the enemy had to fly right into the barrage.

Losses

During the battles around Caen, the unit periodically suffered considerable losses in men and material, due to artillery fire. The losses occasioned by fighter-bomber attacks on the firing positions mostly remained slight, thanks to the defense by close-range and light AA fire. Time and again, however, numerous vehicles were lost during the day, to fighter-bomber attacks, as these latter were even attacking solitary vehicles in movement. The Army in particular could be observed to be suffering heavy losses in vehicles, as it apparently did not prohibit strictly enough unnecessary driving during the hours of daylight.

Reinforcements

Gradually the reinforcements slated for the case of an invasion began to arrive. These consisted of several light AA batteries, partly from the Eastern Front. They were committed on the major routes of supply for the reinforcement of their anti-fighter-bomber defenses. Further, several AA combat teams were also brought up. These combat teams consisted of four AA combat detachments, each having two 88mm guns. They were to be used only against ground targets. Their commitment was envisaged at focal points in the antitank defense system, combined to construct an AA antitank barrier. These AA combat teams, extracted from the AA defenses of the Reich, were unfortunately so little trained for their task, and so insufficiently equipped, that they had, for the time being, to be held back in the area of Trun, east of Falaise, for completion of their training and equipment.

Combat Impressions

1. **The enemy in the air:** The enemy aircraft formations striking the combat area were at first mainly bands of Marauders, of some 20 to 40 planes, with fighter protection, which attacked villages, copses and bridges, and which were suitable, favorable targets for the heavy AA batteries. They were combated very successfully, forced to fly higher altitudes, or to turn back. The number of planes shot down was considerable, but exact details are no longer recalled. These Marauders proved to be hardy machines that could take "a lot of lead" [i.e. could continue flying after being seriously damaged].

    A new task for the AA teams was the combating of enemy combat formations, appearing several times a day, in "scattered bomber formation," i.e. much in the same way as the enemy formations flying over during the night. Now this loose bomber formation was no massed target. Instead it offered many widely separated, single targets. Thereby the AA fire became dispersed, and the concentrations of several heavy batteries onto a single formation, which was always being aspired to, was prevented. The enemy, on the other hand, could not concentrate his bombing, in other words there was no carpet-bombing, but only scattered bomb hits on long strips of terrain, which in general influenced the morale of the troops more often than they caused material damage. Very frequently "Oysters" [small US Army reconnaissance aircraft, L-4s or L-5s], apparently used as artillery observation planes, or for specific close reconnaissance missions, flew over into the field of fire of the heavy batteries. They were easily shot down. A particularly important mission was always the combating of fighter-bombers, which observed every move over extensive areas, throughout the entire day, and often even attacked solitary vehicles.

Frequently changing commitment of the light AA batteries, firing in sudden bursts at medium and short ranges, scored many successes in terms of enemy aircraft shot down. However, the AA forces were far too few for the extensive, wide areas surveyed by the fighter-bombers, even though restricted to the major supply lines only, and paying strict attention to the principle of the point of greatest importance. By night the AA confined itself to the major supply roads, in cooperation with light searchlights. On moonlit nights aircraft were even shot down without the aid of searchlights. Enemy aircraft were particularly sensitive to the tracer bullets of the light AA by night.

2. **The enemy on the ground:** According to personal observation, and to statements made by prisoners of war, the sudden releases of fire from as great a number of AA batteries as possible, directed by the "Normandy" method, proved valuable against ground targets. When carrying out these sudden concentrations of fire, it was important for the overall effect that they started at precisely the same instant. In this manner, limited as to space and time, the 88mm AA, which fired extraordinarily rapidly, attained strong concentrations of fire. What it lacked in caliber it made up for by the number and speed of the hits scored. The extreme traversability of the 88mm guns made the transition from aerial to ground targets, and vice-versa, extremely easy, and caused no loss of time. The successes against enemy tanks were not what they had been in the East; whether attacking in terrain offering good cover, or on open terrain, [the tanks] did so much more cautiously, and under better covering fire, and thus silenced the firing 88mm AA batteries much more rapidly than had hitherto been observed in the East. Nevertheless, decisive successes could also be scored against tanks, especially against those that had penetrated deeply and had erred into the fire of the concentratedly emplaced AA batteries. The AA combat team—i.e. the 88mm team that had been extracted from the heavy batteries and committed further forward—proved itself less valuable, as it was numerically insufficient to cope with the strong Panzer attacks, carried out cunningly and under skillful covering fire. The organization of AA combat teams was therefore rejected as a matter of principle, as the loss in personnel and material, and the undesirable weakening of the antiaircraft defenses, was disproportionate to the expected success. The AA combat teams which were exclusively envisaged for antitank defense did not go into action until later.

Supplies

Despite the initially overextended supply routes for AA ammunition, an almost adequate supply of this was always maintained. Admittedly, the expenditure was rather high. Had the supply of AA ammunition with impact fuzes also been sufficient, then the AA artillery could have participated even more strongly in the ground combat, with surprise concentrations of fire, than it actually did. The necessity for conserving gun barrels, and the limited supply of these, also imposed restraint on participation in the ground fighting by means of surprise-fire concentrations. Supplies of light AA ammunition were adequate, despite the lively combat activity of the fighter-bombers.

Fuel supplies, which were a matter for the Army, were inadequate. For this reason, tactically required regroupings, which would have been highly desirable for mobile commitment against enemy aircraft, had frequently to be omitted. During large-scale withdrawals of whole sectors of the front, the fuel supply often became a serious problem, which heavily taxed not only the Chief of Staff but also the Commanding General, and often led to complicated negotiations with Army offices.

The transporting off of the wounded occasioned no particular difficulties, except for the fact that, owing to the ruthless attacks of the fighter-bombers, which often also attacked vehicles marked with the "Red Cross," some of the wounded could not be moved till the hours of darkness. Many ambulances and medical officers, and many medical personnel, were lost through this.

Messing was almost always adequate. The mail also reached the troops more or less satisfactorily, despite strong aerial interference deep behind the lines.

The maintenance of guns involved continuous, important supply work, which could only be partly coped with by our own repair shops, and required long journeys to other repair shops. The same held true also for the repair of trucks. The resupplying of guns was surprisingly efficient.

Condition of the Troops

The troops, which had initially not been battle-hardened, very quickly grew equal to their difficult tasks, thanks to their exceptional morale, and their exemplary officers. Day by day they become more skilled in cunning entrenchment techniques, in camouflage, and, above all, in standing up to the enemy's versatile methods of attack. Participation in ground combat, to which the troops were not yet accustomed, was also learned quickly, and became daily more important, especially when the Army suffered losses in guns and lacked ammunition, from which lack the Army could be declared to be suffering almost chronically. Many exemplary instances of single combat against enemy tanks and infantry were to be noted, as well as the excellent way the troops stood by their guns and measuring equipment under heavy fire from enemy ground artillery and from aircraft armaments, during their antiaircraft engagements. Despite their frequently high losses, the troops held their own excellently—an example for those elements of the Army which were fighting in the same sector.

Cooperation with the Army and the Luftwaffe

Since the AA Corps was only "directed to cooperate with the Army" but not subordinated to it, the AA artillery officers of all grades were often involved in serious conflicts on the battlefield, especially in emergency situations. These arose out of the belief of local Army Headquarters [or command posts] that they could simply order the AA artillery located in their individual sectors to change their (the AA's) assignments, in particular for the purpose of making them participate in antitank defense and other ground-combat duties. Interference of this sort naturally always hindered the troops in their most important mission, the defense against enemy aircraft. The far superior enemy air forces and the far too scanty number of German fighter planes made it imperative that every gun envisaged for antiaircraft defense was indeed used for this purpose. Ground combat tasks, including antitank action out of the firing positions, without change of position, could also be executed from the same positions, which had always been initially chosen with this double mission in mind. Comprehension of this versatile possibility of commitment of the AA weapons was not, as yet, general amongst the Army officers. On the other hand, the Army units often saw themselves induced, after the heavy losses in guns and the critical situations occasioned thereby, to request a loan of the AA artillery for tasks dealing exclusively with antitank defense, or for ground artillery duty. Generally the AA Corps succeeded in carrying out this double task to the satisfaction of the Army, especially when, on days of strong aerial activity, the aerial successes, in terms of aircraft shot down, and the strong surprise concentrations of fire, were evident to the Army commanders, and showed them that the unit was versatile enough to cope with both tasks. Had the Corps been subordinated to the Army, then the antiaircraft defenses would undoubtedly have gotten the worst of it through incorrect assignment of the AA artillery, to the Army's own disadvantage. A premature expenditure of personnel and material would have resulted. Particularly close was the cooperation with the artillery officers of the Army, who thankfully accepted the superimposed fire of the AA artillery, which was usually better supplied with ammunition.

Cooperation with the flying elements of the Air Force was restricted to the reporting of the relatively weak German fighter formations to the AA artillery, when these were flying up to the front, so as to avoid their being shot at by our own AA artillery, and further the covering by our fighter planes of the areas not protected by the AA forces. Lastly, the aircraft warning service of the AA artillery sent bulletins to the Higher Headquarters of the Luftwaffe several times a day, reporting the enemy points of main effort in the area close to the front.

13 June: 2nd Panzer Division Attacks

by General der Panzertruppen Heinrich, Freiherr von Lüttwitz

For this attack the division committed two battle groups (Kampfgruppen) in the usual combination of the hitherto march groups. Boundary lines between both battle groups were (approximately): Montamy (left)–Jurques (right)–Parfouru-l'Éclin (right)–St-Paul-du-Vernay (left).

The right battle group took up positions in the Jurques area, and the left battle group in the northern sector of the Bois du Homme. The division had to change its course in the darkness of the night. The difficulties in finding the way through the bombed-out towns meant that the division, after moving, was not quite fully assembled.

Since reports of the reconnaissance battalion and reports from the Panzer Lehr Division gave the impression of continuous enemy reinforcement in the gap, the division could no longer wait until all of its units had arrived. The reconnaissance battalion reported the loss of Caumont under loss of the assigned Panzer Jäger Company (motorized). The division, however, awaited here only an enemy push in connection with the advance of the enemy forces on the left wing of the Panzer Lehr Division.

As had been expected, the enemy there had been reinforced. Ancteville was lost. The enemy had penetrated into Villers-Bocage. Therefore the division made the decision to attack at once, with such forces which were on hand. The right battle group advanced generally along the Jurques–Villers-Bocage road, whereby the right battalion of that battle group encountered just before Villers-Bocage, on the bridge across the Seulles river, enemy tank and antitank positions. The same was sealed off and later was destroyed. The battalion then turned off toward the north and attacked Tracy-Bocage on a wide front. Screened towards the north, the battalion began to turn to the east and attacked Villers-Bocage from the west and northwest. At the same time the SS Tiger Battalion began to attack the town from the northeast. In spite of the initial tough defenses, the enemy began to flee. By evening the penetration succeeded into the city and led to the destruction of the enemy.

The left battalion, marching beyond Coulvain, took Hill 198 (two kilometers north of Coulvain). Then it attacked Bruyère from both sides and took the town after partially tough house-to-house fighting. The resistance stiffened considerably. In the attack against Amaye-sur-Seulles, only the first few houses were taken. Hill 193 was taken; from here on the large east–west road, Villers Bocage–Caumont, was taken under artillery fire.

This battle group (Kampfgruppe) had no tanks and only a few (6–8) antitank guns and could barely gain ground against enemy tanks. The bocage terrain, however, lightened the struggle against the enemy tanks with close-combat weapons. Through concentration of heavy weapons upon the right wing, the enemy thrust could still be held up and its spearheads destroyed. One light artillery battalion supported the attack of the battle group, with the main point of effect upon the right wing. Losses were relatively small.

The left battle group, which had to march the furthest, was, on account of air activity during the previous days, more spread out and needed a considerably longer time before its combat units were to some extent assembled in the Bois du Homme. It could start out from its position of readiness only by the early afternoon, and attacked out of the wooded terrain, north of the Bois du Homme, to the town of Cahagnes. Cahagnes was occupied by the enemy, but by concentrating both battalion attacks the town could be taken. While cleaning out the town, there was stubborn fighting for individual houses.

The battle group then noved farther up to the north. The enemy ,who were defending Hill 174, held the city's northern exit under heavy infantry and artillery fire. By getting out the right battalion—moving through houses and gardens of La Croix and Le Temple—it was successful during the late afternoon in overcoming the hill and pushing forward toward evening, almost to the Amaye-sur-Seulles–Caumont road, southeast of Briquessard.

Contact with the battle group on the right was maintained only slightly, by reconnaissance troops. Contact with the reconnaissance battalion, whose wing was at Montmirel, was closer. Fighting by the left battle group was supported by the 3rd (Heavy) Battalion 74th Panzer Artillery Regiment. This battalion arrived relatively late, and went into position in an area south of Hill 309 (west of Bois du Homme), in order to support from here the battle against Cahagnes. Moreover, it did not fire a round, since Cahagnes was taken by then. After the fall of Cahagnes the battalion changed its position, into the area northwest of St-Pierre-du-Fresne, and supported the attack of the 304th Regiment toward the north. It had later also to depend upon cooperation with the reconnaissance battalion.

During a sudden enemy night attack (with tanks) into the town of Caumont, the reconnaissance battalion was forced out of the town. It held on for a while on the southern edge of the town, then withdrew to Le Bourg and Montmirel. The loss of Caumont was reported to the division very late, and it was not therefore possible after the beginning of the attacks by the two battle groups to reinforce the reconnaissance battalion so strongly that the recapture of Caumont would have been possible. There was a complete shortage of armor-piercing weapons, and little support from the artillery and heavy infantry weapons.

During the course of the day two pioneer (engineer) companies also arrived; up to now they had been busy cleaning rubble off the roads used during the march. Their armament consisted solely of nine light machine guns per company. At the beginning of the attack, the division ordered this highly specialized unit (pioneer), for its own disposal, to St-Martin-des-Besaces. Their commitment at Caumont would have had minor success against the enemy's tanks and would have caused unnecessary losses.

A gap of considerable size still existed between the reconnaissance battalion and its left neighbor, the 3rd Fallschirm Jäger Division, and for the time being could not be closed. Strange to say, but in this gap there was no enemy—not even enemy reconnaissance patrols.

During the afternoon the division staff was transferred to Brémoy. Reports received by evening stated that the division's tracked vehicles (tanks, tank destroyers, self-propelled artillery) were being unloaded east of Paris because of enemy air activity, which soon made railroad transport to the west impossible. The commander of the Panzer regiment was ordered to pick up the division's tracked vehicles and to bring the same up to the front under the greatest of care, but still as quickly as technically possible.

PART EIGHT

Summary: Panzers in Normandy

The Panzer units in Normandy were the key to the outcome of the fighting. Their ability to counterattack, whether quickly at the time of the invasion or *en masse*, days later, was seen as the only chance the Germans had to defeat the invasion. In addition, their ability to prevail over Allied armored units that lacked their extensive combat experience (with the notable exception of the British 7th Armored Division, which still initially did not succeed on the battlefield in Normandy and had to rely on the smaller and less capable Sherman tank), was especially pronounced in the weeks of fighting to follow.

D.C.I.

Problems with Panzer Formations

by Generalmajor Fritz Krämer

Strong enemy local attacks frequently developed into fluctuating fighting for individual buildings, small woods, hills, and other terrain sectors, but failed to produce penetrations. They were evaluated by us as enemy attempts to extend his beachhead in order to win ground for the deployment of his forces.

We did not observe any concentration of strong enemy forces for a breakthrough with strategic objectives. We were not in a position to judge the enemy's intentions. Perhaps unexpectedly strong resistance by German formations foiled efforts for a breakthrough. Terrain may not have been suitable for large-scale tank attacks, and this may have forced the enemy to carry out his attacks piecemeal. But he thereby lost time, men, and material—a fact which cannot be stressed too often.

The divisions always reported high losses of lives for the enemy. Our troops may have tended to overestimate enemy losses, but we can safely assume that, in the sector of I SS Panzer Corps prior to 20 June, his losses comprised about 1,000 prisoners and about 300 tanks and other armored vehicles. The fact that the enemy time and again put in breathing spaces between his attacks indicated that he suffered losses.

Many attacks certainly could have been successful if there had been better cooperation between attack infantry, artillery and air forces. We observed, for instance, that enormous artillery activity would start at daybreak and last for several hours. Usually this was considered preparatory to enemy attacks. Sometimes these would not take place, or would start much later with less preparation. We ascertained likewise that air force attacks were not coincident with this artillery fire or the subsequent attacks. As enemy troops gained combat experience, this situation changed. As far as it could be observed from the German side, cooperation between artillery and artillery flyers was excellent; of course, the task of the latter was easy, because they operated undisturbed by the German Luftwaffe.

Naturally, our forces were used up much faster than those of the enemy. Constant local attacks launched by the enemy and similar counterattacks undertaken by German forces caused the latter to dwindle rapidly. Our losses were high. For instance, on 20 June the Panzer Lehr Division had at its disposal only about 2,000 Panzer Grenadiers, including engineer troops, etc. Thus the average strength of a company was approximately 30 to 40 men. If these losses continued, it was evident that the division would be incapable of action in about eight days. At the 12th SS Panzer Division the situation was similar. Many commanders, officers, and many of the trustworthy, battle-tested NCOs and men had been killed in action or wounded. Apart from the events at the front, the chief worry of Corps was to compensate for losses by bringing up men and material.

Corps no longer possessed any reserves of its own for replacements. The telephone battle with higher headquarters over replacements sometimes strained nerves to the utmost. We had to fight for every man, every tank—frequently even for a certain type of ammunition—often spending hours on the telephone.

But higher headquarters also had its problems. Every corps and every division was clamoring for replacements, and the few replacement transport battalions that arrived were quickly distributed. The demolition inflicted on rail tracks and roads by enemy air forces prevented higher headquarters from keeping its promises of reinforcements.

The distribution of replacement transports was under the adjutant's office rather than the tactical services. There were frequent delays, and distributions were made which did not take into account the tactical course of events. Under such conditions only the chief of staff with his tactical assistants should have had the responsibility for replacements of personnel. The divisions frequently had to cover long distances on foot, and men and horses were exhausted upon arrival. Sometimes they were diverted and sent to other endangered sectors. Air attacks on trains or troops on the roads frequently incapacitated elements of divisions and delayed marches. Apart from the loss of life, these attacks resulted in considerable loss of time because it often was necessary to reorganize and wait for equipment or horses.

Under such circumstances the morale of the troops did not improve. There were increasing instances of men going to the collecting points behind the front instead of to the front lines. The fact that these still were exceptional cases gives credit to the German soldiers.

Often it was necessary to commit elements of the divisions in driblets as they arrived, causing premature wear and tear on the troops. Corps attempted to assemble newly arrived formations, give them a few days' rest if possible, and commit them in a front-line sector only after they had had time to acquaint themselves with the terrain.

It was not always easy to follow this rule. No news spreads faster among the hard-pressed troops in a forward line than the report that replacements have arrived or have been sighted somewhere. Frequently there are commanders whose front sectors are about to break down. Inquiries about relief or replacements increase. They tell of frequent enemy attacks, increased artillery activity and new jump-off positions, and tanks are being heard. They plead for anything to relieve their troops, and say the end justifies the means.

Here the commander must remain adamant. Commanders or chiefs of staff can only judge the situation soundly when they are in command posts so near to the advanced line that they feel something of the breath of fighting and are in daily contact and well acquainted with the troubles and real needs of their troops. Long trips between command posts and front lines must be avoided for the benefit of the troops. Besides this, a well-advanced command post discourages visiting firemen from rearward installations, who under such circumstances cannot be of any help but are only wasting time.

Panzer Tactics in Normandy

by Generaloberst Heinz Guderian

12 July 1949: Note by Kenneth W. Hechler, Major, Infantry (Res)

Lt Fye, the historical editor, states that "previous experience of Historical Division officers with Generaloberst Guderian indicated that the latter might not be too cooperative in answering these rather general questions. However, he was quite receptive and cooperated to fullest degree, although he stated that such broad questions could not be answered readily in an interview." I talked with General Guderian in Seckemhein, Germany, in August 1945 and at that time I found him not only extremely cooperative but a very agreeable person. I remember that Dr George N. Shuster, the head of the War Department Interrogation Commission, stated after talking with General Guderian that he could think of nothing more calculated to produce a good strategic history of the German General Staff than to bring Guderian to the United States and install him on somebody's porch up in Connecticut for a summer of casual conversation.

During the period when General Guderian felt that he would be tried for war crimes, however, he clammed up and became extremely disagreeable when asked to prepare material for historical purposes. Apparently by the time Lt Fye interviewed him, General Guderian believed that he would not be tried for war crimes and probably be felt that his best interests would be served by cooperation with the Historical Division, EUCOM; therefore, he decided to talk freely.

The Possibility of Mass Panzer Counterattacks In Normandy

Q. Would mass counterattacks by two or three Panzer divisions have been possible in the bocage country?

A. Yes, they were possible, but only outside the range of naval gunfire, and the Panzer divisions would have had to be broken down into small groups of tanks and infantry, because of the terrain. We had prepared for this eventuality.

Q. How would they have been protected during assembly?

A. With approach marches and assembly at night. This we had prepared for also—the troops were trained for this. Nevertheless, it would have been very difficult to protect the troops and tanks, with such superiority on the side of the Allies.

Q. Could attacks have been made at dark?

A. In this terrain, mass counterattacks were not possible at night. Troops require a very thorough knowledge of the terrain to guide armor at night, and they did not all have this in Normandy.

Q. What losses could have been expected?

A. I cannot answer that—it would have been up to the fortunes of war. At all events, night attacks, if well prepared and guided, cost less in casualties than daylight attacks.

Q. What measures might have been taken to neutralize Allied air forces?

A. (*Interviewer's note: A look of amusement, and a tone of slight sarcasm, accompanied the first part of Generaloberst Guderian's answer to this question.*) The creation of a better Luftwaffe. Also, we should have had more antiaircraft weapons organic to units on the march, as well as in assembly areas, on bridges etc. This would have been possible if Germany had taken measures similar to those of the United States (arming vehicles in convoy with antiaircraft weapons on ring mounts). The Luftwaffe had these ring mounts in excess, but the Army didn't find out about them until too late, after the invasion.

It was absolutely necessary to have sufficient fighters [Luftwaffe planes] to protect troops on the move, but this was not possible; nor was it possible to have the very effective "flak clouds" (*Interviewer's note: By this term, Generaloberst Guderian meant a wall or curtain of antiaircraft fire above convoys.*) because of the shortage of ammunition and weapons.

Q. What objectives would have been attacked?

A. Naturally, the forces of the enemy, particularly his armor and infantry. We would have also attacked reserves, and the flanks and rear of the enemy, particularly Patton's, following his breakthrough at Avranches. Counterattacks to the beaches were feasible on the first or second day after the landing, while confusion reigned, but not afterwards. However, this was possible only if the Panzer divisions were already in reserve, but such was not the case. Generalfeldmarschall Rommel thought the invasion would be in the Calais–Dieppe area, and, therefore, the bulk of the Panzer divisions were assembled north of the Seine. General der Panzer von Geyr and I were in favor of having the reserve on both sides of the Seine. Hitler sided with Rommel, and the reserve went north of the Seine, around the Somme.

Possibilities for counterattacks arose later [following the first few days after the invasion] but either we did not take advantage of them, or the counterattacks made were mismanaged by Generalfeldmarschall von Kluge. He ordered frontal counterattacks on strongpoints, such as Caen; or else they were made by committing units piecemeal and in insufficient numbers, as at Avranches, where no division was employed intact, but only elements of various divisions.

Q. What decisive results could have been achieved?

A. Restriction of the invasion to Normandy. This would have been possible, though, only if we had had a better and stronger Luftwaffe and Navy: they were absolutely necessary to the success of such an endeavor. As it was, the whole burden rested on the Army (Heer), and it was no longer "first class." The infantry divisions were weak and practically immobile, particularly their artillery and supply services. What Panzer and Panzer Grenadier divisions there were, were used only piecemeal. This was a terrible error of the High Command; the fault lay partly with Hitler, partly with OKW, and of course, with von Kluge as well.

Infantry–Tank Team Tactics

Q. What Panzer tactics had been developed for fighting in the hedgerows?

A. Tanks and Panzer Grenadiers [armored infantry] working together in small teams, the infantry protecting the tanks and protected by them. These were not new tactics, but merely a slightly different application of old ones, necessitated by this particular type of terrain, which forbade the use of larger teams.

Q. Did you have specially trained infantry–tank teams?

A. Yes, this was the special mission of the Panzer Grenadiers, and they were trained for this type of work. Their use with tanks, as specially trained troops, was my idea and was incorporated in the German Army before the war. We gained experience from World War I, in which the French had special infantry and cavalry to work with tanks, on a limited scale, of course. This example was used in the organization of our Panzer divisions. From the beginning of training, these Panzer Grenadiers and tanks worked together.

Q. Had you solved the problem of communication between infantry and tanks?

A. The problem had not been solved completely. We were near the solution, with the infantry being equipped with small radios (*Interviewer's note: Generaloberst Guderian could not remember the particular type or types of radios employed, but they were probably the small, portable transmitter-receivers called Feldfunkfernsprecher—literally, field radio telephone.*) to communicate with tanks. The difficulty was maintaining the frequency between the tanks and infantry: the tanks had to communicate with so many in battle—superiors, subordinates, the Luftwaffe, the artillery, etc. This might seem very simple, but it was actually a great problem. However, the communication problem was less difficult with Panzer Grenadiers than with ordinary infantry.

East vs. West Panzer Tactics

Q. In reference to your statement that Panzer divisions were ordered committed intact by Generalfeldmarschall von Rundstedt, was this general armored doctrine in the German Army at the time? (*Interviewer's note: Generaloberst Guderian professed to have no knowledge of having made such a statement and believed it must concern General der Panzer von Geyr. Nevertheless, he attempted to answer it.*)

A. It was our opinion that they should be committed intact, and Generalfeldmarschall von Rundstedt went along with us, in principle at least. But von Kluge cut the divisions to pieces, committing single companies and batteries to action, for which they suffered. And Hitler committed the same mistake. For instance, he ordered just the tanks of the 9th Panzer Division to the invasion area from southern France, over my protests to either commit the whole division or nothing. The tanks were manned with only two-man crews instead of the normal five, in order to save on personnel. Few of the tanks even got to Normandy so manned. (*Interviewer's note: This last, Guderian said with almost disgust and contempt in his voice.*)

Q. What was the practice on the Russian Front?

A. In open country we employed tanks in large units, combined with Panzer Grenadiers who followed the advance. When the tanks came to obstacles, such as rivers or antitank traps, the Panzer Grenadiers came forward under the cover of tank fire, until the engineers could clear the way for further advance. After the first six months, as we got farther into Russia and space became greater and greater, following our heavy losses, and during the winter (the mud was an even greater obstacle than the extreme cold), we had to form smaller Kampfgruppen, for the divisions became responsible for 40–50-kilometer sectors. So actually, for the above reasons, we had to modify our original tactics and lose the important concentration of force.

Q. How far could Panzer tactics as developed in the East be applied to the West?

A. That always depended on the terrain and the enemy dispositions. Generally though, in Normandy we were obliged to split up divisions, while in open country divisions were committed intact where possible. We always employed the same infantry–tank team tactics. But you must remember that every battle, every enemy, and every season has its own factors to be considered, regardless of the theater of war.

Q. What differences were there?

A. There were no great differences; the variations lay in the terrain, the seasons of the year, and, of course, the enemy. The tactics and training were always the same, taken from the service regulations [Dienstvorschriften and Ausbildungsvorschriften – service and training regulations], modified or altered to fit the terrain, etc. Enemy air power did alter our tactics in the West; in the East we could move in daylight and often with great speed, but not in the West.

Q. Did Panzer divisions shifted from the East need retraining in new types of warfare in the West?

A. The Panzer divisions destined to fight off the invasion needed retraining, not so much in new types of war as in new weapons, particularly tanks, which were received in great numbers. The Panzer divisions in the East at this time were equipped with about 40–50 tanks, while those in the West received about 100 new ones and needed training on them. They also required training in night marches, adaptability to the conditions on the coast, small infantry–tank tactics, and antiaircraft warfare.

Q. Did they receive such training in adequate amounts?

A. Not in all cases. We had twelve Panzer and Panzer Grenadier divisions in the West at the time of the invasion, and most came from the east and south. They needed about two to three months' training. Those that arrived before March 1944 received sufficient training, but the last ones arrived just before the invasion and didn't complete their training. Two of the twelve were newly activated SS divisions (I believe they were the 12th SS Panzer Division and the 17th SS Panzer Grenadier Division), and they didn't complete their training either.

Employment of Panzer Forces on the Western Front

by Generaloberst Heinz Guderian

12 July 1949: Note by Kenneth W. Hechler, Major, Infantry (Res)

No record in German was made at the time of this oral interview, inasmuch as it was conducted entirely in English; General Guderian speaks excellent English. I believe that a great deal of credence can be placed in his observations, inasmuch as most of them were of a strategic character, and represented information and analysis which a man at Guderian's level was likely to have within his grasp. He seemed to enjoy the discussion of these questions, even the hypothetical ones. He greeted me genially: "Aha! a fellow armored officer!" Of course, this was just so much soft soap, but I did not have the feeling that he twisted any of his real opinions in order to say what he felt an American would like to hear. He responded quickly to all of the questions, and I do not believe that he was trying to make any particular impression or grind any axe.

Q. What is the reason why armored units were not brought to bear any quicker against the Normandy beachhead?

A. It was a mistake. There was a difference of opinion between Generalfeldmarschall Rommel and myself. I was in France in April 1944 to ask Rommel for his ideas on the employment of tanks, and I proposed withdrawing the Panzer divisions (as did Generalfeldmarschall von Rundstedt and General der Panzer von Geyr) to form a Panzer army north of Orléans. Rommel was of the opinion that he must retain the Panzer divisions on the expected invasion front, which he thought would come at the mouth of the Somme, near Dieppe. Several divisions were placed immediately behind the first line there, on both sides of the Somme estuary, and several others were stationed in southern France, near the mouth of the Rhône. There were, therefore, few Panzer divisions behind the actual invasion front. In consequence of your aerial superiority, much time was needed to bring the Panzer divisions from south of the Somme to the invasion area. I proposed to Hitler in May 1944 withdrawing the Panzer divisions and placing them in the neighborhood of Le Mans, but he refused. This was the real reason that no Panzer divisions were in the neighborhood of the invasion front in time.

Q. Had these divisions been stationed at Le Mans, would they have arrived at the front in time?

209

A. I think so. It was difficult to move during the daytime because of your aerial superiority, but it was possible to march at night with long intervals between vehicles.

Q. After the beachhead had become established during June and July 1944, there were a number of Panzer divisions in the line. Why was this?

A. That was also a mistake. After the beginning of your invasion Generalfeldmarschall von Rundstedt was relieved, and in his place Hitler appointed Generalfeldmarschall von Kluge to lead the armies on the Western Front. Von Kluge had no experience in tank fighting, and he left the Panzer divisions in the first line and executed frontal attacks.

Q. In your position, were you not able to change the tactics of the Army?

A. I could make proposals to Hitler, but I had no right as Inspector General [of Panzer Forces] to give orders. My proposals, prior to and during the invasion, were rejected by Hitler in favor of the opinions of Rommel and von Kluge. Hitler said that the generals in command at the front were right and my advisers were wrong.

Q. Was not von Rundstedt Rommel's superior?

A. Yes, but Rommel was in favor with Hitler, and Rommel's opinions carried weight with him.

Q. What was Rommel's own theory about the use of armor in the line?

A. His theory was to hold the first-line positions, and so he strengthened the Atlantic Wall by obstacles and traps in front of the first line of defense (large cement and iron poles in the water, known as "Rommel's Asparagus"). This was justifiable for defense by infantry and artillery, but was not the place for the employment of tanks. Rommel did much to strengthen the coast defense by neglecting mobile reserves behind the front.

Q. Did he favor keeping these divisions in the front after the beachhead had been established?

A. Rommel had the misfortune of being wounded in an air attack and was only in command of the invasion front for several weeks. He was then sent back home and never became fit for the field again. Rommel had an automobile accident during a fighter-bomber raid and suffered a fractured skull and brain concussion when his car struck a tree.

Q. Had he lost favor with Hitler prior to this?

A. Probably, but not for his conduct of the war. It was because he knew of the assassination attempt but, through his accident, did not have an opportunity to forward the information. Hitler distrusted everybody during the last months of his life, and therefore distrusted Rommel also.

Q. Was Rommel killed in the hospital?

A. Rommel was at home with his wife, and we have heard from the American side that he was forced to admit several unknown men into his home and that he died a few days later. We don't know how he died. We know the story only from an American officer who spoke with Rommel's wife.

Q. Why was von Rundstedt relieved and replaced by von Kluge?

A. Von Rundstedt and von Geyr were relieved on the same day, both because their conduct of the campaign against the invasion did not agree with Hitler's views.

Q. Was there any specific thing that Hitler did not like about von Rundstedt's meeting the invasion?

A. If a battle was not won as Hitler had planned, he sought to blame someone for it. He never found fault with himself, but always with the generals or the troops concerned. Since the invasion had succeeded, he had to find a guilty general, and, in this case, it was von Rundstedt and von Geyr. Von Geyr had made a report about the methods of fighting. This was a collection of reports submitted to him by his troop commanders at the front line and was transmitted to von Rundstedt, who forwarded it to Hitler. After receiving this report, von Rundstedt and von Geyr were relieved.

Q. What was in the report?

A. A recommendation to withdraw Panzer forces from the first line, form mobile reserves behind the front, and hold the first line with infantry.

Q. Did Hitler disagree?

A. Hitler and von Kluge wanted to hold the first line with all troops available and believed that Panzer units were nothing more than infantry. In theory, Hitler knew the difference very well, but in practice, here and on the Eastern Front, he committed a great mistake. I was not able to convince him to the contrary.

Q. Who mentioned where you would put your armor and the withdrawal of the armor from the line? Was there any other point where you disagreed on Panzer tactics with either Hitler or von Kluge?

A. I disagreed with the opinions of Rommel and von Kluge. I conferred with Hitler about the matter and was sent to France in April 1944 to speak with Rommel, who did not change his opinion. Hitler then said that the man in the front command must know better than the general on the staff; one uses theory, the other has practical application.

Q. How strong were your Panzer divisions in the West?

A. We knew we were inferior in the air, and that this inferiority could not be made up, since we had lost two years in the race for airpower. Planes were under construction, but they were not used; it perhaps was a mistake of Göring not to use them. Our Navy was also inferior and could not engage the British Navy, which was bombarding our front lines. It was difficult for our infantry, weakened as it was with its third-rate units. Newly formed divisions had restricted mobility and were made up of older, second- or third-class soldiers. The Panzer Lehr and 11th Panzer Divisions in southern France were excellent, and the 116th and 9th Panzer Divisions, divisions from the Eastern Front, fought well. The infantry, however, consisted of second- or third-rate divisions, and this weakness of the infantry and artillery was all-important. In addition to the faulty employment of Panzer divisions, there was a great shortage of troops which could not be made up; hence Patton, in his race across France, found no real resistance. He saw a good opportunity and made good use of it.

Q. Had you opposed Patton, what would you have done?

A. I would have put the armor on the left wing. Patton still might have succeeded; there is an element of chance. But it would have been much more difficult for him.

Q. What about the counterattack towards Avranches by the Germans? What caused it to fail?

A. It did not take you by surprise. The removal of Panzer divisions from further east was not accomplished rapidly enough. Also, Generalfeldmarschall von Kluge did not concentrate them at one time on the left wing, but sent them one after the other. He did not succeed in assembling all his forces at the critical point. I believe he had only four divisions in all at the time, whereas he could have had eight.

Q. Do you think that, with the strongest German forces around Caen, the German left wing was weakened before our breakthrough to Avranches?

A. It was always too weak, even from the beginning, because the commander did not succeed in reinforcing the left wing in time.

Q. Was that because the British were at Caen?

A. Hitler had ordered the reduction of the bridgehead at Caen, expecting that the British would attack towards Paris.

Q. Was that better tank country?

A. Much better. The rear was good for tank employment. The terrain further west was very bad. We could not employ strong units in the West, but used a single tank combined with infantry instead.

Q. Did you have any of your armor directly attached to infantry divisions?

A. Generally, no. Our Panzer division contained several battalions of armored infantry specially trained to work with tanks [Panzer Grenadiers], and it was our idea from the beginning to have the infantry and artillery specially trained for tank operations and tank fighting. That was the reason for creating Panzer divisions rather than having tanks work with infantry.

Q. Looking back over the whole war, what operations stand out in your mind as being good ones?

A. Those of General Patton were well conducted. He was very quick. The essential thing in Panzer command is speed. His best operation was that after Avranches, since he had the greatest resistance there. Later, he had practically no opposition and it was very easy for you to win the rest of the war. For you, it was a supply and communications problem only. After arranging your supplies, victory was easy.

Q. Did you have anything to do with the Western Front?

A. Only with reference to tanks. I was Inspector General of Panzer Forces, and in that capacity I had a right to speak, but not about operations as a whole.

Q. Were any of your recommendations carried out regarding armored employment in the West?

A. I recommended, in the fall of 1943, putting a number of Panzer divisions on the Western Front in view of the anticipated invasion. This was not done until spring of 1944, and it was up to me to remind Hitler every day, at every conference, to move these divisions from the East to the West. Finally, we had twelve divisions on the Western Front, most of which had come from the East. We reorganized and improved them, and they were well-trained and good fighting divisions. This much influence I had. When I tried to make further arrangements for these divisions, I did not succeed.

Q. After Normandy, what recommendations did you make?

A. I practically made daily recommendations that dividing the Panzer forces into two parts should be avoided. Von Kluge, however, actually split the Panzer divisions into several parts. He separated the tanks from the Panzer Grenadiers and artillery, employing them with infantry units not trained in Panzer warfare; therefore, he failed to get favorable results. This was a great mistake throughout the whole war.

Panzer Tactics in Normandy

by General der Panzer Leo, Freiherr Geyr von Schweppenburg

The Possibility of Mass Panzer Counterattacks in Normandy

Q. Would mass counterattacks by two or three Panzer divisions have been possible in the bocage country?

A. Definitely yes.

Q. How would they have been protected during assembly?

A. By concentration of forces and all other troop movements during the night. The road net permitted this, and the cover was there. Under my supervision, the Panzer troops had been trained in these tactics.

Q. Could attacks have been made at dark?

A. Yes, we would have used the one to two hours of dawn and dusk and attacked with limited objectives during these hours. I suggested these "Tiger tactics" to Hitler. If the attack had been successful, effecting a breakthrough, we would have gotten in among the Allied forces, forcing your airpower to quit its attacks, which were a constant menace to Panzer forces. Our supply routes would then have suffered from air attacks, but the success would have been worth it.

Such a night attack with two Panzer divisions did take place on 10 June 1944, at Caen, the 21st Panzer and 12th SS Panzer Divisions each employing a Panzer regiment in its attack element; but, as you know, the attack never really got under way and was called off when my staff was destroyed by air attack.

Q. What losses could have been expected?

A. (*Interviewer's note: Here General der Panzer von Geyr threw up his hands and shook his head in a very helpless gesture. For the first time, he waited for a few moments before answering, as if groping for a reply.*) I can't tell—I can't foretell that answer.

Q. What measures might have been taken to neutralize Allied air forces?

A. Only passive ones. The only measure we could take was using dusk, dawn, and night for all operations.

Q. What objectives would have been attacked?

A. That depends on the situation, of course. Generally, one thing is sure—we would have made the enemy artillery our first objective. I had always taught my troops the Napoleonic principle of "s'engager, puis voir" [a free translation would be: "Engage the enemy and then we shall see"], get into the enemy lines, lose the enemy air striking force, and take advantage of any opportunities that arise.

214

Q. What decisive results could have been achieved?

A. The fate of Panzer attacks you could't foretell. If a breakthrough had been achieved, perhaps complete success; if failure to achieve a breakthrough, perhaps complete failure. (*Interviewer's note: Here, in an effort to pin down his term "complete success," I asked General der Panzer von Geyr if by it he meant a drive clear to the beach and the ultimate ejection of the Allies from the continent, as Hitler anticipated. He answered: "No, it would have been impossible to push you into the sea, in my opinion. And we would have stopped short of the beach, out of the range of your naval artillery, for which we had a healthy respect—this we learned at Salerno. We would have attempted to split up your forces and create havoc in your rear, disrupting communications, etc."*)

Infantry–Tank Team Tactics

Q. What Panzer tactics had been developed for fighting in the hedgerows?

A. This, too, depends entirely on the situation and terrain. In very bad terrain, where only forces in platoon or company strength could be committed, our Panzer Lehr Division decided on the tactics of joining up a Panzer company, a grenadier platoon or company, and a pioneer (engineer) company. This would result in only local action, though, for if you disperse forces in this way, there is much local fighting, you lose control, and no big success is achieved—contrary to the opinion of the Panzer Lehr Division commander, who believed and put in writing that with such tactics the enemy could be thrown into the sea. This violates the principle that Panzer tactics require concentration of force.

Q. Did you have specially trained infantry–tank teams?

A. We trained these troops for cooperation even in night fighting. I checked myself on these night tactics to see that liaison and communication worked well, but I wouldn't say that this difficult problem was completely solved below battalion level. Another difficulty that arose in our infantry–tank tactics was the lack of armored personnel carriers to make it possible for the infantry to keep up with the swiftly moving tanks.

Q. Had you solved the problem of communication between infantry and tanks?

A. We had solved the problem in an even greater aspect in training. I had subordinate commanders who from their mobile command tanks could direct their divisions or regiments and coordinate their actions with that of the infantry, the artillery, and the air force—all by radio. However, this was all on battalion level or above; below that level, I would not say that the communication problem between the individual tanks and infantry was ever solved. We were forever concerned with our radios; as long as they functioned, cooperation among the various forces was possible. We were afraid of their being jammed though—tactics which the British employed very successfully in Africa.

East vs. West Panzer Tactics

Q. In reference to your statement that Panzer divisions were ordered committed intact by Generalfeldmarschall von Rundstedt, was this general armored doctrine in the German Army at the time?

A. There was no overall armored doctrine in the German Army at that time! This order came out through my instigation, but it was not practiced or carried out. Panzer divisions were committed piecemeal or had elements lent out and attached to infantry divisions on orders from Generalfeldmarschall von Rundstedt when he thought the occasion demanded it.

Of all the German generals, Generalfeldmarschall von Rundstedt knew the least of Panzer tactics—he was an infantryman of the last generation. He and his staff were armchair strategists who didn't like dirt, noise, and tanks in general. (As far as I know, Generalfeldmarschall von Rundstedt was never in a tank.) Do not misunderstand me, however: I have the greatest respect for von Rundstedt, but he was too old for this war. I had a free hand in the training of Panzer forces in the West, and Generaloberst Guderian [at that time Inspector General of Panzer Troops] and I saw eye-to-eye on this. I should have been allowed to employ these forces as they had been trained. Hitler, with his 1918 ideas of trench warfare, also was responsible for the incorrect use of Panzer forces.

Q. What was the practice on the Russian Front?

A. On the Russian Front, as elsewhere, the only rule in Panzer tactics was that there was no rule! In Russia, I myself broke many basic Panzer principles because of this. Normally, however, divisions were committed intact in the East. (*Interviewer's note: General der Panzer von Geyr clarified this as follows: A Panzer division was given a definite sector to operate in and functioned under one commander, normally, rather than having elements parceled out and attached to other units.*)

Q. How far could Panzer tactics as developed in the East be applied in the West?

A. This question is too difficult to answer in short. Briefly, the tactics were entirely different. I wouldn't say they couldn't be applied at all, but generally the fighting and tactics were entirely different. Space is endless in the East, limited in the West, and this makes a big difference in Panzer warfare.

Q. What differences were there?

A. I could write a book on this. There was little to compare between tactics that were successful in the West and those in the East. Complete differentiation was made in training for the two fronts. New problems arose every day in the West, a new front. Enemy airpower was something to be reckoned with seriously for the first time. Rocket-carrying planes were a menace that continually harassed our tanks; I recommended that fully one-third of our tanks in the West should be primarily antiaircraft weapon carriers. Whether you realize it or not, it was British rocket-carrying planes that halted our counterattack at Avranches, not your 30th Infantry Division. (*Interviewer's note: Here, in attempt to draw General der Panzer von Geyr out more on these differences between the East and West, I asked him if enemy artillery in the West was not also a more serious consideration than in Russia. "Do not underestimate Russian artillery for a minute," he said. "You had good artillery that could adjust quickly on point targets, such as tanks, and bring down sudden concentrations, but the Russians ccould too. When I was in Russia in 1941–*)

42, their artillery was not this proficient, but the Russians learn quickly and reports that came to me near the end of the war indicate that Russian artillery had improved immeasurably and was capable of any tasks put before it.")

Q. Did Panzer divisions shifted from the East need retraining in new types of warfare in the West?

A. Entirely new training, most of all in leadership. In the West, divisions had to be kept together, their power concentrated, while in the East they had to be broken down and formed into combat groups [Kampfgruppen] to try to cover the vast spaces. Here, the basic principle of concentration of force had to be habitually violated. The troops had to be trained more for consciousness of airpower in the West; although the Russians had Lend-Lease planes in great numbers, they never employed them as effectively against tanks as they were used in the West.

Q. If so, did they receive such training in adequate amounts?

A. (*Interviewer's note: General der Panzer von Geyr, after losing his command in the West, became Inspector of Panzer Troops and was responsible for the training of all Panzer troops—a task for which he obviously had a great deal of enthusiasm and in which he took great pride. Therefore, this question was almost a personal one, and he laughed a little self-consciously before answering.*) They got all that was humanly possible to give. Those troops already in the West had received very thorough training before the invasion. You would have won anyway, I feel quite sure, but you would have had a harder time, I am equally as sure, if we had been able to employ these troops as we wished—as *Panzer* troops.

PART NINE

Summary:
The Reasons for the Defeat

The reasons for the German defeat are quickly limited to the "usual suspects." While all are politically convenient for the writers, they all are largely true. Allied control of the air is cited time and time again as being decisive. That Allied material superiority should in the end prove decisive should not have come as a surprise to German officers, many of whom came of age at the first invention of the *materielschlacht*, at Verdun in 1916.

Their perception of Allied—especially American—tactical inferiority, while also self-serving, contains elements of truth, especially in Normandy, where the Allied divisions were either green or war-weary. Only grudgingly do they admit the evolution in Allied battlefield capability that they saw over the course of the Normandy fighting. Certainly they might have thought their US Army captors would have liked to have heard better about themselves, but this is not reflected in these writings.

D.C.I.

Forces Brought Up
During the Normandy Battle

by Generalleutnant Bodo Zimmermann

At the command of Army Group B or Seventh Army, the following were moved up to Normandy from the Army Group B area:

77th Division, from the vicinity of St-Malo;
12th SS Panzer Division, from the vicinity of Lisieux (after release by OKW);
Panzer Lehr Division, from the vicinity of Chartres (after release by OKW);
17th SS Panzer Grenadier Division, of First Army (after release by OKW);
II FS Corps HQ and 3rd FS Division (Seventh Army area, with OKW approval);
346th Division, of Fifteenth Army;
XLVII Panzer Corps HQ, of Army Group B; and
LXXIV Corps, of Seventh Army.

Therefore, Army Group B at the critical moment gave up only one division (346th Division) of its main body, whereas according to OB West's estimate it could have released at least seven divisions.

The following were readied for an early transfer:

353rd Division, of Seventh Army;
Kampfgruppe 265th Division, of Seventh Army;
Kampfgruppe 266th Division, of Seventh Army;
9th Panzer Division, of Nineteenth Army; and
I SS Panzer Corps HQ and 1st SS Panzer Division, of Army Group B.

The following were alerted to anticipate transfer:

LXXXVI Corps HQ, of First Army;
LXXX Corps HQ, of First Army;
LVIII Panzer Corps HQ, of Army Group G;
16th Lw Feld Division, of Wehrmacht District Netherlands;
276th Division, of First Army;
708th Division, of First Army;
271st Division, of Nineteenth Army;

221

272nd Division, of Nineteenth Army;

277th Division, of Nineteenth Army;

338th Division (in the gravest emergency), of Nineteenth Army; and

2nd SS Panzer Division, of Army Group G.

In the further course of the Normandy battle, it also became necessary to move to Normandy the 85th Division and 89th Division from Fifteenth Army, and 84th Division from Seventh Army, after they had been readied for combat. The same was done with the 2nd FS Division of Seventh Army (after it had been readied for combat) and the elements of the 5th FS Division that were ready for action.

During the first days of the invasion, Generalfeldmarschall Rommel still thought he could not release the 2nd Panzer Division and 116th Panzer Division, which were standing by in the area between the lower Somme and the Seine. He was unwilling to release them because of his well-known opinion in regard to a second major landing along the Channel coast with its main effort near the Somme estuary. Apparently, at this time his belief was still supported by OKW and Fifteenth Army.

During June, OKW brought up to OB West from the Eastern Front II SS Panzer Corps HQ, with the 9th and 10th SS Panzer Divisions, and, later on, the 363rd Division, for the Normandy battle. Both of these Panzer divisions had to be unloaded from their trains at about the Verdun–Nancy–Dijon line because of the transportation situation, and proceed to Normandy by road march. (This was at the end of June.) It is easy to understand what that meant, in view of the difficult fuel situation, and what it did to the condition of the armored vehicles! Nevertheless, this large-scale movement went off comparatively smoothly, due to careful organization and planning as to the routes, halt areas, and antiaircraft defense. Rail transportation, on the other hand, was no longer dependable or predictable in any way. Only in the very first days of the invasion might the forward displacement of units by rail still have been perhaps "conditionally" feasible—particularly of Fifteenth Army units to, or via, Paris. Due to the conflict of opinions already mentioned, this valuable time and opportunity was not utilized, and the enemy was given a unique strategic opportunity. In subsequent days and weeks, the condition of roads, railroads, and important bridges changed increasingly to our disadvantage.

Critical Summary

by General der Flakartillerie Wolfgang Pickert

The assembly of III AA Corps, for the repulse of the long-awaited invasion, appeared unfavorable. When the Commanding General, arriving from the East approximately on 24 May 1944, assumed command of the Corps, he immediately made application for a strict concentration of the forces in the area around Paris, so as from there to be able rapidly to reach the possible landing area east or west of the mouth of the Seine. This application was rejected. However, the alternative request of the Commanding General, at least to withdraw Corps from its rigid commitment and to give it an opportunity for training in mobile fighting, was accepted. Should, however, as now appears certain, the invasion have been expected in all probability to be about to occur in Normandy, then III AA Corps should have been placed behind this coastal sector.

III AA Corps' state of training was insufficient for the severe mobile battles that were to be expected. The troops were insufficiently trained for these [sic]. They had been committed for many months, almost uninterruptedly in fixed positions, on airdromes, etc. The techniques of entrenchment during mobile combat, of position reconnaissance and camouflage, and of training in ground combat were not mastered to the extent which the heavy fighting that was ahead would in all probability require. The reasons for this backwardness are not going to be entered into here. Still, the ten days of mobile commitment on the coast—short as they were—astride the mouth of the Seine, which were permitted effective 25 May, had the effect of a ground maneuver with live bullets. The troops learned much that they were soon desperately to need. Nevertheless, it was incorrect to let three or four regiments "exercise" at the mouth of the Somme, if the highest command apparently expected a landing to take place in all probability in Normandy. The destruction of all the Seine bridges between Rouen and Paris, as well as that of the many Oise bridges, could almost certainly be expected to force a time-absorbing, fuel-consuming detour via Paris, which did actually happen later. The allocation of the fourth regiment into the Isigny–Bayeux area was necessitated by the heavy air activity over this region, and the urgent need for AA protection. However, by this commitment, the AA Corps lost one quarter of its combat strength. This fourth regiment only rejoined the (bulk of the) Corps several weeks after the beginning of the invasion.

The forces of III AA Corps were inadequate in view of the width the enemy landing could be expected to take. Twice, if not three times their number could have been regarded as a minimum requirement. With the forces available, strong AA protection could be offered at best only to one Army, and even then only to a limited extent.

The organization of the supply facilities also did not take into proper account the size of the enemy landing expected in Normandy. Otherwise ammunition and fuel depots should have been readied behind this sector at a commensurate distance from the coast, to quite a different extent than actually happened. The supply routes for AA ammunition were too long, at least in the initial weeks. The same, in my estimation, can also be said for the supply routes of the artillery ammunition of the Army, and those of fuel.

Moreover, the supplies of a place like Cherbourg, exposed as it was, and particularly endangered by a landing in Normandy, were insufficient, at least as far as AA ammunition was concerned. This I learned from an appeal for help from the AA commander there, with whom I was personally friendly. Shortly before Cherbourg was encircled he contacted me, through an officer specially sent to Caen for this purpose, bearing an urgent request for AA ammunition. Although he was not subordinated to me, I would gladly have helped him, but this was beyond my means.

Coming from the East after two years of heavy fighting—advance from Kharkov to Stalingrad, attack on Stalingrad, "pocket" of Stalingrad, Kuban bridgehead and Sebastopol—to the Western Front in 1944, a comparison between the Eastern and Western enemies is noteworthy.

Particularly noticeable in the West were the extraordinarily carefully attacking enemy tanks, which only went into action under the best possible covering fire, and then almost reluctantly, but which overpowered our defenses including the antitank AA much more quickly that I had seen it in the East. Perhaps my troops in the East were more experienced and skilled in this sphere of combat—a supposition borne out by the high numbers of tanks put out of action through AA fire in 1942 and 1943 in the East.

Compared to the Russian artillery, good as it was, however, the enemy artillery in the invasion front had an overwhelming effect, owing to its abundance of ammunition, its caliber, and its long range. The Russians appeared to be much more generously equipped with mortars and knew how to use these to best advantage. Smokeshell firing, which had also been observed in the East, was used by the enemy in Normandy to a great extent, mostly successfully. The enemy infantry appeared less active, and tough on the attack, than the Russians often were.

Particularly great, of course, was the difference in the aerial activity between the Eastern Front and Normandy. Even though the Russians often sent in a sizable number of warplanes over the focal points, this was as nothing compared to the enemy air activity over Normandy. Even the excellent German information leaflets about the battles in Africa and Italy could not give, even to a lively imagination, that picture of reality which Normandy then offered. It may well be said that the enemy's fighter planes helped him decisively to win the battle of Normandy. The losses in vehicles, weapons, and men, through air attacks on the field of battle and on the rear of line areas close behind the front, were almost overshadowed by the indirect effect, which was that of a prohibition of all major troop movements by day, and sometimes even of solitary driving of single vehicles during the hours of daylight. Just the destruction of fuel transports repeatedly had an extremely unfavorable effect, as the fuel was often insufficient even for tactically absolutely necessary transfers. The bulk of the traffic, and of the troop movements, had consequently to be crowded into the unfortunately very short summer nights. It was lucky for us that the enemy abstained from destroying our most important supply roads through bombing at the most suitable places (in soft meadows, near steep slopes, etc.) which he could have done shortly before nightfall, without difficulty, considering the strong air forces he committed. Our nocturnal traffic would have been seriously impeded hereby, which would have caused grave tactical disadvantages for troop movements and supply transportation. The repeated destruction of villages with road intersections, where detouring was possible only with difficulty, often had a very disturbing effect. These attacks, which could not be prevented with the weak AA forces available, undoubtedly brought the enemy much success, even though they caused the civilian population particularly much suffering.

The attitude of the population throughout the entire battle was definitely not hostile. It alternated between reserve and amicable neutrality. Sabotage, by cutting of telephonic communications, and certainly also by reports of agents, occurred. But partisan activity, for which the Normandy terrain, with its hedges and forests, is particularly well-suited, could not be observed. It was very regrettable that the fleeing civilian population, though marked by white sheets, etc., was also attacked by fighter-bombers.

Critically summarizing the commitment of III AA Corps, comparing its losses with its successes, it may be said that, as far as I recall, some 500 planes and 100 tanks were put out of action by the AA batteries. Further, the lively participation in the ground fighting, with surprise-fire concentrations or with observed fire guided by forward observers, caused the enemy quite significant losses, and often decisively helped the Army fighting side by side with us.

The battles in Normandy were amongst the most severe I have ever participated in, even counting the First World War, and the heavy battles I participated in in the Second World War. At any rate, the courageous troops held out in an exemplary fashion, in heavy fighting, against a superior enemy, so that, after replacements of men and material had arrived, the survivors, toughened by experience and under heavy fire, and their new comrades, could be committed again a short time later in the autumn battle for Aachen, in the winter battle in the Ardennes and in the final battle for the Rhine.

Opinion on the Treatise by General der Flakartillerie Pickert, Wolfgang, on "III AA Corps in the Normandy Battles"

by Generalleutnant Max Pemsel

An excellent piece of work, with a clear, frank expression of opinion, and critique.

The AA forces located in the West and later committed on the invasion front, were far too few, to compensate even to a small extent for the weakness of the German air forces. In Normandy, even before the invasion, we should have committed:

1 AA corps in the Caen region; 1 AA Corps in the Cotentin peninsula; 1 AA Corps in the center of Normandy for mobile commitment.

In actuality the invasion was opposed by:

1 AA regiment of the Air Forces Administrative Command Headquarters (Luftgau-kommando) Western France, for the protection of the V-weapons north of the Cotentin peninsula; 1 AA regiment of III AA Corps, north of Isigny, to protect the artillery group stationed there.

The application repeatedly sent in by Seventh Army before the invasion—to have the AA forces stationed at the submarine bases transferred (insofar as they were mobile) to Normandy, for commitment—was always rejected. It was obstinately expected that the U-boat would stage a comeback.

The invasion was not—as the writer states—expected to take place in Normandy. Proof of this is furnished by the author himself:

a) Commitment of three-quarters of III AA Corps, shortly before the beginning of the invasion, in the Somme region;

b) No organization of AA ammunition stockpiles in Normandy.

It was a tactical mistake to shift the AA corps out of the area of greater Paris to the Somme, in anticipation of the invasion, however much the protection of important objectives in this area, and reasons of training, were in favor of it. Time, equipment, and personnel were lost on the long march from the Somme via Paris to Normandy, after the beginning of the invasion.

By the commitment of III AA Corps (minus one regiment) near Caen, and the almost exclusive commitment of the German air forces over this area, a definite center of gravity of the Luftwaffe came into being here, both in the air and on the ground. However, this correct commitment did not have a significant effect against the enemy air supremacy.

The commitment of III AA Corps at Caen was especially effective in ground combat later, toward the middle and the end of July, when the British attacked. The unstable

226

front of the divisions 270 [*sic*] and the burnt-out Panzer divisions received considerable support from III AA Corps with its rapid, versatile fire from its excellent 88mm guns.

It was a mistake to direct III AA Corps to cooperate with the Army. Only a subordination of III AA Corps to the Army in command of the sector in which the corps was located, in all respects, even that of supplies, could have worked. However, questions of prestige decided this problem. The author, who is himself an Army man, overcame the friction that arose.

I agree with the comparisons between East and West, and with the critical observations.

Fighting in Normandy:
The 3rd FS Division

by Generalleutnant Richard Schimpf

Reserves

The establishment of a tactical reserve was only possible to very limited degree, since the division was not compactly thrown into the Battle of Normandy and later it became necessary to greatly extend the division sector in the course of the engagement for St-Lô. A certain reserve formation existed only due to the fact that the division retained the regimental reserves behind the regimental sectors for commitment (usually one company, but also up to one battalion). This important weakness in the formation of reserves, of course, had a very bad effect. Many recognized favorable opportunities to carry out counterattacks or to exploit the results of successful counterattacks had to remain unutilized.

Use of Artillery

During the first combat weeks the division had at its disposal only *one artillery battalion.* This battalion was committed behind the center of the division sector in such a way that it could concentrate its fire in front of the 5th FS Regiment (region of Bérigny) and, furthermore, could cover with its fire the area before the front line of the 9th FS Regiment (to the left) and partly in front of the 8th FS Regiment (to the right). Therefore, until the arrival of further Heeres (Army) artillery reserves, a heavy antiaircraft battery was employed in support of the 8th FS Regiment for firing at ground targets, and was directed to cooperate closely with it. The high rate of the fire and precision of its weapons and fuzes nearly equalled the firepower of an artillery battalion. The disadvantage of the flat trajectory was less apparent in Normandy, because the hilly terrain offered sufficient suitable firing positions. The troops liked to cooperate with this antiaircraft battery, because the concentrated fire, which, for the most part, immediately hit the target, had a powerful effect. Furthermore, the flak was mostly supplied with ample ammunition.

After the arrival of a second Heeres artillery battalion about the beginning of July 1944, and of a Heeres Werfer (mortar or rocket projection) brigade about the middle of July, the antiaircraft battery could again be used for firing against air targets. The Heeres artillery was committed without special tactics.

The terrain, in which the line of vision was greatly impeded by hedges, rendered observation extremely difficult. The complete lack of airplanes, which would have made possible firing with air observation, had, therefore, especially troublesome effects. Land observation from elevated points proved to be only a poor substitute in this terrain where the line of vision was restricted.

Nightly harassing fire on localities where troops were billeted and road targets, etc., was limited by a scarcity of ammunition. At first one advanced observer, later two, were assigned to each battalion. The contact with the artillery battalions was established by telephone and radio. The first was mostly disturbed by enemy fire, the latter often hindered by the characteristic nature of the terrain and dampness of the ground. The troops were of the opinion that the short-wave apparatus of the advanced observers was located and placed under fire by the enemy. Therefore, they did not like to see radio stations in their vicinity. The radio personnel denied the possibility of finding positions by means of short-wave apparatus. The question remained open.

Characteristics of the Hedgerow (Bocage) Terrain

The characteristics of the Normandy terrain offered considerable advantages for defense—good camouflage and cover, as well as limitation of the mobility of all enemy vehicles, including tracklaying vehicles, off the roads and streets. The only disadvantage was the very restricted possibility of observation for artillery and infantry heavy weapons.

The terrain hindered the attacking enemy from fully developing his air and tank superiority. This was very helpful to the division, which for the first time took part in the fighting. The value of the individual as a fighter immediately became evident. He could evade the effect of bombs and shells by skillfully utilizing the available camouflage and cover, and soon recognized that tanks could be destroyed from ambush. (Even in this terrain, so unfavorable for the use of tanks, the American infantry did not dispense with them as a steady infantry escort.) The tank's psychological danger was quickly overcome. Over 360 tracklaying vehicles were annihilated by the division in close combat, which is the best proof for it.

Next to courage and skill, it was the terrain of Normandy which enabled the division to retard for so long a period a disproportionately stronger enemy who was lavishly equipped with all weapons of modern warfare. Here it should be mentioned that the enemy only seldom made use of the possibilities of covered approach for the purpose of attaining victory through surprise attacks. He mostly forewent this advantage due to the betraying noise of the accompanying infantry tanks. The only exceptions were the later-mentioned raids in platoon or company strength. The choice of a suitable main line of resistance was difficult for the defense. The fields surrounded by embankments and hedges were mostly so small that the repelling fire effect—even of the light machine guns—could not be fully utilized. The advancing of combat outposts was possible only to a limited extent, because it was easy for the enemy to eliminate them without being seen by German troops or from the neighboring posts. Due to the insufficient supply of portable radio apparatus, the advance of the combat outposts was only done for short distances, and only where visual contact existed.

On the whole, the outpost area was secured by frequent use of reconnaissance patrols, observation posts, and snipers in the trees. However, these covering parties could not prevent unnoticed enemy approaches, sporadically carried out in platoon or even company strength, as near as 70 meters from the main line of resistance. This fact required a constant and the strongest possible occupation of the main line of resistance, a high degree of preparedness, and the movement of local reserves to move immediately behind the main line of resistance.

It is obvious that these conditions were a strain for the troops. The mortars were the most effective heavy weapon in this bush warfare. Unfortunately, at that time, the German side did not have at their disposal the necessary number of guns and ammunition and radio equipment, not to speak of artillery observation airplanes. (At the turn of the year 1944/45 only was one mortar battalion assigned to the FS divisions.) Computation of firing data was also difficult during the first six weeks, due to the lack of special maps. The troops were compelled to draw firing maps by hand, which sometimes delayed the full effect of a plan of fire up to 48 hours. Moreover, the same map shortage existed for subordinate commanders and combat and reconnaissance patrols. Captured maps (1: 25,000) with marked-in embankments and hedges were in great demand in the infantry.

Finally, I would like to mention that the best protection against enemy mortar fire was covered foxholes. Whenever time afforded even the slightest chance, the infantry entrenched itself up to two meters deep, directly behind the embankments, and covered the holes with beams three deep. For the narrow entrance into the foxholes, it was important to construct a suitably strong cover out of wooden boards and beams. The infantry entrenched in this manner had hardly any losses, even during concentrated mortar fire. Only in isolated instances, where shells with time-fuzing or phosphorus grenades were fired, were the casualties increased.

Counterattacks

Due to lack of reserves, no counter*attacks* could be executed in the sector of the 3rd FS Division. However, enemy penetrations were often sealed off and cleared by local counter*thrusts*.

Road Nets and Signal Communication Lines

In the rear of the combat area, all roads and streets were fully made use of in spite of enemy fighter-bomber activity and artillery fire. Only the points covered by especially severe artillery fire were avoided (in some instances by detouring), and were marked accordingly. In the advanced combat area, traffic during the daytime was carried on, avoiding as much as possible motor vehicular traffic, by using the numerous concealed roads and defiles. At this point, it was our experience that narrow defiles were not under fire. Comparing the captured map, it was ascertained that the defiles were not marked in as "roads" but as "hedges" (most probably a mistake in the interpretation of aerial photographs). German troops made use of this fact many times, with fine success. In general, it has to be stated that the streets and roads, as far as they did not provide full cover, could, during the *daytime*, be used only by single vehicles, because the traffic was constantly under enemy observation due to his air superiority. This limited use of the roads was a very troublesome obstacle to the control of supply traffic.

Because of its well-equipped signal battalion, the division was not dependent on the county telephone system. Naturally, available lines were used whenever necessary. However, with the increasing violence of the battles the telephone net lost more and more its value and importance, so that, finally, only radio communications and the use of motorized messengers were possible.

Estimate of Their Strength,
and Criticisms of American Tactics, Their Troops and Equipment

It had indisputably been ascertained, through interrogation of prisoners, that the strength of the enemy forces consisted of three divisions in front of the division sector (without counting the strategic reserves located in the near). Furthermore, it had to be taken into consideration that these divisions—as was likewise determined—continuously received replacements and were relieved after a comparatively short period of commitment, whereas, on the other hand, the German division received replacements only once and in insufficient strength, and never was relieved during the whole fighting period in Normandy. The purely numerical proportion of power was therefore estimated to be 1:4 to 1:5.

It is impossible for me to offer any criticism, as a division commander, of American *strategy*, because for this I lack the necessary data. With regard to the American *tactics*, I am of the opinion that they differed fundamentally from the German conception. I would like to state that, principally, their tactics were much more schematic and inflexible than the German, which fact often gave the defensive troops the opportunity to take appropriate countermeasures.

Enemy surprise assaults were extremely rare. Therefore, in spite of the only very weakly occupied defense lines, the defenders often succeeded in repelling enemy attacks merely by being able to assemble, in time, local counterattack reserves at the likely points of enemy attacks by weakening quieter sectors.

Another difference from the German conception consisted in the fact that they only decided upon extremely *limited* objectives, and failed to exploit achieved successes by continuing their thrusts in depth, which, due to the weak defense, would have been quite opportune, and would have resulted in very serious consequences for us. Therefore, it was nearly always possible to establish new defense front lines.

I cannot follow the reasoning that these tactics were supposed to have helped avoid bloodshed, as I was told by captured American officers. For, although losses on the *day of attack* could be kept comparatively low, on the other hand the *total* losses suffered through the continuous minor attacks, launched over a long period, were surely much heavier than would have been the case if a forceful attack had been conducted into the depth of the defense front, which would have led to an encirclement battle already at the town of Vire (instead of later near Falaise).

It is to be noted that the equipment of the American troops was excellent and efficient. The conduct and the effect of the very strong artillery, and especially of the mortars, was good and because of its mobility caused considerable losses to the defensive troops. Its effect could be lessened only by skillful tactics, in the use of terrain, and by immediate entrenchment in the respective defense line.

The enemy air force seldom appeared over the division front line. However, it harassed the supply in the rear of the front line to such an extent that a heavier traffic during daytime was hardly possible. The almost complete lack of German fighter formations and inadequate number of antiaircraft forces made this easy for the American Air Force.

Losses in men and material were high during this six weeks of defensive fighting, that had to be endured without a break, and during which the losses were replaced only inadequately. It is impossible for me, however, to give a numerical estimate without the help of my war diary.

Commentary on the Report by Generalleutnant Dipl. Ing. Schimpf, Richard

by Generalleutnant Max Pemsel

A very good and clear work. The author is a highly qualified officer with a technical career and practical parachute experiences.

The fighting power of the 3rd FS Division was equal to two German standard divisions. The weakness of the division lay in its artillery equipment. As the division only had one artillery battalion at its disposal, it had to be reinforced by Heeres artillery.

In order to have this valuable division near the expected invasion front line—Normandy—Seventh Army proposed in December 1943 the commitment of this division in the area of Rennes. OKW, however, for the protection of the important town of Brest, wanted to commit—in addition to one stalling (static) division—two reserve divisions (among which should be the 3rd FS Division) near the fortress.

It was remarkable that the division suffered hardly any losses in men and material (due to enemy air force activities) on its ten-days' march from the extreme west of the Bretagne to the front line in the Normandy. The reasons were a good organization of the marches and insufficient enemy observation from the air and by agents in the area.

The attack aimed at capturing the Forest of Cerisy, as proposed by the divisional commander, might have been successful, but it had to be carried out with insufficient forces. The danger of completely exhausting the division during the attack was great, as the division was poorly trained for attacks. Therefore, Seventh Army prohibited the attack.

The strength of the FS division rested in defense, because the division was well trained for it. The parachutist felt at home in this bocage terrain and as an individual fighter felt himself superior to the enemy's matériel.

In the defense, the division was fortunate to be able to extract reserves up to battalion strength. The Army had no anxiety about the sector held by the 3rd FS Division—in spite of its width—and the division justified the confidence placed in it.

Summing Up

by Generalleutnant Joseph Reichert

The defender will never be able to prevent the initial successes of a large-scale attack, particularly so if the attacker succeeds in keeping secret the chosen attack area. Since the so-called "Atlantic Wall" at most parts had been nothing but an insufficient cloak of security—equipped with numerous reinforced fortifications and defensive weapons it is true, but not at all sufficiently manned, with one weak division holding a sector of 40 kilometers in a double (even three- or fourfold) position against an invasion, carried out under the protection of concentrated fire from the sea and air and with an additional threat to the coastal garrisons by airborne troops—any landing attempt was bound to succeed, no matter where it was taking place. The choice of the place was of importance only so far—whether one was prepared to put up with minor or heavier losses in view of the operations envisaged later on.

In view of this situation, the questions which were mostly discussed regarding the defense of the coast—whether it would be better to build a few, heavily fortified strongpoints and have them cover a larger depth, or a continuous line of small pillboxes; [and] whether one ought to fight from the inside of pillboxes (therefore to construct loop-holes) or to continue open warfare after enduring the bombardment in the pillboxes—were of little importance.

Coastal defence alone was never in a position to hinder an enemy large-scale landing: it could only harass the enemy and report. The High Command, no doubt, had realized this too, and from the very beginning had expected the total loss of the coastal divisions affected by an enemy large-scale landing operation. They nevertheless fulfilled their purpose of harassing and weakening the enemy and furnishing reports about the operations. The coastal divisions on the whole were relieved of the anxiety about a threat from the rear, inasmuch as available forces permitted, because reserve divisions were held ready in the near hinterland.

Thus, in my opinion, no serious mistakes had been made in the organization of the coastal defense and in the conduct of battle which would have facilitated the landing of the enemy. The task for the coastal defense—to prevent an enemy landing, applied to the case of a large-scale operation—meant asking for the impossible, in order to get all the results possible.

After the successful landing, the most difficult stage of the operation for the attacking forces was not a speedy initial landing but the formation and holding of the first

234

strongpoint on land, with the view of securing further landings and a continuous flow of necessary supplies. In my opinion, only the immediate employment of tanks, which for this purpose had to be held ready near the coast, would have been able to solve this problem successfully against this landing. I know that, conforming to Rommel's point of view (despite the views held to the contrary) by OB West, the 21st Panzer Division on D-Day was held ready for action in the rear of the 716th Infantry Division. I do not know, however, whether and at what time it launched a counterattack and, if so, which were the reasons for the failure of this counterattack.

Nevertheless, the mistakes made in this respect were not a decisive reason for the failure of the defense, neither was the fact that the mentality of the enemy was obviously too little understood by the German Command; [the cause was] the typical German way of reasoning prevailing in the beginning—that at this spot, apparently so unimportant strategically, the main operation had been launched by the enemy, in consequence of which steps for the transfer of forces from other parts were taken very reluctantly.

In my opinion the cardinal weakness of the German defense could be compared with a man who had been stripped of everything; who, due to the lack of equipment, had to direct all his thoughts to the trials and tribulations of the invasion itself because no adequate preparations had been made to shield him in some degree from its terrible effects, and from the onslaught of an enemy who had already achieved a bridgehead on land; instead of being able to lay his finger on the real root of all his woes, and the most sensitive one—namely, the enemy's armor, his fleet, which assured him of his supplies of men and material. If we could have gained a decisive success here, it would have been a trifle to get the upper hand of the landed forces later on. Only two weapons would have been able to achieve this—the Navy and the Luftwaffe. The German Navy practically no longer existed. One of the first suppositions for the success of all invasion forces from the sea was certainly the invention made by the enemy to eliminate the danger of the U-boats. Unfortunately the Luftwaffe also existed only as broken fragments. In spite of all that, one should have expected that everything that was still left of the Luftwaffe, in all theaters of the war and in the homeland, would be assembled together with everything that was still worthy of the name of "Navy," in order to launch an attack against the enemy fleet. Against this, only minor attacks took place with a weak bomber wing, which at night and with individual planes only tried to release its bombs on the enemy fleet or drop mines into the approach route. The Navy made use of its small arms, until even the last man was lost.

Today I do not know how badly off the Luftwaffe was at that time and whether neglect had occurred, but it was absolutely impossible to get together even the minimum of forces necessary for such an undertaking.

That things could have come to such a state was due to mistakes made on the part of the Germans, but the bulk of the deficiencies was certainly due to the Anglo-American air force, which untiringly smashed the production plants, wore down the people, and completely paralyzed traffic.

Whoever, as I did, witnessed the continuous raids of British and American four-motor bombers at the periphery of the invasion's area—for hours on end the whole sky vibrated with deep sounds: up to one thousand planes were counted at times and then the counting was given up as a bad job, because nobody could see the end of it—realized that no troops could stand any longer, where this blessing had come down.

Thus the invasion was successful neither because of mistakes made on our side nor because of its prompt execution, which had been carefully planned by the enemy to its smallest detail, but because after five years of war, with all its consequences on our front and in the homeland, the weapons which alone could have enabled us to banish the danger—the Navy and the Luftwaffe—were almost non-existent. However, these were at the disposal of the Anglo-American forces to such an extent that it is hardly too much to say that it was like pitting two peoples against one another, one with bows and arrows and the other with firearms.

Comments on the Manuscript of General Reichert, OC 711th Infantry Division

by General der Panzer Leo, Freiherr Geyr von Schweppenburg

General Reichert comes from the Infantry, where he served in World War I. He is 55. General Reichert had been in command of the 711th Infantry Division for about two years, beginning from April 1943.

The report has an agreeable and personal touch. It gives a vivid picture of the outlook, as it presented itself to an average divisional commander of an infantry division, which at the crucial time was obsolete in organization and suffering without a fault of its own from the consequences of preconceived strategical ideas adopted by higher authorities.

The German Seventh Army and its subordinated corps commanders, most of all the OC LXXXIV Army Corps, were well aware of the danger to the Cotentin and relentless in pointing it out. However, the High Command, C-in-C West, and Fifteenth Army were more inclined to expect the center of gravity of invasion to come later on and north of the Seine, if this event were to materialize at all. Since they didn't want to be fooled by the enemy, the outcome was halfhearted measures and tactical patchwork of the worst type when the blow fell. The idea of invasion possibly being a large-scale bluff only had spread even down to this divisional commander.

The tactical ideas of the German military mind were and have always been in danger of being slow to adopt *revolutionary* changes. While the German Navy had learned the lesson of artificial smoke and its importance, this was not the case with the Army. The importance of the reverse slope in modern battle had been realized within the British Army by 1935. This was and had to be linked up with the decline in importance of the range of sight (Schussfeld) in infantry fighting, which the enemy might shorten by smokescreens whenever he chose to. It is therefore very typical when General Reichert writes that most of the pillboxes were built in closest proximity to the strand and to the very waterline.

Rommel's obsession for digging fortifications and erecting obstructions of the 1918 type resulted in the dwindling of the training idea, the outcome being failure and serious losses.

The conclusions of General Reichert may be approved save one exception. Unbiased historical criticism by military experts will have to state that the defense of France resulted in catastrophies not because the teachings of Moltke and Schlieffen were erroneous. They were meant for a different, bygone military period. The men with the power behind them to enforce these principles were ignorant or unmindful of these teachings. This has nothing to do with the corollary fact that the technique of modern battle had undergone a revolutionary change because of the advent of overwhelming and decisive airpower.

The commitment of the 711th and 346th Infantry Divisions as well as of the 21st Armored Division in counterattacking the 6th British Armored Brigade, most of all the complete lack of coordination in their activities, is likely to offer a very useful lesson for military students in the future.

The Failure to Deploy Reserves

by Generalmajor Rudolf, Freiherr von Gersdorff

The German Command realized that every day and every hour were of paramount importance after 6 June—and that time would have to be exploited to the very extreme to destroy the enemy forces which had landed, in order to make the invasion a failure for him. Aside from the great psychological effect of delays, on both friend and foe, every inch relinquished to the enemy increased our danger. The weakest moment for the enemy was when he landed—and the further this moment slipped into the past, the stronger his foothold would be.

This realization moved Field Marshal Rommel to issue his orders to the effect that the enemy be destroyed before reaching the beach. His orders—which stated that all weapons and men, including the reserves, be massed along the coastline, and that the defense front slightly to the rear of the coast be filled up with troops as much as possible at the expense of the occupation by troops in the depths of the terrain, so that not one coastal position was to remain unoccupied—were not carried out for some inexplicable reason in the defense sector where the invasion struck land, which was within the framework of the Seventh Army area. The sector of Fifteenth Army, however, was secured according to the orders of Field Marshal Rommel. From the commitment maps of the 716th and 352nd Infantry Divisions—with which I was thoroughly acquainted— I saw that areas as large in extent as four kilometers had been left unoccupied.

These open areas were located between strongpoints, and enabled the enemy to set foot on the beach at certain spots without being noticed—and where he could then push forward into the interior. The counterthrusts made by our weak reserves were so scattered and disorganized that they had no useful effect: our troops merely attacked and then disappeared into thin air when they reached their target, the enemy invasion force. The operational reserves stood so far from the coast, and were organized and spread out over so wide an area, that it was impossible to bring them to the front in compact fighting forces on the first day. The securing of small bridgeheads by the enemy could therefore not be prevented on the first day.

This was the first ice cold bath for the German Command. The first weak moment of the enemy had not been taken advantage of, and this would now be a matter of the past which could not be remedied. After realizing this misfortune, an energetic reaction should have taken place, and countermeasures should have been employed immediately. This was impossible, however, for now the Allied air force proved that we had estimated

239

its strength wrongly. We had formerly thought that it would not be able to intervene while friend and foe were closely interlocked in combat. This state of affairs led to a repeated attack over and over again by assault groups on our part, which, after reaching their zone of commitment, were able only to restore the situation where the danger had become very grave. The decisive results which were expected to be the fruits of these attacks hardly ever became reality. Up till the time when a sufficient German force had been organized and prepared for commitment, the smaller combat and assault groups— which had made individual attempts to pin the enemy down while the main force was not yet ready—either had been knocked out or were completely exhausted.

Apart from our estimate of the overall situation, in which we reckoned that large-scale landings would occur on other coasts, we had estimated the strength of the enemy forces which had landed between Le Havre and Cherbourg with approximate accuracy. The German Command therefore ordered that strong bodies of reserves be sent in immediately—which, as it appeared later, were not adequate in strength after all, and which, seen by a shrewd enemy, could not put up an effective defense with regard to the situation at sea and in the air, and their suitability for fighting. We see here a fault which was a characteristic of Hitler's command. He never understood how to build real strongpoints. This trait of Hitler's command may be seen throughout the entire course of the invasion.

Four armored divisions (21st, 12th SS, Panzer Lehr, and 2nd, of Panzer Gruppe West), which had taken over the sector of Caen during the night of the fourth day of the invasion and had remained in command there up till 13 June, and one infantry division (346th) were sent in against the British bridgehead. During the same period, one Panzer Grenadier division (17th SS), four infantry divisions (243rd, 91st, 77th, and 3rd Fallschirm), one brigade (30th Mobile), and three combat groups (of the 2nd Fallschirm, 265th, and 275th Divisions), which altogether amounted to an approximate force of six divisions, were committed against the American bridgehead. In addition to these there were also two coastal divisions in each sector—the 711th, 716th, 352nd, and 709th— which, however, had suffered acutely during the very first few days of the invasion.

Despite the fact that one German division was stronger in numbers of troops than the Americans had in their bridgehead for a large-scale battle, the Americans had weapons which were much more suitable and effective, and our Panzer divisions had been committed in the eastern invasion sector. The German Command thought that the prime operative danger was in this sector during the first period of the invasion, for it embodied a threat in the direction of Paris.

In the event that both these enemy bridgeheads, therefore, could not be eliminated, the German Command planned to destroy the British bridgehead in the eastern sector first by concentrating heavy attacks on it, and, after that had been achieved, it would concentrate on the bridgehead in the western sector. In order to carry out these plans, however, it would be a matter of great importance to prevent the enemy from uniting both these bridgeheads. Cherbourg would also have to be secured. These three necessities—a destruction of both the bridgeheads, one after the other; the sealing off of smaller enemy penetrations; and the maintenance of Cherbourg by our forces at any cost and under all circumstances – were the sole aims of the German Command in its planning during the first phase of the invasion.

The principle reason that every one of these three aims failed was that the reserves were brought up only sporadically, and we could therefore, at times, throw these into the fighting at only one-battalion strength, so that, on the whole, we never really succeeded in organizing a wholesale force. The fact that the reserves arrived bit by bit and so very slowly is mainly to be credited to the Allied air force, which, aside from intervening effectively by attacking and destroying our paths of approach, saw to it that we could execute large-scale troop movements only during the night. Railroad transports had to be unloaded early in most cases, so that it soon became necessary to carry out all troop movements by motor truck. We soon did not have the necessary trucks, however, and our fuel supply was also inadequate.

The following table will give quite a clear picture as to how slowly our reserves were brought up. The following units arrived on the following dates:

21st Panzer Division	6 June
12th SS Panzer Division "Hitler Jugend"	7 June
Panzer Lehr Division	8 and 9 June
346th Infantry Division	8 and 9 June
77th Infantry Division	11 June
2nd Panzer Division	13 June
3rd Fallschirm Division	13 June
353rd Infantry Division	16 June
1st SS Panzer Division "Leibstandarte"	18 June

The same was true also of the other detachments, such as artillery reinforcements, assault guns and mortar brigades. The result was that, instead of being able to launch a counterattack on a large scale, we could only seal up gaps which the enemy had made, and the Allies were consequently provided with the initiative all along. It was, however, impossible to bring all these forces up at once—we could not afford such, for the Allied air force was alert. The German Command could have smoothed out this disadvantage by disregarding the safety of its troops, in other words by drawing all its forces from the other coastal sectors to the scene of the invasion, at the same time exposing them to the enemy air force. No decision could be made at this time, however, as our command did not have a clear conception of the strength of the enemy air force.

It is true that Field Marshal Rommel did suggest, on 7 June, that all available forces be rushed to the invasion front immediately, especially those stationed in Brittany, but he could not convince OB West and the Supreme Command that this was the wise thing to do. During the first phase of the invasion, for example, Fifteenth Army, to which six divisions were subordinated for a long time, had to give up only one division for the invasion front; the same was true of the forces in southern France, but here we were almost certain that another landing operation would occur, and no forces were therefore extracted from this area. Nevertheless, those reserves which were destined to fight against the enemy invasion army were brought up very reluctantly, and sent in very slowly. And thus was born the tragic scene for us, namely that the decision was being wrought in our disfavor in Normandy while the main body of the German "Westheeres" watched idly—and while an inadequate German Army was fighting a despairing battle against a superior enemy.

During this period of dire need, in which the decision of this war was fought out, the differences of opinion remained among our highest commanders. The competition conception between them still led to a chaotic issuing of contradictory orders. The Heer was not authorized to draw troops—and might not issue orders to same—of the Luftwaffe or the Navy. It all had to be kindly requested first. It was therefore impossible to exploit fully the possibilities and means at our disposal; for example, transportation was disarranged.

Going back to the actual events, it can be established as a fact that the counterattack by I SS Panzer Corps on 9 July in the sector of Caen was handicapped by a lack of forces and was therefore brought to a halt by the enemy, just as all attacks which were carried out later were also stopped on either side of the Orne. These attacks achieved small successes in the beginning, but were then doomed to failure.

Furthermore, when considering the attack which was planned for II Fallschirm Corps—which, at the time of these plans, was was made up of the 3rd Fallschirm and the 77th Infantry Divisions, and which never became reality because the assembly activities and preparations were taking too long—the situation which was rapidly developing into a very critical state compelled the corps to commit its divisions among other places in Carentan and Valognes.

The enemy was inconvenienced by the weather on 9 and 10 June, but this advantage on our side could not be exploited— in other words, the Germans could not launch counterattacks on those days in which the enemy air force was grounded because it did not have the necessary forces.

Our troop commanders realized as early as 10 and 11 June that the original plan of battle had become obsolete, and that the first matter was now to assemble as many troops as possible, and as soon as possible, in order to be able to carry out the necessary countermeasures.

On 12 June Hitler ordered that the enemy bridgeheads be cleared off the mainland sector after sector, starting from east of the Orne. Attempts were made to execute this order, but they failed. In order to strike harder, we would have to wait for II SS Panzer Corps, which was under way from the East, and the 2nd SS Panzer Division, which was under way from southern France at this time. We did not expect them to arrive sooner than the end of the month, however. The forces which we were able to muster immediately—the 116th Panzer Division, the 319th Division (which was on the Channel Islands), the 326th and 331st Infantry Divisions (which were near the Pas de Calais), the 84th and 85th Infantry Divisions (between the Seine and the Somme), and the 2nd and 5th Fallschirm Divisions (in Brittany)—were to be left alone in accordance with an order from the Supreme Command.

Seventh Army had requested several times that at least strong portions, if not all, of the 319th Division, on the Channel Islands, be sent in against the enemy invasion force. This request, which was of course also supported by the Heeresgruppe and OB West, was rejected every time by Hitler. It must also be mentioned here that the so-called fortresses were to remain at full strength according to orders issued by the Supreme Command, so that here also here strong German forces were pinned down for a useless purpose.

This question became a very painful one after the surrender of Cherbourg in the middle of July. In order to strengthen this harbor as much as possible, Seventh Army had sent in comparatively strong forces southeast of Cherbourg—the 709th, 91st, 243rd, and 77th Infantry Divisions—which were now threatened with being cut off by the American forces which had broken through to the west coast of the Cotentin peninsula. LXXXIV Army Corps and the Seventh Army therefore requested at an early date that this group of divisions be reorganized in order to remove the danger of being encircled. These requests were, however, all rejected with regard to the Cherbourg fortress—and strict orders were continually issued to the effect that not one inch of ground was to be surrendered.

When, on 15 and 16 June, the last-mentioned Army and Corps decided to reorganize and shift their forces on their own initiative—more towards the south in order to prevent the enemy from breaking through near St-Sauveur, and to withdraw the garrison out of the fortress of Cherbourg—Hitler's order was rescinded and, after a lot of wavering back and forth for forty-eight hours, was made retrospective. The result was that the Americans broke through our weak front near St-Sauveur, and destroyed the four divisions. Owing to an order issued by Rommel on his own initiative, and the successful breakthrough by portions of the 77th Infantry Division, it was possible to save at least some weak forces.

Despite that fact that the inconsistency of the countermeasures carried out by the German forces at this time was one reason that our efforts failed, there were also other facts which handicapped us, namely, on 13 June, that portions of the 21st Panzer Division were still in the Bois de Bavent while other portions of the 2nd Panzer Division near Caumont had not yet received their tracked vehicles, as well as portions of the 17th Panzer Grenadier Division near Carentan which were engaged in a local counterthrust which led to only a slight success, as could have been expected.

The first counteraction of a stronger nature carried out by us was an attack by I and II SS Panzer Korps on 29 and 30 July southwest of Caen, which, after achieving preliminary successes, stuck fast owing to the superior British land and sea artillery as well as the effect of the Allied air force. How far the reproaches so often raised with regard to this—errors of strategy on the part of the leadership, and the unreadiness of the formations for commitment, as well as a lack of the proper knowledge of how SS units ought to be trained—are valid, I am not in a position to judge.

Critique

by General der Infanterie Günther Blumentritt

(Interviewer's note: This section was written by Blumentritt with direct reference to the Historical Division General Brief. The questions on the brief have been included in the report for clarity.)

Q. Describe any changes in orders given or received, with the reasons therefor, and any actions taken on our initiative.

A. OB West could not, on its own initiative, alter orders issued by OKW. Naturally, however, developments in the actual situation often forced us to deviate somewhat in the execution of orders as planned from a map in East Prussia, (for example, the north and south wheeling movement in the combat for Cherbourg). The subordinate commands, such as Seventh Army, Corps, and divisions, often had to take action different from that which had been ordered. The responsible officers concerned can offer the best information on this subject.

Q. Give the time, place, and reasons for commitment of reserves.

A. In my opinion, OKW did not know on 6 June 1944 whether the events in Normandy were the expected invasion and were to be taken seriously, or whether they were only a diversion. This was probably the reason OKW was reluctant to release the only two reserve units available. Until eight to ten days after 6 June, OKW still seriously considered a second invasion in the Channel-coast sector of Fifteenth Army. Consequently, reserves in the Fifteenth Army sector were transferred very reluctantly and in two cases even recalled to Calais... The 1st SS Panzer Division (near Brussels) was released about 8 June and was moved toward Normandy. However, the division was halted for a short time in the Fifteenth Army sector because OKW still expected a second invasion. II SS Panzer Corps (9th Panzer and 10th SS Panzer Divisions), coming from the East, had to detrain at the German frontier because the destroyed railroads to Paris would not permit further transport. Only the tanks could be transported to Paris by rail. Bringing up reinforcements was thus accomplished very slowly after the mechanized infantry. Because of the effects, further divisions of all types for other areas of France and from other armies were very slow and difficult. The Allies were able to transport strong forces from England to their artificial harbors much faster than we could bring up reinforcements to Normandy.

Q. State changes in flank units and/or higher headquarters.

A. Not applicable to OB West.

Q. Describe special tactics or techniques of the infantry, tanks, SPs [self-propelled guns], artillery, engineers, and so forth.

A. This question can be better answered by the tactical commands. The hedgerow terrain of Normandy often forced us to commit tanks individually. Infantry without tanks and assault guns was just as ineffective as it had been in Russia in 1941.

Q. Describe the road nets used and the types and performance of communications.

A. We utilized all roads leading to Normandy. However, the use of these roads was very limited in the long summer days because of the air threat. Signal communication from OB West was in order; there were no particular difficulties.

Q. How did supply and reinforcement agencies function?

A. The most serious problems of supply were the effects of Allied air superiority and the lack of convoy space.

Q. What was the effect of German air support?

A. There was one German plane to 25 Allied planes. This meant that there was practically no support for the ground troops. The few available squadrons performed well. (The same may be said of the few E-boats, destroyers, and one-man submarines of the Navy.)

Q. Give a personal eyewitness account of conferences attended, engagements observed, and so forth.

A. The conferences I attended as Chief of Staff OB West were naturally many and interesting. Only these conferences could give an insight into why certain actions were ordered and what such men as von Rundstedt and von Kluge actually thought and believed. These considerations are much more important from the historical and psychological viewpoint than the heaps of "dead" orders and documents. A report on these factors, however, would also fill volumes.

I was with the combat divisions at the front several times. My impression at that time, after nine and half years of world wars, was that even very brave and willing troops can do nothing against superior matériel, especially in the air. (The same was true in World War I after 1916, with the equipment then in use.)

Q. Discuss the effects of the Allied air attacks; ground attacks, both tank and infantry; artillery; the weather; and the terrain.

A. The air force dominates a war on land and will probably do so even more in the future with newer weapons. Pattern bombing will break the worst and the best divisions, and no bravery or high degree of morale can prevent it. The air force can hinder and prevent troop movements, concentrations, shifting of forces, artillery displacement, and movement of supplies. It can paralyze railroads, knock out bridges, and delay or prevent rapid strategic movements. Only a strong friendly air force can counteract these effects. The Allied air force played absolutely the largest part in the success of the war.

The naval heavy artillery made more of an impression on the morale of the troops than we had previously thought possible. Thus naval artillery can be of valuable support to a landing up to 25–30 kilometers inland. The technical aspect of the landing was well organized. For a time, the Allied tanks had to cope with the same peculiarities of the Normandy terrain as we. (There could be no mass commitment of armor.) Panzer experts (Bayerlein, von Geyr, Hauser, von Lüttwitz, von Manteuffel, etc.) will be able to give more detailed information.

The Allied infantryman, on the average, was young (20–30 years old), had a fairly long period of training, was equipped with the best of modern weapons, and was rested. These characteristics no longer applied to our own army in 1944. The Allied infantry fought hard and bravely, but in the interests of the British and American infantry I must say that the British, Americans, Germans, and Russians were all brave, even though there were small differences due to nationality. However, in a modern war of technical development and material, even the best infantry cannot achieve success in large-scale combat without planes, tanks, and assault guns. I believe that the American and British officers also discovered that their infantry can fight successfully only if these means are available.

Our troops were always deeply impressed by the accurate fire of the artillery. Part of the credit is due the artillery liaison planes, of which we had very few in World War II. Our troops were baffled by the great amount of ammunition expended by the Allied artillery. In general, the weather was good, so that the Allied air force naturally dominated the combat area. The hedgerow terrain of Normandy demanded a high degree of small unit training (platoon and company).

Q. What and where were the critical times and places? Why?

A. The critical moments of the Normandy campaign were (a) 0100 to 2400 on 6 June in the landing areas; (b) 6 and 7 June at Caen; and (c) consolidation of the beachheads at Arromanches about 9 June. (The encirclement of Cherbourg was anticipated and therefore is not considered a critical moment. Naturally, critical moments occurred constantly in the tactical situations of Seventh Army, Corps, and divisions.) The breakthrough in the West by invasion obviously had a decisive effect on the final victory of all the Allies, for without an invasion in the West our power of resistance in the East would have been greater and would have lasted longer.

I presume that the Western Allies wish not only to gain historical value from these reports, but also to obtain lessons and experiences for the training of their officers and men. My personal opinions after two world wars, schools, and an examination of war histories are as follows:

a. **Politics and War:** The politicians must decide policy and accept responsibility. The soldier is only the instrument of politics and therefore cannot be held "responsible." If a soldier were to answer for the actions of the responsible political leaders, then his initiative as a soldier in future wars would be considerably handicapped. The corresponding consequences to the nation are obvious.

b. **Strategy:** Modern weapons and matériel are built for speed. The engine dominates both the air and the ground. These means should never be employed solely for static warfare. Strategy is characterized by freedom of movement, with a bold but deliberate spirit and sense of responsibility. It is the prerequisite either for fighting under favorable conditions or for putting the enemy out of action without a decisive battle. The latter can be accomplished only by cutting off the enemy communication of supply, which is the most vital part of a modern technical army. "Operations" involve "movement" in every advantageous direction—forward, laterally, or sometimes deliberately to the rear. A famous doctor once said, "Movement is life; quiescence is death." Modern strategy must utilize mobility in the same manner as Alexander, Hannibal, Genghis Khan, Napoleon, and the great North American cavalry leaders of the War of Secession conducted strategic operations with the old matériel of their respective periods. Many lessons can be learned from these operations and from the mobile operations at the end of the nineteenth century and in the twentieth century. Mobility permits one to maintain a broad front, to deceive the enemy as to the main effort, and to effect a last-minute, rapid concentration of force in the direction desired. After 1943, these principles were forbidden in Germany. The guiding doctrine was that of a rigid defense—the quietus of leadership and mechanization.

c. **Tactics:** Tactics dominate both the battle and the local actions. From the profusion of tactical problems, I would like to discuss just one: "Use of Streams and Rivers as Obstacles." The attacker can almost invariably surmount the obstacle. In ten and a half years of war (1914–18 and 1939–45) both friend and foe have defended and attacked river lines many times. Eventually, the attacker has always effected a crossing. This all goes to prove that a rigid defense of the bank is not possible. One must maintain a flexible defense, utilizing strong, mobile reserves behind the river line. Pattern-bombing and new aerial weapons can smash any rigid position, however strong it may be. The position becomes a field of craters and shell holes. Only dispersion and movement afford a certain degree of protection.

d. **Air force:** The air force is decisive. Combat with armored and mechanized divisions on the ground and with the fleet at sea cannot succeed without air support. Only the air force can permit the movement of strong mechanized forces on the ground.

e. **Leadership:** The political leaders designate to the commander his mission and establish his political limits. They should take care that the soldier does not have to do everything and fight on all sides. They should intervene when the strategic plans of the soldier appear to jeopardize politics. Apart from that, however, the commander should be allowed a free hand. Only this confidence, this inner freedom and knowledge of full responsibility will give a capable leader the inner strength he needs!

Index